WILLIAM SKIDMORE

Theoretical thinking in sociology

CAMBRIDGE UNIVERSITY PRESS

CAMBRIDGE

LONDON · NEW YORK · MELBOURNE

Published by the Syndics of the Cambridge University Press
The Pitt Building, Trumpington Street, Cambridge CB2 1RP
Bentley House, 200 Euston Road, London NW1 2DB
32 East 57th Street, New York, NY 10022, USA
296 Beaconsfield Parade, Middle Park, Melbourne 3206, Australia

© Cambridge University Press 1975

Library of Congress Catalogue Card Number: 75–2715

ISBNs: 0 521 20716 9 hard covers
        0 521 09932 3 paperback

First published 1975

Printed in the United States of America by Vail-Ballou Press Inc.,
Binghamton, New York
Typeset by Radnor Graphic Arts, Radnor, Pennsylvania

to

The Anchorage

and

All Its Inhabitants

Contents

iii

Preface

Experience suggests that students of sociology at all levels have much in common. They need, on the whole, to be convinced that sociological theory is worth studying for its own sake, rather than as a requirement toward a degree. They need to know something about how to judge theory – how to tell good from bad in the conceptual world of sociology. They need, above all, to know the objective of theory: *to explain social order*, so that they can better see what the whole enterprise is aiming for and gauge progress.

When someone takes up the study of sociological theory he does not want to be smothered in detail, nor to be insulted by superficiality. He seeks a substantial overview of theory, so that further work in the field can proceed according to solid preliminary understandings. Most students would also like to know the bearing of sociological theory on research, and to have concrete examples of how theory and research contribute to each other's success. Finally, to gain perspective, students ought to know that all theories are deficient in at least some respects, and that theoretical thinking includes a proper appreciation of critical remarks about each competing viewpoint.

Theoretical Thinking in Sociology attempts to speak to these requirements. The first three chapters consider the idea of sociological theory and its use, examine some methods of theorizing and some theoretical problems, and set out basic understandings from the philosophy of social science about the relation of evidence to theory, the logical structure of theory, and the methodological procedures appropriate to various theoretical styles. These first three chapters outline the distinguishing marks of the three kinds of theory to be described later on: deductive theory, pattern theory, and perspectives.

Chapters 4 through 6 examine these more closely. Chapter 4 describes deductive theoretical structure, using exchange theory as an example. Chapter 5 examines pattern theory, describing functionalism. Chapter 6 describes symbolic interactionism as a perspective. Finally, Chapter 7 outlines other activities of sociological theorists and returns to the question of social order by describing how ethnomethodology deals with this problem. These chapters are independent enough to be read separately, and in any order; but it is the author's hope that the book will be read through from start to finish, or at least that the first three chapters will be familiar to the reader before any of the following four. This is because the later chapters are intended as examples from active theory of the strengths, weaknesses, and thought styles which the first three chapters introduce. The book delineates the thinking of the theoreticians it discusses, not just their conclusions.

In writing any book, one incurs many debts, to teachers and students, to colleagues known and unknown whose ideas one has absorbed, to family. I wish to acknowledge the very considerable critical and editorial help given me by my wife, who has also typed the whole manuscript through twice. In addition, the University of New Brunswick kindly provided a grant to support the preparation of this book, and my colleagues in the Department of Sociology and Anthropology at U.N.B. maintained the usual congenial and encouraging atmosphere.

W.S.

The Anchorage
May 1974

1 Sociological theory

I. *The term 'theory'*

The term *sociological theory* has a variety of meanings and usages. This variety has on occasion led to confusion among sociologists and persons studying sociology, because two or more persons may not agree about the theoretical meaning of an idea. Because of such misunderstanding, the idea itself may be lost or misinterpreted. It is a good idea, therefore, to have a firm understanding of the variety of things the term 'theory' can refer to in sociology, and a grasp of the main differences between these things.

Theories come in various packages. They may be clearly and succinctly stated, or they may be implied by less precise statements. Actually, most theoretical work is in some measure ambiguous on at least one point, and therefore there is almost always room for interpretation and re-evaluation of the exact meaning of any one theory. There will be more said about this as we progress in our examination of sociological theory, but for now it ought to be emphasized that seemingly detrimental ambiguity in theoretical statements is very often a positive point, since it is as a consequence of the mental work of reinterpretation and evaluation of theory that we really make advances in theoretical work in the social sciences.

The rise of academic sociology in universities and colleges has been accompanied by the more or less systematic study of sociological theory as such. But this was not always so. Formerly, the more usual case was that theories came about as a consequence of someone's trying to understand something that puzzled him. Theories grew up around themes that we might call theoretical problems. Sometimes these were immediate, practical problems, as well. Such problems as the advent of urban crime, or the increase in the birth rate, or the nature of social solidarity were involved. Concern for issues like these actually transcended the immediate practical importance which gave rise to interest in them. Consequently, such issues formed the bases of systems of thought which came to be called theories; these systems went much beyond the problems that started them on their way.

The solution of a theoretical problem does not necessarily mean that the practical problem associated with it has also been solved. Anyone who has ever noticed the number of theories of crime and the rising crime rate knows this. But theoretical problems do have solutions in the sense that the ideas in a theory, and their interrelations and structure, can give answers to the theoretical problems. That is, the problem of how properly to conceptualize social class, for example, is solved by the generation of other related concepts and ideas. When these ideas are put together and systematized, the result turns into something beginning to look like a sociological theory.

Theories formed in this way obviously could take many forms and exist in various states of relative consistency or inconsistency, clarity or obscurity. They might also be mixed with some amount of simple narration of fact or perhaps ideology. For this reason, it is sometimes hard to discover the actual meaning of a theoretical term, since it may be unclear whether its inventor means his reader to take the term as description, plan of action, or mainly for its usefulness in understanding something. There will be more about this later.

From the rather loose collection of ideas suggested above as one pole of a continuum, we can suggest the opposite pole. Theories can take the form of precise presentations of ideas, in which the concepts and processes suggested by the theory are clearly and definitively spelled out. This, of course, is an ideal for many sociological theorists, who generally wish to clarify theoretical issues and problems. But since this ideal state of affairs is not often reached in actual practice, we must expect to find examples of real sociological theories falling somewhere between the loose-construction and precise-construction poles.

II. *Theory and practice*

At first glance, sociological theory often seems like a separate entity, alone unto itself, and something to master since, like the mountain, it is simply there. This approach to sociological theory usually ends in frustration, since it is not based on a reasonable understanding of what we can expect to get out of sociological theory. In general, the strength of theory is in its ability to bring a great deal of thought and information to bear on a specific problem or set of problems, and thereby go far beyond unsystematic thought in the detail and precision of subsequent concept formation and manipulation. Theories work out and hold ideas ready to be used at a moment's notice.

The idea of a theoretical problem has already been introduced. We may conveniently divide the ways in which a theory comes to grips with a theoretical problem into four categories and discuss them separately. These four are:

1   Theory may suggest additional ideas in the course of solving some given theoretical problem.
2   Theory may suggest models of the subject matter, so that a kind of schematic description results. The description can be thought of as a pattern into which ideas may be placed for convenience and clarity.
3   Models may suggest theories.
4   Theory may suggest hypotheses.

A. *Theory as suggestive of ideas*

Thinking of theories as suggestive of ideas more or less corresponds to the loose-construction approach to theory described above. A single concept is not a theory. Social class may be felt or experienced, in some sense, but there is no theoretical meaning in the term alone. It is only when the idea of social class is put together with additional ideas that it begins to be explained and accounted for or to take part in explaining something else. For example, the understanding of what social class is has altogether to do with the meaning of social structure, social relations, power, privilege, obligation, authority, and many other ideas as well. What this means in practical terms is that to understand social class, one is obliged to develop clear definitions and conceptions of these related ideas. In doing so, it is probable that even more ideas will be suggested, and the search for understanding they require will further illuminate the idea of social class, as well as the other ideas which grew up around the first one.

Ideas and concepts which seem to spring up around an initial problem or object of thought do not do so at random. They develop principally because (1) the definition of one concept suggests another, or (2) some observation indicates that an idea or concept is needed. In the first case, we may say that the loose collection of concepts with which we started implied relationships among the concepts which must be discovered. For example, the idea of social class suggests that there is more than one class, and that the characteristics of these classes are not the same. Thus specifically setting one class off from another helps in understanding both. In the second case, we are asking a question of how well an initial conceptualization seems to 'fit' the facts. Again using social class as an example of an idea, it is possible in principle to have many concepts of class, only some of which will appear to have any ability to describe or suggest something about real social classes. The ones that seem to have this ability will be preferred.

To continue the example, we see at once that any definition of social class (whatever specific one we may care to choose) immediately implies a division of something 'social' into categories called 'classes'. Starting with an idea of 'classness' we have generated the need to discover the relatedness of one class to another. In the process of doing this, we have also had to define social class in such a way that there is a clear distinction between one class and another. We have begun the job of constructing theoretical categories. Since these classes are in the process of becoming distinctly defined as this theoretical work goes on, the problem of their relatedness comes to the fore and requires attention. This is also happening because whatever we started with which we understood as 'social' is also in the process of being defined in terms of 'classness'. The relatedness of these classes as they form a 'social' unit ought to be of interest to us. The nature of this relatedness would likely form the basis of a general idea about social structure.

In this example, we have seen that a theoretical approach to one idea led quite naturally to the creation of other ideas which helped to clarify the first one and define its relatedness to others. It is in something like this way that theories tend to become developed in their logical structure, since before long, ideas that are logically incompatible with each other will probably be discovered. Then, this logical incompatibility will require the theorist either to change the ideas or alter the whole theoretical structure in some way, hopefully resulting in a more coherent idea system.

We also ask directly empirical questions as a result of having them suggested to us by theory. If our understanding of social class developed to a point where specific relations between classes were suggested, it would be proper to try to find out if these relations indeed existed, or to find out more about whatever relations between classes we actually did find. There are vast problems involved here, which will be covered more thoroughly in the sections of this book on specific theories and on verification. Let it be said, however, that in principle it is possible to generate an idea by examining something empirically, and to work this idea into the web of ideas called a theory.[1] If we did not believe this principle to be true, there could be but scant hope of ever applying sociological theory, even if the theorizing process did begin with interest in an empirical problem.

B. *Theory as suggestive of models*

There is, unfortunately, no clear distinction between models and theories. The idea of a model is often confused with that of a theory, and

---

[1] Generating ideas from empirical observation is usually described as the process of *induction*. This requires the observer of facts to notice that certain things in reality 'go together' and then conceptualize these things according to some unified entity or process. It is unfortunate that, logically speaking, there are no rules to follow in doing this which would ensure proper concept formation. Thus we must take it as a matter of principle that concepts can be generated from experience and do have value in describing and accounting for experience.

sometimes the two terms are used interchangeably with no attention given to the differences between them. One theory might serve as a model for another.[2] In essence, theories without models explain directly; models explain by analogy.

It will be useful to describe the concept of models before returning to the ways in which theory may suggest models and what is gained when this happens. A *model* of a thing is, by definition, not the thing itself, but something that has a resemblance to the thing of interest. It is precisely in the resemblances that the utility of models is apparent. If the model bears resemblance to the real thing in certain ways, but not in others, the ways in which the model does resemble the reality is the sense in which the model is analogous to reality. A model may be useful in pointing out these elements of similarity and in developing a better understanding of why the model resembles the thing. Again, an example might be helpful. Everyone knows that a model airplane and a Boeing 747 are not the same thing. But in what ways are they similar? If the model flies as a result of being thrown, the action of the air on the wings of the model as it moves holds the plane in flight. Because flight has occurred as a result of the action of air on wings, the shape and structure of the wings and their relationship to the rest of the structure are analogous in some ways to the flight of the 747. If we are interested in understanding the action of air on the wings of the 747, we can investigate it by investigating the action of air on the model and drawing an analogy to the real plane. But we could not do this to discover the cause of movement through air, since we tossed our model. The model is analogous to reality in some important sense, and not analogous in another. The model is useless if what we want to understand is why the real airplane moves, but if we are interested in why it stays up, the model might be important.

Of course in this example we already knew that the model was not analogous with respect to cause of movement, and this lack of correspondence between model and reality caused no difficulty. But we sometimes build up models of reality to better understand it, and then fail to notice the ways in which the models do not correspond to reality. Or, to take a related problem, we may define parts of reality which are poorly understood as though they were analogous to the parts of the model, knowing that this is risky. In the field of economics, for example, how people allocate a given amount of resources among hundreds of choices has long been a puzzling concern. Since the theory of this kind of activity must emphasize choice and choosing, one kind of model which has grown up is that of the Rational Man or Economic Man.[3] This model amounts to a series of assumptions about how choices are made, based

---

2 For a fuller description of models in science, see Abraham Kaplan, *The Conduct of Inquiry* (San Francisco: Chandler Publishing Co., 1964), Ch. 7.
3 The concept of rationality is not limited to use in economics, and we will have occasion to examine the concept in more detail, especially in Ch. 4.

on the principle of maximization of benefit. The immediate question about this model is, of course, is it true that real people behave according to ways the model suggests and maximize their benefit from a given level of resources? Also of interest is the related question of whether or not people are motivated to act in the way assumed by the model. Now, taken literally, the model is 'wrong' in the sense that it is probably not a description of how real people actually go about allocating their resources. Obviously they do not spend entirely on the basis of egoistic benefit, and they often spend resources unwisely. But remember that they do not spend chaotically, and they usually do spend with the objective of receiving value for money. And do not forget that what we wanted initially was a model of the resources allocator, not a model of Emotional Man or Altruistic Man. It is probable that Economic Man, as a model, is quite useful in emphasizing aspects of economic behavior that are of interest, even though this model is oversimple and does not resemble 'real' man in very many details. The intelligent use of a model like this involves understanding the analogous points between reality and the model while not supposing that the model explains too much.

C. *Models as suggestive of theories*

Models may suggest theories or additions to theories. This can be very helpful when the theory is more poorly worked out than the model. A theory may predict that there is a certain relationship between two ideas but say little about the relationships between these ideas and some other. By finding a model which seems to approximate the relationship between the first two ideas, it may be possible to see by analogy that there are other ideas and relationships implied. Thus the model has suggested additions to the theory. An example of this situation can be found in sociological theory. It is sometimes held that the process of social change through time is analogous to the process of biological evolution.[4] In fact, a very important branch of sociological theory in the nineteenth century (which is by no means completely outmoded today) said precisely this. Such theory uses our knowledge of the evolutionary process, a biological phenomenon, as a model for understanding social change. Among the things suggested by this approach to social change is that while there may be intense conflict on the part of discrete social units in the short run, among individuals, classes, interests, or whatever may have been

---

[4] A good short treatment of how this principle affected the work of William Graham Sumner and Lester Ward is found in Richard Hofstadter, *Social Darwinism in American Thought* (Boston: Beacon Press, 1944). The concept of evolution has been applied at many levels of generality. In a fairly recent work, Talcott Parsons uses the idea to help explain the general pattern of world social development in *Societies: Evolutionary and Comparative Perspectives* (Englewood Cliffs, N.J.: Prentice-Hall, 1966).

suggested by the particular version of the theory, the long-run result of the conflict is not destruction of society, but rather a reshaping and redevelopment of it. Note that this constructive aspect was not suggested by a knowledge of instances of social conflict; the idea of benefit arose from the biological model.[5] In this case, preliminary suggestions that social change might be analogous to biological change and evolution produced the idea, derived by analogy, that social conflict is productive in some way. It is not appropriate here to try to resolve the issue of whether or not social conflict is beneficial, but it is important to see where we got the idea of its being so. We used a model, and the idea came from the model, not directly from observation. The use of this analogy could go much further. For example, we have already warned that in the absence of any solid proof, the limits to which analogies may be taken are unknown. It would be important to know, therefore, exactly how 'social evolution' resembles biological evolution, and if the resemblance is essential or superficial.

It should be emphasized that sometimes the desire to understand reality better drives us to define it in terms of models. In the present example, if we say that social evolution is just a particular kind of biological evolution, then we are saying by implication that whatever is 'social' resembles the biological world in essential respects. This amounts to making an array of assumptions about the social world in the same terms in which the naturalist makes assumptions about the biological world. Done within bounds, this can be productive of useful theory; but it can lead to absurdities as well. For example, it might be instructive to imagine society to be a web of complex, interrelated functional parts such as a living body is; but it is probably absurd to go on and attribute 'life' to this web in anything like the sense in which a body lives.[6] Models are usually better understood and more complete than the social facts they are taken to represent. Hence, when the intention is to know reality by analogy through a model, extreme caution should always lead us to question the extent to which models are really applicable and the value of learning too much too easily by taking over too grand an analogy.

D. *Theories as productive of hypotheses*

In the discussion of models and theories, we have gone more or less on the intuitive idea that a sociological theory is some kind of arrangement of ideas which 'tells us something' about the social world. But the way in

---

[5] The source of the idea is a matter of some controversy, since it might have been borrowed by the natural sciences from political economic studies. The point remains, however, that in the present example the idea of evolutionary change was borrowed by sociological theorists from the naturalists.

[6] When life is attributed to sociological entities, as in 'the living city', this mistake is dangerously close.

which it tells us this may be very important. One way of doing it is to produce hypotheses, although this is not the only way. In the discussion of the structure of theories, we will see which form of theory is best at producing hypotheses.

An *hypothesis* is a statement of a relationship between two or more ideas or classes of thing. The important point about this preliminary definition is that, by itself, it could also be the definition of a scientific law, or just a guess. To take up the latter possibility first, the important difference between hypotheses and simple guesses is that the hypothesis is in some way conceptually related to the theory from which it comes. In the strongest relationship between theory and hypotheses, the hypotheses are deductively derived; that is, they follow directly as a matter of logical extension from the generalizations and concepts already established within the theory.[7] A theory can generate hypotheses if it is applied to some specific theoretical or empirical problem. If we have a theory concerning social solidarity and religious practices, as Emile Durkheim did in his book *Suicide*,[8] we may be in a position to create hypotheses, or statements of possible relatedness between religious practices and some societal problem, suicide in this case.

Durkheimian theory holds, in general, that the individual is entirely dependent for his life, including his individuality, on society. Collective society gives him his identity, stabilizes him against the buffeting forces of everyday life, and sustains him in a spiritual, as well as a material, sense. Society is represented in each person's mind by the 'collective conscience', which may be concrete or abstract, depending on the state of societal development.

But what we are interested in now is, how can an hypothesis be derived from Durkheim's theory? Wisely, Durkheim chose suicide as a problem with which to test his theoretical scheme. He reasoned that if he could show a social influence on this, the most individual of individual acts, he would be a long way toward proving his point that society is of prime importance to individuality. But how to do it? It was easy to discover the statistical records and show that in certain places in Europe at certain times the suicide rate varied, went up or down, from some median level. Durkheim reasoned that if he could account for the changes in suicide rate entirely by reference to states of social solidarity, he would have his answer.

According to the generalizations of Durkheim's theory, the greater the social solidarity of a population, the more likely it is that individuals will

---

[7] Deduction is often defined as reasoning from the general to the particular. Fundamentally, the deductive process follows the form of the syllogism: a major premise states a generality, a minor premise gives a statement of a specific case, and a conclusion states the relationship of the specific case to the generality.

[8] Tr. J. A. Spalding and G. Simpson (New York: Free Press, 1951).

experience meaningful social support in times of stress, and the less likely, therefore, will be their suicide. Religion enters the picture at this point. Durkheim reasoned that the Roman Catholic faith provided stronger social solidarity than did Protestantism. This seemed to be so because Catholicism at Durkheim's time of writing tended to take a more collective and integrative approach to the individual, and it more often emphasized commonality and similarity to others. Protestantism, on the other hand, was much more individualistic. With their doctrines of direct participation in some of the sacraments, the emphasis on reading the Bible for oneself, and, in some cases, democratic control of church affairs by the congregation, the Protestant faiths were associated with a less tightly knit and less solidly integrated social system.

Here Durkheim had his answer. To demonstrate a relationship between social solidarity and individual behavior, Durkheim needed real indications of each. He had indications about individual acts, *par excellence* – suicides. He had to account for them. He had Catholicism and Protestantism with which to do it in terms of social solidarity.

His hypothesis, therefore, was that in areas of Europe where Catholicism was strong, suicide rates would be lower than in areas of Europe where Protestantism was predominant. It is important to spend a moment on what Durkheim's hypothesis meant. It meant, in its most obvious sense, that he expected a relationship to exist between suicide rates and religious affiliation. But he did not guess this *ad hoc*. He derived it from a theory about something much broader and potentially important: the relationship between social solidarity and individuality. The fact that Durkheim's prediction (his hypothesis) was by and large confirmed suggested that his theoretical scheme relating social solidarity and individuality was valid. If his research had not tended to confirm his prediction, his theory of social integration would still be a theory, and the logic of suggesting the probable distribution of suicides in Europe would still be intact.[9] However, it would not enjoy empirically derived evidence of its validity.

It should be pointed out that Durkheim's general theory of social solidarity and its relation to the individual suggests other hypotheses as well. For example, it implies the primacy of society in matters of morals and professional ethics, and Durkheim did research in this field, again gener-

---

9 This may seem confusing but it is really simple. Durkheim's hypothesis might not have been confirmed, but there are a variety of reasons which could account for this: his statistics might have been wrong; he might have made a mistake in calculation; some other factor which had an effect on social solidarity might have temporarily influenced his results. Thus, hypotheses are usually cautiously related to reality in terms of 'weights of evidence' or 'tendencies' to confirm or disconfirm a given hypothesis. Of course, all the things that could have led to a failure to confirm Durkheim's hypothesis might have contributed to its confirmation as well.

ally confirming his main theory.[10] More than one hypothesis can come from a theory, and the number and variety of hypotheses derivable from a given theory are part of the measure of that theory's worth.

The definition of an hypothesis has not yet been differentiated from the definition of a scientific law. Again, more detail will have to be postponed until the discussion of the structure of theories. But it can be said now that if a given hypothesis seems to be confirmed by experience over a wide range of events and in a wide range of situations, the hypothesis can be 'elevated' to the status of a law. This means that those who work with and know an hypothesis in all the forms it takes, and have sufficient confidence that its predictions are true, will begin to feel less of a need to constantly test it against experience each time they use it. They will instead begin to use the hypothesis as a generalization or principle from which to deduce new hypotheses. It will, thus, become a law.[11]

The general form of the statement of relationship between two ideas does not necessarily change when the statement ceases being an hypothesis and starts becoming lawlike. Neither would the form necessarily change if the statement were just a hunch. The distinction between hypothesis, law, and hunch comes in the state of logical relatedness and weight of confirmatory evidence that builds up between the statement of relationship and the rest of the theory, on the one hand, and the statement of relationship and evidence on the other. If a statement of relationship is clearly and logically linked to the theory, it is an hypothesis rather than a guess. If the statement is supported by a quantity of evidence, it may be called a law rather than an hypothesis.

III. *Types of theory and typologies of theory*

Obviously, there is more than one theory in sociology. This does not mean either that all but one of them are 'wrong', or that any of them are 'wrong'. When theories have grown up around problems, as has been suggested, they group themselves naturally into types of theories related to this issue, theories related to that issue, and so on. To some extent this actually prevails. But as we have seen, theories have a tendency to expand their scope by subsuming hypotheses; and also, they suggest other hypotheses that go beyond the initial interest of the man who first proposed the theory. Thus, over time, there has been an overlapping of theoretical 'territory', so that now there are many theories which offer explanations of approximately the same phenomenon. This gives rise to

10 Emile Durkheim, *Professional Ethics and Civic Morals*, tr. Cornelia Brookfield (London: Routledge and Kegan Paul, 1957).

11 A considerable literature in 'the philosophy of science' has grown up, partly around the question of laws. See Kaplan, *Conduct of Inquiry*, Ch. 8, and N. R. Campbell, *Foundations of Science* (New York: Dover, 1957), Part I, for further discussion on laws.

the need to classify theories and sort them according to some rational criteria. The attempt to do this has sometimes led to problems and confusion.

One way to classify theories is to attach dates to them, according to the eras in which they were first proposed or first came into relatively wide use. Then the theories can be discussed in temporal order. Courses in sociological theory which take an 'historical' approach often do essentially this. The advantage of this procedure is that it shows repeatedly that a given idea has had the power to spawn other ideas, and that idea systems evolve as they are thought through again and again. By looking back at the course of time, new and different ideas can be traced to old ones. The disadvantage of this approach is that is is sometimes difficult to grasp the reasons why theories change, and rise and fall.[12]

Another scheme that has been used with some success is to group theories according to the country in which they were proposed and used most widely. This approach has led to some fairly stable classifications of theory, in sociology as well as in other disciplines. For example, German sociology of the middle and late nineteenth century tended to be distinguishable from sociology in England or France of about the same period. Probably the similarities among German theories were the result of common cultural themes and points of view shared by the German theorists. This is not to say, however, that these theories were all the same. Far from it. Nor is it to say that theories produced in other countries did not resemble German theory. This happened. In fact, good cases can be made for the resemblance of, for example, Durkheim's theory of social solidarity, developed in France, and German theories of folk spirit and the importance of cultural heritage. It could also be shown that rather similar ideas were in use in England at the time. Nevertheless, the national classification method has been used as a convenient labeling technique, and 'German sociological theory' still has a reasonably precise meaning.[13]

A more defensible method of classifying theories has been to analyze them according to their main concepts and assumptions, and to group those that are similar, no matter when or where they were formed originally.[14] This method has the distinct advantages of showing the logical similarities of various theories, and of showing how a given theoretical

---

[12] The master at showing historical precedent for sociological ideas is P. A. Sorokin. See his *Contemporary Sociological Theories* (New York: Harper, 1928), *Sociological Theories of Today* (New York: Harper and Row, 1966), and *Fads and Foibles in Modern Sociology* (Chicago: Henry Regnery, 1956).

[13] Examples of this approach are: Howard Becker and Harry E. Barnes, *Social Thought from Lore to Science*, rev. ed. (New York: Dover, 1966), III, and Raymond Aron, *German Sociology*, tr. Mary and Thomas Bottomore (New York: Free Press, 1964).

[14] See Don Martindale, *The Nature and Types of Sociological Theory* (Boston: Houghton Mifflin, 1960).

group differs from another group on conceptual grounds. Taking this approach is especially appropriate if a comparison of the possible value or usefulness of theories is desired, as it shows clearly what we can expect from a given group of theories. However, there is a danger in classifying theories according to main concepts and ideas which ought to be pointed out, since it is the cause of much confusion. When theories are classified according to the similarities of their main ideas, concepts, predictions, and types of explanation, there is a temptation to see all of the theories in one group as being the same. They are not the same, but the fact that certain similar aspects of them have been emphasized, partly to satisfy the categorical approach, gives this impression. This often leads to the belief that there is one theory corresponding to the name of the category in which several theories are placed.

The most obvious example of this mistake is that of 'conflict theory'. In more than one text now in use, several theories are grouped together because of the fact that they all have something to say about social conflict. But when the differences among the theories are blurred, the result is the impression that the theories are similar in essentials. For example, Marx's ideas concerning modal social relations among classes in capitalist society are sometimes found grouped with ideas of Darwin and of those who used Darwin's ideas of natural selection to argue a basic conflict model of society. But we almost never see Marx's ideas grouped with those of Simmel, who also had a considerable amount to say on the subject of conflict. Similarly, Adam Smith's rationalist theory could be considered a conflict theory just as well as it could be considered a theory based on the variety and interdependence of human needs. The classification of Smith with Marx would emphasize certain things, while classifying Smith separately would emphasize others.

It is important to appreciate that the study of theory is the study of ideas, related in such a way that they are suggestive of explanations, models, and hypotheses, and that the classification of these ideas is merely for convenience. In other words, names of classifications of theory are not names of theories.

One more way of classifying theory which has something to recommend it has been proposed rather recently. This scheme emphasizes that, to have a theory of something, the thing must first be precisely defined, and then it can be accounted for. This attention to definition absorbs much sociological theory. The upshot of this is the proposal to group theories together which take a similar approach to the definition of 'the social' and then examine these categories to discover how the theories in them explain 'the social'. Theories that define and explain in similar ways are placed together for convenience; those that have substantial differences are placed apart.[15]

15 Walter L. Wallace, *Sociological Theory: An Introduction* (Chicago: Aldine, 1969).

It will probably be true that no scheme of classification of theories will provide categories into which a single theoretician's work will fit in its entirety. This is because the categories are often rigidly consistent with respect to a few criteria, while a theorist, working over a lifetime, may have developed a variety of ideas and worked them all into his scheme. That is, a theorist's early work concerning some explanation may belong in a different category from his later work on the same issue or problem. This resistance to categorization leads to the last method of organizing the study of social theory, which is really no scheme at all. It is to study the work of men who have made substantial contributions to sociological theory, and try to become so familiar with their efforts that the knowledge of several of them provides sufficient background for us to say we know something about sociological theory in its entirety.

IV. *The objectives of theory*

Why theorize? Is there an alternative to theorizing? These are reasonable questions to ask, especially if one is at first uncomfortable with theory and wants to get on as quickly as possible to 'the facts'. But the truth is, we do theorize whether or not we realize it, and we do interpret facts in the light of thoughtways that give facts their meaning. Sociological theory in the formal sense, with which we are here concerned, is simply a more thorough, more careful, and better understood form of theorizing than the naïve theory we all employ in everyday life.

Most people already know a lot of sociological theory, and the key terms of sociological theory often turn up in daily language. Let us see how one common term is in fact a key word for social theorists. One often hears people speak theoretically about 'role', as in 'the role of women today'. What may or may not be understood when this term is used, however, is that role is a key concept in several sociological theories. Used in its functionalist theory[16] sense, the idea connotes a set of rights and duties accepted by a role player. The player believes in the legitimacy of these rights and duties as defined and sanctioned by the system in which the role is found. The idea of role in this context is given meaning by the webs of rights and duties. These collectively constitute a system that can be thought of as accomplishing something, having systematic effects, or functioning (hence the term 'functionalist theory'). Thus, 'the role of women' really connotes not only something about women, but something by implication about the various roles of men and all the other roles with which someone playing the role of woman might come into contact. These interconnected roles are viewed in functionalist theory as constituting natural clusters making up functioning groups. Thus the family is

---

[16] Of course, every functionalist is a bit different in emphasis and style. The exact meaning of 'functionalism' is not settled. Sometimes the term 'structural functionalism' is used in the way 'functionalism' is in this example.

viewed as a set of legitimate relationships among two or more complementary roles concerned with the functions of family life, e.g. mutually supporting and caring for persons of special relatedness, legally procreating, raising and training children.

Additionally, the term 'role' is often used in everyday language in quite another sense. If someone says he is 'playing the role', meaning he believes he is doing what the other expects of him while he himself might not view this behavior as actually appropriate to him, he is emphasizing the 'self-presentation' or 'impression management' meaning of the term 'role', theoretically speaking.[17] This approach emphasizes the 'self' as a conscious entity which uses symbols to convey meanings and impressions to others who, in turn, do the same. The term 'role' is used here as analogous to the behavior at the front of a stage on which the presentation is made, while the 'other' is the audience. Behind the stage are found all the production facilities that make it possible for the stage-front action to proceed. Social organization, in this way of thinking, has not so much to do with the functional interdependence of roles in some system as it does with a kind of 'negotiated order' in which each actor is working out his part as he goes along.

Clearly, in these two examples the actual meaning of the term 'role' is intuited by the innocent user according to the idea he wishes to convey. It is the job of sociological theory not only to point out the different meanings, but in addition to point out what other concepts and processes are implied when one uses a sociological term or idea. Theory study emphasizes that it is in a conceptual and logical context that a term like 'role' gains its initial meaning. Sometimes these contexts are enormously complicated, but enormously interesting and rich. They open up many avenues for exploration and thought as well as criticism and reasoning. In one way, this is what theorizing is for.

There is really no alternative to theorizing. If we did away with it, we would be left with a chaotic mass of data and impressions which would only cry out for ordering and interpretation. But how would we order it? If we had no idea of the possible orders available, or no notion of how to start, we would really be powerless to give the raw material meaning. For the ways in which facts and impressions gain meaning (and therefore sometimes imply the need for action) are precisely the methods by which they are recognized as having relationships to other ideas and concepts of process. Finding relationships among facts brings them into some coherent conceptual order. The construction and analysis of these orders, usually with considerable attention to the ways in which these conceptual orders 'fit' the facts, is the process of theorizing.

Putting it more formally now, theory introduces theoretical order into a

17 See Erving Goffman, *The Presentation of Self in Everyday Life* (New York: Doubleday, 1959).

situation for the purpose of explaining something, or a range of things, to which the theory is relevant. The theoretical order it introduces is the order which relates the concepts in the theory together. In the example of the use of 'role', a theoretical order related concepts like 'role', 'system', 'function', 'legitimate', 'rights', 'duties', and so on, together. This conceptual order is actually the 'sense' made by a given arrangement of these terms, and their connected definitions. Defined differently, and placed in a different context, they would make a different kind of sense. Used in addition to other concepts which emphasize some other aspects of the social world, still another kind of sense would result – a different kind of theoretical order, but an order nonetheless.

When these conceptual orders are grasped, it is possible to put them to work explaining. A description of some of the different modes of the term 'explanation' will have to wait until the chapter on the structure of theories, but it can be said at once that to explain is the main goal of sociological theory. In essence, this explaining consists in relating somehow a conceptual problem or set of observations to a theoretical construction of reality which fits it. If no theoretical scheme is available that seems to do this reasonably well, the desire to have the problem explained satisfactorily is really the desire to set things in order by inventing some scheme of ideas which gives a convincing definition and understanding of the problem at hand. This is theorizing. If some scheme does seem to fit the facts or problem, then the act of demonstrating this by logical analysis, or by showing that the theoretical order is a good analogy to the real order, is 'explaining' the situation in theoretical terms. In both cases – relating existing conditions to existing theory, and constructing or modifying theory to fit the conditions – the objective is the same: to explain. Explanation is the main objective of sociological theory.

But the utility of sociological theory does not stop at explanation. It is possible that, knowing theory, one might be able to predict something about the future. Prediction is entirely a matter of theory since, strictly speaking, there can be no empirical data on the future – it hasn't happened yet. But what will or might happen can often be foretold with reasonable accuracy by consulting theoretical studies. These can furnish ideas and suggestions of processes assumed to be as valid for explaining the future as they are for explaining the present. Realistically, prediction is what would happen if the theoretical basis for prediction were entirely adequate. There is considerable controversy as to the validity of the claim that prediction in the social sciences is possible, and more will be said on this in later chapters; but the fact is that attempts to predict and to control behavior are being made now. As government and business become increasingly committed to long-range social planning, community development, economic management, and so on, they are at the same time relying on the ability of social scientists to manipulate models and theories so as to suggest the results to be expected from the expenditure of millions of dollars on given efforts. This is not idle ivory-tower prediction, and we ought to be keenly aware that such social prediction has its basis in sociological theory and explanation.

In addition to noticing the challenge and prospects of theoretical work in sociology, we ought to make a realistic appraisal of the state of development now achieved, and come to some conclusion about possible development in theory in the near future. Sociological theory is in a constant state of change and reformulation. But this does not mean that, at some point in time, a theory will necessarily be arrived at which explains everything, and then all additional development and interpretation will stop. As new problems arise and new needs press, theoretical interpretations of the social process will be altered. Facts and ideas which seemed satisfactorily accounted for will suddenly become a problem again, as new emphases are required or new arguments arise. Thus theoretical work not only develops toward more subtle and accurate formulations as time passes; it also reshapes itself as it goes.

KEY CONCEPTS

theory	theoretical order
hypothesis	explain
model	predict
law	analogy

TOPICS FOR DISCUSSION

1   If an hypothesis does not actually describe observed reality, what is the implication for the related theory?

2   The same theoretical terms can have different meanings, depending upon the theories in which the terms are found. Discuss.

3   Is there one 'conflict' theory? Why or why not?

4   What is the possible benefit of theoretical ambiguity?

5   What differentiates guesses, hypotheses, and laws?

6   What are the strengths and weaknesses of the various ways of classifying theories?

7   What would life be like if no one theorized?

8   What theoretical ideas and kinds of assumptions would you say are implied by everyday terms like 'instinct', 'conditioning', 'free will', 'system'?

9   What is an explanation?

10   How is it that a 'theoretical problem' can be 'solved' and the related practical problem remain unsolved?

ESSAY QUESTIONS

Describe how an idea like 'human nature' really depends on theoretical thinking, models, and concepts.

Examine the ethical questions involved in using social science to predict or control social events.

FOR FURTHER READING AND STUDY

Aron, Raymond. *German Sociology.* Tr. Mary and Thomas Bottomore. New York: Free Press, 1964.

Banton, Michael. *Roles: An Introduction to the Study of Social Relations.* London: Tavistock, 1965.

Braybrooke, David. *Philosophical Problems of the Social Sciences.* New York: Macmillan, 1965.

Goffman, Erving. *The Presentation of Self in Everyday Life.* New York: Doubleday, 1959.

Hofstadter, Richard. *Social Darwinism in American Thought.* Boston: Beacon Press, 1944.

Kaplan, Abraham. *The Conduct of Inquiry.* San Francisco: Chandler Publishing Co., 1964.

MacIver, Robert M. *Social Causation.* New York: Harper and Row, 1964.

Nettler, Gwynn. *Explanations.* New York: McGraw-Hill, 1970.

Ryan, Alan. *The Philosophy of the Social Sciences.* London: Macmillan, 1970.

Wallace, Walter L. *Sociological Theory: An Introduction.* Chicago: Aldine, 1969.

2   Key theoretical problems

The main goal of theory is to explain. But what is to be explained? It is not enough simply to assume that since this book is about sociological theory, something sociological will be explained. This chapter examines some issues connected with the question of what is to be explained about society and how to do it, as well as taking note of some of the problems involved.

The issues to be discussed in this chapter are listed below. In each case, the way an individual theorist resolves these problems has a lot to do with the form and content of the theory he eventually builds. The issues are:

1   The problem of how to conceptualize social order and the related concept, social change. Whether or not different theories are needed to cover these two major ideas is discussed.

2   The problem of how properly to conceptualize the subject matter of a sociological theory. This is the polarity between the objective and subjective approaches.

3   The problem of the proper focus of sociological theory. Here the question is, how does the idea of the individual fit into the web of ideas called sociological theory?

4   The problem of how to understand cause. The section on function and cause discusses some of the variety of things we might mean by the term 'cause' and the special meaning of that word usually associated with the concept of function. In this section the question of how to apply the scientific idea of cause and effect in sociological theory is discussed.

5   The problem of values. Here are considered how, and to what extent, the theorist's values ought to shape his conclusions, and whether or not he ought to try to keep his values from influencing him. This problem currently goes under the name of the 'value-freedom problem'.

6   The metaphysical problem of the repeatability of human events. Here the question of whether or not there is sufficient similarity between human actions to make theorizing possible is introduced.

The related problem of uniqueness of social events in this context is considered.

I. *Order and change*

A. *Order*

The main problem for all sociological theories, and the main objective of theorizing in sociology at all times, is to explain social *order*. It is important that this be appreciated, since confusion about the general objective of all theory is usually at the root of specific confusions about specific theories.

The idea of social order, therefore, because of its central place in theoretical work in sociology, should be examined more closely. Theorists do not use the term in the sense of 'law and order', where order is conceived to be more or less identical with repression or conflict. Nor is 'order' meant to denote authoritarian order, such as rules barked by a drill sergeant, which are followed because of some strict penalty system. 'Order', in the sociological sense, refers to any patterned action, or any regularity displayed in people's behavior. In this usage, social order is analogous to the order described by the periodic table of the elements in chemistry, or the observation that water runs downhill: some things behave in similar ways, patterned ways, which in principle might be either simple or complex, in given situations. The main business of sociological theory is to conceptualize the circumstances in which certain orders result, and to discern the reasons why these circumstances are associated with these orders.

We must be careful not to speak of social order in a narrow and restricted sense, however. Order may be quite abstract, rather than observable. It may appear at one level of analysis and disappear at another. It may pertain to a given subunit of a population or sample and not another. The idea of order in sociological work may be founded directly on some experience of ordered things, but when order is used as a general idea it means the patterned events that may be explained regardless of whether or not observations suggest order to the naïve observer.

Thus the idea of order itself is abstract, and covers much more ground than simply the instances of ordered things we discover about human behavior. Sociological theory, at the same time as it is trying to give reasonable accounts of given concrete instances of sociological fact, is always developing in the direction of a general statement on the causes and consequences of social order. This is because it is developing explanations of the principle causes of order itself, and not just explaining instances of it. Theories tend to become general statements on the nature of social order, and they tend to expand. We noticed in Chapter 1 that theories might subsume other theoretical problems and explanations as they expand. The principle on which this expansion is based is the explanation of social order as a general idea.

What kind of order is there in society? This is a reasonable question, and one with several answers, since differing points of view exist on the issue. Society may exhibit many fairly obvious kinds of order. For example, birth rate, which has important consequences for social planning, economic speculation, and so forth, can be seen to vary with given influences. It is notable that the birth rate in most Western countries has been steadily dropping for the past ten years or longer. The reasons for this are varied, and have different force in different places, but the main idea at present is that the rate, calculated by dividing the number of live births per year by one-thousandth of the population, constitutes an example of order. How is this fact pertinent to the idea of order? In the first place, one might want to try to see why in certain countries the birth rate is fairly high, while it is rather low in other countries. Without regard to changes in birth rate, that is, taking the rates as stable for the moment and comparing them, how could such variation be accounted for? One answer is that some aspect of the belief system might be an influence. Persons believing it is virtuous to have children may have them more often than those not believing this. Another explanation might be that the type of economy dictates it – much land to cultivate requires many sons.

The point here is to show that when a given order, birth rate regularities, is explained, the explanation goes beyond the simple account of the order itself, by suggesting that the things which cause this order may themselves be ordered. For example, there may be some general relationship between type of economy and land use patterns, on the one hand, and birth rate on the other. This speculation suggests the possibility not only that birth rate exhibits order, but that the influences on it also are ordered in some way, and furthermore that there is something ordered and regular about the relationship of these two facts. Perhaps the relationship between land use and birth rate follows some pattern. Suppose the influence of a given kind of land use on birth rate, other things being equal, is always the same or similar. This similarity of effect (given similar circumstances) is not observed directly, but abstractly grasped, since what we actually observe are instances of birth rate, and what we are talking about is a principle which relates all birth rates to given causes. We have moved one step away from explaining our particular problem and one step toward the 'general level' on which all finished theory exists.

But what of the fact that in the Western countries, generally speaking, the birth rate is dropping? Is this contradictory to the speculative theory relating birth rate and land use that we have been considering? In other words, in addition to noting order in birth rates, and their ordered relationships to characteristic patterns of land use, we are now introducing order in the form of a trend: something is causing the birth rates to go from previously higher levels to new lower ones. How is this accounted for?

It might be explained by considering whether or not the causes of the previously high birth rate are collapsing, and if they are, whether or not these are being replaced by something that would result in a new, lower birth rate. In the example, the patterns of land use were hypothetically connected to birth rate to explain its being high ('much land to cultivate requires many sons'). But if this pattern of land use is itself changing, perhaps into one in which extensive mechanized agriculture is more important, and if the movement of sons from the land to the towns becomes more prevalent, would we not expect birth rates to drop? Could we not reasonably relate the changes of given birth rates and the rates themselves to some third trend or force, which might be called industrialization or mechanization or urbanization?

Of course there is more to social order than birth rates or other kinds of demographic facts and figures. Consider, for example, the concept 'authority' and how authority might exhibit order. Max Weber, in an important work on the nature of social and economic order, suggested that there were characteristic types of authority.[1] These types he related to the different types of reasons people had for following rules made by authorities. For example, *zweckrational* authority is that arising out of situations in which persons accept the authority of others because their acceptance brings some rationally sought benefit to themselves. This is the sort of authority we let our doctors have over us in matters of health. It is usually strictly limited to aspects of the relationship directly relevant to the objectives of those involved, and does not spill over into other areas. But 'traditional' authority, on the other hand, is much different. We may accept the traditional authority of a chief or elder because either it has 'always' been right to do so, or we can conceive of no reason not to do as has 'always' been done. Characteristically, authority of this type is far more wide-ranging, and covers more of the activities of those accepting it. It would be easy to relate such types of authority to types of social situations and to social needs for efficiency or production, and thus to predict that rational coordination (*zweckrational* authority) would come to characterize a society with extreme division of labor, and that societies with less of this might remain more traditional in authority patterns. Actually, Weber did something like this in his famous work on bureaucracy.[2]

[1] Max Weber, *The Theory of Social and Economic Organization,* tr. Talcott Parsons (New York: Free Press, 1964), Ch. 1.
[2] *Ibid.* Ch. 3, Part 1.

In the example using birth rates, we had something to count as our basic datum (births), but in the example from literature on authority we have nothing so easy before us. Authority is an abstract quality that has to do with a relationship in which one person gives directives and another takes them. And except in cases of compulsion, he who takes instruction from authority does it with some degree of willingness. Thus, abstractions concerning social relations such as authority are just as potentially ordered, and just as important in sociological theory, as things we can more easily see and measure. Most of the social order that sociology is concerned about is of an abstract kind, and must be understood in abstract terms. Most of the operative ideas surrounding things like authority, role, social structure, culture, and so on are not visible directly, and they thus must be inferred and understood as ideas concerning the concrete order that we do observe.

Let us have an example to show this. In the previous chapter we used an idea of the 'role of women' to show that the concept 'role', which most people know well, was in reality a theoretical term. Now let us show that it is also an entirely abstract term. Recall that the idea of role involves, in the example about married women, a consideration of what may be called the duties of the role and the rights associated with it. Also recall that the idea of role implied the existence of other roles which had some bearing on that of women. What one woman could consider duties, someone else could consider rights, and what were the rights of one woman were the obligations, duties, of someone else. The relationship between these compatible sets of rights and duties is the important meaning of the term 'role'. But how to observe a relationship? What one observes is behavior. We do not see the relationship composed of rights and duties; we see only what we can use as data from which to infer the relationship. We see concrete behavior which we may take as evidence – but we do not see the relationship as if it were itself observable.

Most of what sociological theorists propose as the causes and consequences of social order have this abstract character, and therefore the subject matter of sociology itself is abstract. This is not radically different from the situation in other disciplines which make use of theory, but it is often harder to grasp in sociology, where because we are so used to social relations, we tend to think about them as more concrete than they are and to look in vain for concreteness in things which are by nature abstract. Thus we have an order to account for – usually an abstract one.

B. *Change*

It is important to distinguish between change and chaos. The term *change* applied to social arrangements means some kind of alteration in patterns of social relations. If there were no patterns at all, there would be no change, but chaos instead. Thus it is true to say that change is a kind of order, and it was with this in mind that the example of decreasing birth rates was given as an example of order. Order of one kind was responsible for birth rates being at a certain level, and a different kind of order seemed to account for birth rates shifting to a new level.

All this is another way of saying that any sociological theory is capable of accounting for change if it is capable of accounting for order. This is not universally recognized. Some argue that separate theories for order and change are needed. The point being put forward here, however, is that any theory which accounts for order in social relations does so by pointing out the forces making things 'ordered'. Order, or social stability, is taken as something remarkable, a kind of dependent variable. The question in the mind of the theorist accounting for order is, 'Why should this aspect of social relations be patterned in this way, and not chaotic, or not in all the other ways that it might be patterned?' Now, when he has satisfactorily answered this question, he has built up a set of concepts and ideas about social relations which account for things as they are, to the best of his ability. But notice that the theorist has also built up a set of concepts and ideas which can account for change, in exactly parallel terms. This is so because, according to his analysis, order is obtained because of a certain relationship of social elements; in the absence of some of these, or if one or more of them is altered, the theorist must predict social change as the result. Moreover, this would also be the case if a thinker started from the viewpoint of trying to explain social change. If he did, in fact, explain change by citing basic processes and facts of social life, we would be faced with exactly the above problem, but in reverse: every appearance of stability would be a special problem, to be accounted for only by the adaptation of his change theory.

For example, an old and important branch of sociological theory explains social order in terms of shared values. Thus it puts particular emphasis on the centrality of certain broad values, and considers the moral acceptance of these a key factor in shaping society. This explanation in the simplest terms says that when there is substantial consensus on values among the members of a society, there results a moral order. The order is explained in terms of the consensus on values. Now, this kind of thinking can just as easily explain change, by resorting to the same key term: value consensus. By suggesting that imperfect consensus, or a failure of consensus, exists in certain situations, the main explanation of order is removed and the theorist must expect change instead.

The same argument can be demonstrated in yet another case. Suppose that a certain theory posited change as the major fact of all society, and that it located the reason for this in a continuing struggle among the oppressed to become 'free'. This theory would immediately be faced with the fact that all are not presently 'free' in the sense meant by the theory, and the next step would have to be the proposition of a reason why. Clearly, this theory would need to identify a series of constraints which prevented freedom, thus bringing in a form of 'anti-change agent'. However unexpected this might be, such a theory would eventually do it; it would have to give a theoretical account which included the idea of order, even though the theory emphasized change initially.

Now, it is true that sociological theories meet with different degrees of success in explaining order or change, in both the empirical sense and the logical sense. Some theories are quite limited in the kinds of things they can explain, while others are broader. Some theories seem to work with a minimum of logical complications, others with more. In the context of a discussion of order and change, it should be noted that the logical status of the theory and its empirical coverage are not affected when it is altered from an explanation of order to an explanation of change. For example, if the concept of 'equilibrium' is not an operational concept (one which can be detected and measured) in the service of theories of stability, neither is the concept of 'disequilibrium' in theories aimed mainly at explaining social change. The logical and empirical status of both is just the same.

We can now better understand the considerable controversy in sociological work today concerning the problem of how theory ought to explain order and change. Some of the controversy could be resolved if it were fully recognized that theories conceptualize processes and account for them mentally. (Note that this does not contradict the notion that theories produce hypotheses and suggest social action.) There is misplaced concreteness in theoretical discussions, as in cases where one proponent wishes to argue that the basis of social life is order, while another argues it is change. It should be emphasized that these concepts are just that, concepts, and as such are capable of rendering something more or less understandable depending on how they are accounted for. In this connection, we might remember the argument between the professors. One said that man's nature was to make war, because he made so many. But the other professor insisted that man's nature must be to make peace, since man did this every time he had a war.

II. *Subjective and objective*

The subjective–objective dichotomy is very old, going back in the history of thought far beyond the foundation of sociology. It is still with us. In basic outline, this dichotomy suggests that there are two fundamentally opposite ways to theoretically treat man and his social organization. One is the *objective* way. This views man and human society as basically similar to other aspects of the physical world. By doing so, it suggests that even though man may be complex and intricate, in principle his actions ought to be explained in the same fashion as any other aspect of the natural world. Defining human behavior entirely objectively leads to two sets of concepts, one set defining social relations in objective terms and the other set giving the explanation of these relations in terms of objective forces. It is this kind of objective thinking that leads some psychologists to conceptualize all human behavior in terms of some physical process (for example, stimulus and response), and to suggest that this conceptualization, if rigorously applied, could explain all human activity, including creation of social organization and culture.

The objective viewpoint can also be taken in a slightly less 'scientific' sense, but the kernel of meaning is the same. When someone suggests that objective forces outside the control of individuals are at work, he is suggesting the reality of these forces, but he may or may not be saying in addition that these forces are properly conceptualized as aspects of the physical environment. For example, we might take the existence of social classes as an objective fact; the class system may be concretely real enough, but it is probably not possible to explain its existence in purely scientific objective terms.

There is good reason to seek objective terms in which to conceptualize human behavior. Objective things are things which in principle can be measured, counted, observed, and correlated according to their behaviors. This is an advantage to a social scientist who wishes to make the strongest possible empirical case for his theories, and to use observable facts to do it. There is also a formidable argument that there is no alternative to the objective approach. We know nothing about people's behaviors that we do not learn by treating them as objects of our senses. There is a cliché that 'talk is cheap'. The confirmed objectivist classifies any non-objective contention about behavior as 'mere talk', and pays little attention to it.

For example, some would argue that a considerable amount of what people do is dependent on their states of mind or on their attitudes. But do these things exist? Is there 'mind'? If so, what is it and where? What does the 'mind' do that cannot eventually be understood entirely in terms of objective physiology and chemistry? Even though at present we do not have an explanation of 'mind' entirely in these terms, the objectivist will point to examples of research on animals which indicates that the 'emotions' might be controlled and explained by electrical impulses in the physical brain. He will point to the advances in genetic research which suggest it is possible to produce animals and people having definite predictable traits, once thought of as matters of upbringing.

What of the concept of 'attitude'? Is attitude more than a convenient fiction, a word for the 'stuff' which seems to be in the mind? There have been many clever attempts to objectify the concept 'attitude' and to measure it. But these attempts have met with only mixed success. For instance, we do not always act the way our attitudes suggest we 'ought' to act. Does this mean that a theory of human behavior based on attitudes is based on a fiction?

Questions like these have led many to abandon research into the 'mental' or subjective aspects of human behavior and to concentrate on the objective aspects of action. But a problem soon arises if this is done. Exactly what is entirely objective about human behavior? The no-nonsense answer is that there is very little of human behavior that makes much sense when considered entirely from the objectivist perspective. We might consider population and migration studies to be an exception to this, as long as all we wish to know about these things is what people do, and not why they do it. For example, we can take census data and immigration data and draw up statistical pictures of age distributions, sex and occupation distributions, and the movement of people from place to place. But such things are only descriptive. When we start to ask the theoretical question, 'Why are these objective things the way they are and not otherwise?' the objective perspective does not carry us very far. For as soon as an answer to one of these questions comes in terms of will, choice, belief, value, and so on, we are out of the realm of purely objective things and face to face with the problem of trying to understand these human motives and forces in objective terms.

Thus it is that the *subjectivist* position gains its strength. It argues that, fundamentally, social behavior must be understood in human terms, and that it is fruitless to begin with knowledge about humanity and, in effect, try to explain away this humanity in objective terms. A subjectivist might start with a concept of the will as his basic data, as Tönnies did,[3] and develop a theory of types of social organization based directly on these types of will. Or, following Weber, we might wish to understand types of social organization by considering the characteristic reasons why people tend to follow behavioral rules or, in his terms, the types and kinds of legitimacy present in specific kinds of social arrangements, and the reasons why people find these acceptable.

To some, it sounds almost subversive to suggest that there is anything wrong with the subjective view. Naturally, persons studying human organization want to understand it in terms that seem uniquely applicable to humanity. But as the objectivist would argue, there is in principle no way of verifying the propositions made about human society and man in subjective terms. Verification depends on the outward demonstration that something is true, and the very essence of subjectivism is that it is the conceptualization of inner experience, which is capable of being described to others, but never demonstrated. Often, subjectivist theory

---

[3] Ferdinand Tönnies, *Community and Society*, tr. Charles P. Loomis (New York: Harper and Row, 1963).

tends to take an 'ideal type' character, and the theories themselves must be taken as conditional statements: that is, we must say, to the extent that people experience their world in subjective terms such as those in theory, certain results are expected. Consider Weber's idea of bureaucracy as an example. Weber's interest was to understand bureaucracy as a form of social order and to show why it was growing in importance. He found bureaucracies had several characteristics which tended also to define them as bureaucracies. He built up an ideal type (a mental construction) characterizing bureaucracy according to these main features.[4] He then explained the behaviors of particular persons and of organizations as though their views and motives fitted those of his ideal type. Now then, to apply this in research, one would have to argue that a specific example of social organization fits the ideal type. To the extent that it fits, Weber's conclusions using the ideal type would be appropriate to the specific case. Note that we did not try to verify the ideal type, that is, we did not verify the theory. Instead, we used it as a guide to discover something real in a particular case. The ideal type, based on subjective criteria developed through description, was not verifiable, but only useful. And the usefulness of it was not in its 'rightness' or 'wrongness' but in Weber's ability to describe his experience in a meaningful way to us.[5]

All sociological theoretical work must take account of the subjective–objective polarity. We cannot get around it, and if we take a stand on one side of it or the other, we are bound to be open to criticism from the opposite side. Probably the best plan in this case is to be conversant with the reasoning on both sides and be able to use whichever kind of theoretical attitude seems appropriate. But a final word about consistency is now relevant. If we slip from one side to the other of the subjective–objective polarity in an effort to 'explain everything', we will eventually find that the mixture of concepts and procedures developed as a 'theory' will be muddled, and more confusing then enlightening. It is better to settle for a clear explanation of some of the truth than a confused account of more of it.

III. *The place of the individual in sociological theory*

Sometimes a loose definition of sociology contains elements that we might call 'individual' as well as some 'sociological' ones. But precisely what is the domain of sociological theory? Is social theory to confine itself to society *per se*, or is the individual the focus of interest, or per-

[4] Max Weber, *Max Weber on the Methodology of the Social Sciences,* tr. Edward Shils and Henry Finch (New York: Free Press, 1949), Ch. 2.
[5] Weber, *Theory of Social and Economic Organization*, Ch. 3, Part 1.

haps is some combination of these two the proper arena? In fact, historically speaking, the great thinkers of social philosophy and social theory
have very often made questions like these the center of their work. It is
not as easy as it might appear to have a theory which adequately and
convincingly treats both society and the individual. It will become
obvious in later chapters that, depending on which we emphasize, or how
we combine the two, we come out with quite different social theories.

Of course the goal should be to develop an acceptable theory which handles the individual and society equally well. But the problem is that
usually theoretical attempts along this line have explained one in terms
of the other. This might be done simply or subtly, but the problem
remains. For example, the belief is not unheard of that society controls,
shapes, and directs the individual. In extreme form, this argument leads
to the conclusion that virtually whatever society wishes to make of us, it
can. And furthermore, that the individual has no power of resistance to
society. Thus, schooling is sometimes criticized by the allegation that it
'conditions' individuals, meaning that the experience of school (which
represents society in the larger sense) forms students so completely that
they evidently are thought to have no ability or judgments outside those
which were given them at school. Therefore they must not be held
responsible for their behavior.

It would seem that there is a substantial amount of truth in this social-
determinist argument. Certainly young people experience, in the process
of maturing, very considerable social formation. In a sense, the society
forms, molds, and shapes attitudes, behaviors, morality, and so on. Also,
it is easy to see that this process continues throughout life, for 'fitting in'
is often the prime requisite for a rewarding and comfortable social life,
and the main agent of this fitting-in process is society.

But can we say, because of this, that society has all power of constraint
and formation over the individual? Are we not insulting the intelligence,
ability, and judgment of individuals when we say that individuality consists basically of doing what we are told by society? If we take this objec-
tion seriously, we see that it implies the negation of most of the previous
argument, for if individuality consists of abilities, reason, judgment, and
character not entirely attributable to society, then we have demoted
society from its previous theoretical position of omnipotence over individuality.

We might wish to go further in this vein, arguing that, indeed, the whole
idea of society is just a fiction. Instead, there are only individuals, people
of uniqueness and character who find it necessary for a variety of reasons
to get along together. The getting along accounts for society, but the
operative force is really individuality. Theoretically speaking, whatever
we may wish to explain on the level of society can be explained by
making reference to the quality, character, or activities of indivduals.

This is an appealing position, for every person likes to feel this is true in his daily life; he wills his own actions and reasons out his attitudes.

But now all that we thought before about socialization and the shaping force of society comes back to haunt. If we have taken a very individualistic viewpoint, how can we adequately explain the 'facts' about society which previously seemed true? These include the force of society itself in the lives of individuals – how society forms, controls, and molds. If we have trouble accounting for the influence of society's dictates, as we surely will, then we might feel the need for an intermediate position on the society–individual polarity.

Actually, it is overly simple to conceive of this distinction as a polarity. It does not, in fact, present a continuum on which we might be able to find the 'right spot', combining features of individualism and sociologism⁶ in just the right proportions. Remember what was said above concerning consistency; mixing incompatible ideas will lead to a conceptual muddle. So it is here. Taken literally, the idea of the individual as the main operative force in sociological theory tends to destroy the reality of the concept 'society', and vice versa. This is so because, from either point of view, there is an implicit explanation of both society and the individual, but taken together these explanations are not compatible. No amount of mixing of terms which imply each other's negation will produce an acceptable theory containing adequate accounts of such terms.

Keeping in mind the difficulty caused by 'individuality versus society' in sociological theory, some additional points concerning concepts and method should now be made. We often speak in terms of 'levels' of analysis in sociological theory. Usually, this term means the individual, the society, or some intermediate position, such as primary groups or institutions. Depending on the level, some aspect of the society–individual problem is probably being emphasized. Usually this means that some other aspect of this problem is being ignored. Thus, we might wish to know the 'functional prerequisites' of society, i.e. what things must social organization accomplish for society to exist? This is a macro-sociology question, or one at the level of society. In other words, the question pertains primarily to the society, and while all kinds of questions about individuality come into this, they are in effect being set aside. Similarly, ideas about face-to-face interactions in specific situations usually take almost no account of society as such. 'The situation' may be relevant, as may some aspects of the history of individuals participating, but this discussion is mainly at the level of the individual. Thus, sociologists slide up and down a scale of levels, depending on what they wish to emphasize and explain. The advantage of doing this is that the specific nature of the

⁶ This is a term sometimes used to designate the point of view emphasizing collective factors in the explanation of individual acts.

problem at hand can be made fairly clear; the disadvantage is that implications of what is said at one level may lead to absurdities at another.

We can bring together aspects of the individuality–society problem with the objective–subjective problem to show another difficulty facing sociological theory. Plainly put, the problem is how do we observe, measure, or count anything uniquely pertaining to society without reducing this to individuals? If we wish to determine something at the level of society we ought to focus our methodology there. But we have seen that society is something which defies direct observation at its own level. We can only infer things about society from the behavior of individuals, even though we may not believe that the behavior of individuals as units explains everything. This methodological individualism which is forced upon us makes us adopt a subjectivist position about society – one which we may or may not wish to adopt. If society is considered an objective reality, in principle as real as anything else in the natural world, yet is not directly observable (it can only be inferred from the behaviors of individuals in it), the necessity to infer a knowledge of society leads away from objectivism toward subjectivism. Society is in our experience only as an inference, not as an observation – so it asks to be considered subjectively. On methodological grounds we cannot be strict objectivists where society is concerned, even if we may have good reason to be objectivists on theoretical grounds.

This problem can become a wedge driven between types of sociological theory, and the resultant gap is bridged only occasionally. One side, emphasizing methodological concerns, has tended to de-emphasize the objective nature of things which are not directly observable; hence it has tended to settle on the individualistic side of the individual–society question. The other side, less concerned about methodology of the purely objective kind, has tended to be more impressed with the substance of society, and hence has taken the society side of the polarity. As one might expect, each side has tended to develop unique explanations of that which it has not initially emphasized. Thus those on the individualistic side may be seen to be using concepts like 'psychological reduction' of society to individualistic terms, or 'individual interests' as mutually compatible or shared forms of individuality, on which to base explanations of stable patterns of social behavior. Those emphasizing society as a reality of its own have often had severe problems with empirical methods. Thus they have tended to use concepts heavily dependent on imagining ideal types, which can be supported by subjective insight, as Weber suggested.

IV. *Function and cause*

The words 'function' and 'cause' are very troublesome ones in sociological theory. This is so in part because they are often confused with each other, so that when one person says 'function', a listener may somehow hear 'cause', and vice versa. A variety of learned essays and books have been written to elucidate what we mean when we use these two words, and the arguments in them run the gamut of plausibility. One is that cause does not exist except in the minds of those who believe they see causes in action.[7] Another says that whatever the problems with conceptualizing and verifying cause, we still cannot seem to do without the idea of causation; hence the term has gone underground, but the basic idea remains.[8] Some descriptions of sociological methodology use the idea of cause openly, arguing that there are ways of inferring cause from statistical procedures.[9] Concerning function, it has been claimed that 'functional analysis' is really the only method in use in sociology and anthropology.[10] At the same time, some thinkers have tried to get rid of the whole idea of function by arguing that it is too rigid and implies a social system that is too structured to be realistic.[11]

What is the trouble with these words? Begin with *cause*. The common usage of the term is not very precise, even though some precision was introduced by Aristotle, who was interested in the term in its strictly logical sense.[12] He showed that 'cause' usually means one (or more, simultaneously) of these:

1 that for the sake of which – the purpose, or teleology;
2 that in which – assumptions, concepts or the logical context;
3 that by which – the technique of making something happen; methods;
4 that out of which – the material context; the stuff from which an effect springs.

If we claim the first type of cause we are saying, in effect, that the purpose for which something happens lies in the future, or that some end state of things is guiding the current reality. But usually what people seem to mean by cause has to do with the cause first and the effect later. The first kind of cause seems to be opposite to this cause-before-effect sequence, for the future state of things (purpose) somehow determines what happens in the present.

7 Bertrand Russell, 'On the Notion of Cause', in *Mysticism and Logic* (London: Allen and Unwin, 1963), pp. 132-51.
8 Robert M. MacIver, *Social Causation* (New York: Harper and Row, 1964), Part One.
9 Hubert M. Blalock, Jr., *Causal Interferences in Nonexperimental Research* (Chapel Hill, N.C.: University of North Carolina Press, 1964).
10 Kingsley Davis, 'The Myth of Functional Analysis as a Special Method in Sociology and Anthropology', *American Sociological Review*, xxiv, no. 6, pp. 757-71.
11 Daniel Foss, 'The World of Talcott Parsons', in Maurice R. Stein and Arthur Vidich, eds., *Society on Trial* (Englewood Cliffs, N.J.: Prentice-Hall, 1963), pp. 96-126.
12 Aristotle, *Organon: Analytica Posteriora*, Book 2, Ch. 11, in Richard McKeon, ed., *Basic Works of Aristotle* (New York: Random House, 1941), pp. 170ff.

The second type of cause has exclusively to do with the logical context and the logical necessity of drawing certain conclusions, given certain premises. For example, the sum of two and three must be five, and hence five in the example is 'caused' by the addition of two and three. Five is the result of the logic and assumptions involved in 'two', 'plus', and 'three'.

The third type of cause has to do with making something manifest itself, given that it is possible to do so. That is, if we ask, 'What were the causes of the French Revolution?' when we really mean, 'What were the techniques by which the changes in government in France in the revolutionary period were brought about?' we are thinking of cause in this sense.

Finally, the last type of cause is that about which we may want to know if we are interested in data first. It asks the question, 'How could this have been the case, given the actual circumstances at the time?' From the data, we seek to discover how the data did come to exist. Note that this usage more or less ignores the questions raised by the other kinds of cause.

It should be clear by now that when one seeks a sociological explanation of the cause of an event, he could have a varity of questions in mind. A theorist's choice out of this variety has a lot to do with where and how he seeks his causes, and how he constructs his theory or evaluates someone else's attempts. Does he pay particular attention to the logical structure of the theory, to the techniques and principles of its working, to the actual specific situation in which the theory is applicable, or does he look for a theory which will tend to explain in terms of a growing unity or evolving structure which seems to be heading in some direction?

Actually, as one would expect, some sociological theory has grown up around each of these understandings of the term 'cause'. Bypassing the first one for the moment, we have theories which have paid particular attention to finding cause in the structure of a logical argument. An exercise of this kind is: deducing the event from general statements, after forming these statements into propositions which, when manipulated properly, produce the event to be explained as a logical deduction. Formal attempts to write theory in this fashion have paid attention to the second of our meanings of cause. Similarly, there is theory devoted to understanding the techniques by which something happens. For example, theories of processes in race and ethnic relations which propose a series of stages or steps toward assimilation emphasize that an end result, assimilation, is 'caused' by a series of stages beginning in hostility.

Also, primarily inductive theories, ones which examine each material or social context for a plausible explanation of given events, make use of the fourth type of cause – the one which emphasizes the possibility or non-possibility of an event's occurring in a given context of material or social action.

Why has the first type of cause been omitted in this discussion? It is closely related to the idea of *function,* and the two will now be discussed together. 'Function' is a word which has a variety of meanings, but it is rather restricted in sociological work. Basically, 'function' denotes the dependence of one or more units on each other, so that each unit is maintained and so that the relationship between the units tends to remain relatively unchanged. The units in sociological theory are often called 'structures'. These can be roles, groups, institutions, or perhaps other units of analysis, as we will see in detail in Chapter 5, but in functionalism the idea is always to discover the relationships among units, and to see how these units, via their relationships, form some kind of system.[13]

The idea of cause enters the picture at this point. We may wish to ask why a given set of units (roles, institutions, or the like) have clustered together in the way they have and not otherwise. If we seek a functionalist explanation for this clustering, we are asking a question about the nature of the total cluster, and also about the functions of each unit in this cluster. This is perfectly proper to do, and it is legitimate to construct a functional theory around this question. It is this that Davis argues we all do in sociology and anthropology, although we may complicate the matter. If we answer the question about the nature of a cluster of functioning units by saying something to the effect that, in order to operate as a total cluster, some specific arrangement of units is required, then the question as to why they are so arranged has been answered causally by referring to the final state of the relations of the units. They are so clustered in order to enable the total to perform adequately to maintain the whole, that is, the end state is a cause of the ordering. But how could the units have known this in the process of forming up, except by some ability of the total system to get the message to them? This question is not satisfactorily answered within the confines of sociological theory, but some suggestions may be made via example. One popular solution to this kind of dilemma is to say that 'evolution' toward the most satisfactory state of organization is a natural process, and that it will work to determine which functional arrangement of social units persists. Another solution has been to posit some kind of rationality on the parts of the units making up the functional whole, along with the argument that this power of insight will cause men to arrange their affairs so that the whole can function in unity and harmony. Cultural arguments have been proposed, saying essentially that common values and beliefs will lead men in common situations to similar solutions, and that the result is a workable, functional whole. No matter which tack we take, for present purposes it is important to note the relationship of functional analysis to the concept of cause. If we try to explain how a functioning whole (society) came to be so well organized, we have to dream up some theo-

13 Robert Merton, 'Manifest and Latent Functions', in *Social Theory and Social Structure* (New York: Free Press, 1957), pp. 19-84.

retical entity or process (evolution, rationality, insight, culture) which gives a causal account of the 'cooperation' among the structures in society.

The term 'function' also has a less metaphysical meaning in sociological theory. This meaning is somewhat related to the points just described, but it ignores them to focus on specifics. A question in the form, 'what is the function of X?' usually means, 'what is the result of X's having happened?' If the idea of function is confined to specific effects of events, then accounts of social arrangements may be built up with little or no regard for larger theoretical problems associated with the meaning of the term 'function'. An example of this is Merton's classic discussion of bossism in American cities.[14] His argument is that, in days before large-scale publicly sponsored welfare, persons out of work or newly arrived in the country could agree to vote in a particular way, and in return the political party in office (the machine) would 'find' them a minor office, a job on the public payroll, or some form of assistance. The theoretical importance of this is to show that a clear need on the part of a fairly large number of people was being met, and the result of this need's being met in this way was the assurance of the continuation in office of just the people meeting the need. Hence, a 'functional' relationship emerged between the political machine and a group of people which tended to assure the existence and continuation of both.

V. *Sociological theory and values*

Since sociology is one of the disciplines which try to explain aspects of human life, it is natural that it would be sensitive to discussion about the values and moral questions involved in theorizing. In general the argument for 'value-freedom' in sociological theory has run as follows. In order to discover what 'is', and to properly conceptualize what 'is', it is necessary for the sociologist to bring no personal prejudice or bias concerning proper social relations to his study. This does not mean that he ought not to be a moral man, but for purposes of description and theory, if one wishes to know what is, then one must observe, describe, and theorize dispassionately. If disinterestedness is not maintained, what one believes ought to be may get in the way of what is; dogma would interfere with thought.

This position on value-freedom arose, curiously perhaps, among those who took a subjective approach to sociological problems. It has since been taken over largely by the objectivists, but in the beginning it was felt that if proper understanding of society required inferences from data and an interpretive appreciation of abstract human relations, value-freedom was essential. Since data were, they believed, obtained only in this

[14] *Ibid.*

way, the observer would have to hold his own feelings in check, 'bracket' them, for the duration of his observation and conceptualization period. Certainly, after this had been accomplished, the sociologist could freely comment on the acceptability of society from a moral standpoint, but he had no right to impose his values in the conduct of sociological analysis. Since all data-gathering was subjective in nature, if there were no attempts at value-freedom the sociological enterprise would surely break down into controversies of opinion. In short, this group thought the sociologist ought to describe things as they are to the best of his ability, keeping values out. He should pass judgment only as a person, not as a sociologist, on the things he observed. For the objectivist, the sociological theorist who wanted to describe and systematize ideas about that which he could see, the value-freedom position took the form of seeking the best methodological tools available. He needed techniques that would actually measure the things he wanted to measure, and not fool him by measuring something else. This is an impersonal form of the same hope voiced by the subjectivist.

As long as the objective of theorizing was description and explanation alone, the question tended to rest at this point. If the intent of theorizing was not overreached, then the problem of being biased could be solved by men of good will if they simply tried hard. At least, so it seemed. But this kind of argument eventually leads to a new attack on the proper goal of theorizing, one which blurs the distinction between explaining something and altering it.

The attack tends to point out that explaining things as they are tends to put emphasis on the forces leading to stability and *status quo,* and to direct attention away from what perhaps might be possible by way of improvement. Indeed, if ideas like evolution or structure are taken too seriously, runs this argument, it may appear that there is no alternative social organization possible. At times, people who argue in this vein have also impugned the motives of sociological theorists, arguing in effect that they gave value-free interpretations of things as they are in a surreptitious effort to justify them and keep them that way. A less personal version of this same line of attack points out that sociological theorists who are intimately familiar with a given society will have biases and viewpoints peculiar to that society which they might not be aware of, but which will nevertheless influence the things they tend to see and explain. Hence, the attack on value-freedom usually ends up, for one reason or another, by advocating a biased viewpoint in sociological analysis, not an unbiased one.

What alternatives to value-freedom are possible? One option is for the sociologist to become frankly normative about what he says. By subtly changing the objective of theory from explanation *per se* to 'criticism', one can present things in a different light. This does not mean that the critic fails to explain. He must do that, and thus explanation remains the first intent of sociological theory. But by 'critically' explaining, he shifts the emphasis from what 'is' to what might have been or what could be. By making one's biases clearly open, one's explanation takes on a reformist tinge. The matters needing reform are clearly indicated by the points at which the sociologist's opinions of what is proper differ from what, in fact, is in existence. Done in this way, the no-value-freedom option accomplishes mainly the same thing as the value-freedom approach, but with a different emphasis.

Alternatively, the sociologist not wishing to be value-free could turn sociological theory into propaganda – arguing that existing theory is only a tool of the *status quo*, and that new theory, which might make different assumptions and come to different conclusions, will pave the way for new modes of social organization. Such theorizing could have the intent of social reform, or it could be promulgated in the cause of some movement or dogma that might not have the good of society as a whole as an over-riding intent.

The value versus value-freedom controversy need not involve politics, although the two are usually intertwined, since altering social organization is the object of social and political planning. Indeed, taking a value stand for or against something one is studying can make certain things clear which might not be so otherwise. Many who try to understand poverty have felt that a clear sympathy with those one studies is an advantage in getting a proper feeling for the ways the political order bears on poverty. Without this, they believe the resulting theoretical information would be of less value. Also, it is often argued that to understand a culture, it must be experienced from 'the inside'. This involves taking onto one's self the values, beliefs, and themes of that culture to experience the ways these things actually affect behavior. It is in this vein that Black sociologists in the U.S.A. argue that none but other Blacks can adequately interpret the experience of being Black.

These examples and contentions lead to the recognition of a problem behind the controversy. What is the proper understanding of the term 'explanation'? If the objective of theory is simply to explain what people do, and to deduce these explanations from descriptive data organized into concepts, then the value-freedom problem does not really arise. This is because no matter what one's values with regard to the subject matter, the same results will obtain. If, on the other hand, to explain means not only to derive explanations in this manner but also to 'understand' or to have insight into the situation, perhaps in some allegedly unique human terms, then the value problem will arise. When it does, the distinction between theory *per se* and bias or politics is blurred. One becomes intentionally biased, then, at the risk of prejudicing the accuracy of his results. But this risk is sometimes worth the price in terms of the quality of insight rendered possible.

VI. *History and sociological theory*

The final problem to be considered in this survey of theoretical muddles confronting the sociological theorist is whether or not theory is really possible. Because we are sociologists and not historians, we have all taken a decision on this matter already. It is well, however, to understand the decision we have in fact made, and to understand some of the logical reasons why this decision is open to question.

When we consider drawing up a theory about something, we are actually saying that it is possible to conceptualize this thing in general terms – the essential qualities of it, and its causes and consequences. The statements we make become a theory, and serve to provide the explanation for all such events. When theory has been formed, then it is automatically alleged that the theory is applicable to many events of the same type as the events which led to the theory's being formed. It is alleged and not proven, remember, but nevertheless the allegation holds.

The problem here is simply this: we cannot know, and will not be able to find out empirically, the exact extent of the similarity between situations. Because of this inability to know just how much likeness there is, we can never be certain that one situation resembles another enough, or in essential ways, so that the generality covering a class of events actually covers more than just one. If such a generality is justified by the existence of classes of events, problems remain; but they are simpler ones than would obtain if it were not justified. Our duty in this situation is simply to keep working at theory until we have examined events in enough detail to make our genneralization stand up. It will never be possible to completely prove theoretical similarity of events, but as complementary data and details build up, the case for similarity could become stronger.

If it is not true that one event can resemble another in essential or sufficient ways for a class of events to be established, then the whole exercise of theory building is useless, since in principle a theory could apply only to one case. Such theory would be useless to us as a guide in other situations. This question of the uniqueness of human events is the reason for comparing sociological theory with history. History is the record of unique events together with theory occasionally borrowed piecemeal from the other sciences. In general, historians describe what happened, and account for it by narrating what happened earlier – by describing previous situations. Sociology, on the other hand, is a fundamentally theoretical account of social events, relying on historical-like data for its information. The emphasis of history is not theoretical in this sense; the emphasis of sociology is theoretical. The essence of the difference is that the theoretical study arrives at general conclusions about types of events while history does not.

Now it is true that some historians have developed theories of history.

There is nothing sacred about the convenient boundaries between the departments of learning. But the point is that whenever an historian, or anyone else, asks a question about the reason why a class of social events occurs, not why one event alone occurs, he is asking a question which has its basis in social theory.

Drawing up a defensible and enduring list of the classes of things which may be sociologically explained has been one of the continuing headaches in sociology theory. The headache could be taken as evidence that the historians are right about the possibility of having social theory in the first place. Nevertheless, it seems we need and use the idea of classes and categories, and thence comes the support for the idea. 'War', 'revolution', 'bureaucracy', 'family', – all of these are names of things which are identifiably of a type. Although to precisely define the types may be a problem, these things are social forms in terms of which we order our thinking, and in terms of which we often try to theorize regarding causes and functions. These types of social relations, and many more, are the objects of all sociological thinking. They are the classes of events about which we make the assumption that it is possible to theorize in sociology.

Thus, while we recognize that the assumption of the similarity of some social events is not without its critics, we make the assumption and proceed to theorizing. While we recognize that there are philosophical questions about the real existence of these essential similarities, we provisionally decide the issue in the positive when we make the decision to study sociological theory and to theorize. Making the opposite decisions denies our obvious and natural tendency to think in types and explain by classes. To go on to do sophisticated theorizing, it is necessary to make this decision and understand what it entails.

In summary, it should be emphasized that all of the problems examined in this chapter – order–change, objective–subjective, individual–society, function–cause, values, and uniqueness – are not simply issues in the history of social theory. They are problems still very much alive. As appealing solutions are worked out and found wanting, new approaches are tried. These and other issues are the stuff of which controversies and dialogue are made; they make sociological theory change, grow, and advance.

KEY CONCEPTS

social order	role	value-freedom
social change	chaos	levels of analysis
abstract idea	value	ideal type
subjective	function	individuality
objective	causation	teleology
class of events		
uniqueness of events		

TOPICS FOR DISCUSSION

1   What do we mean by saying that we wish to 'explain social order'?
2   Can the same sociological theories be used to understand both social order and social change?
3   What is the difference between objectivity and subjectivity?
4   Could the future state of society be the 'cause' of its present state?
5   What might we mean by saying that X is the cause of Y?
6   How does the historian depend on the social theorist?
7   In what ways does the sociologist use the data found by historians?
8   How do we know that one event resembles another enough to be 'like' it?
9   What properties of sociological theory cause it to change and develop?

ESSAY QUESTIONS

Why is the term 'role' an abstract one?
If we 'know' something because we ourselves believe it is true, is it necessarily 'objectively' true?
What are the relative merits of maintaining value-freedom in sociological analysis?
Describe the ways the terms 'cause' and 'function' might become confused in sociological theory.
What are some of the things that a sociologist might be interested in explaining which one might call aspects of 'social order'?
What is the controversy between the free-will concept of the individual and 'sociologistic' accounts of the force of society?
Why, when we attempt to deal with 'classes of events', must we do it theoretically?

FOR FURTHER READING AND STUDY

Isajiw, Wsevolod. *Causation and Functionalism in Sociology*. New York: Schocken Books, 1968.
MacIver, Robert. *Social Causation*. New York: Harper and Row, 1964.
Merton, Robert K. *Social Theory and Social Structure*. New York: Free Press, 1957.
Rudner, Richard. *Philosophy of Social Science*. Englewood Cliffs, N.J.: Prentice-Hall, 1966.
Russell, Bertrand. *Mysticism and Logic*. London: Allen and Unwin, 1963.
Stein, Maurice and Arthur Vidich (eds.). *Sociology on Trial*. Englewood Cliffs, N.J.: Prentice-Hall, 1963.
Tiryakian, Edward A. *Sociologism and Existentialism*. Englewood Cliffs, N.J.: Prentice-Hall, 1962.
Tönnies, Ferdinand. *Community and Society*. Tr. Charles P. Loomis. New York: Harper and Row, 1963.

Weber, Max. *Max Weber on the Methodology of the Social Sciences*. Tr. Edward Shils and Henry Finch. New York: Free Press, 1949.
   The Theory of Social and Economic Organization. Tr. Talcott Parsons. New York: Free Press, 1964.

3 Types of theories in sociology and the problem of verification

I. *Introduction*

In Chapter 2 we saw that the would-be theorist of social behavior faces a bewildering array of problems requiring attention before meaningful progress toward explanation in sociology can be made. If attacked systematically, these problems might yield up an easier and more obvious task for the social theorist. But it would take a long time, and perhaps no final solutions could be reached at all. Actually, either theorists have tended to ignore certain problems of explanation to focus on others, or they have tried to solve their problems as they went along. The result has become a collection of varied literature we call sociological theory. This body of literature takes different logical forms and different views on the task of explaining social phenomena. In this chapter are discussed some of these kinds of explanation, with special attention to their logical forms and the related issue of how one goes about confirming a theory which is written in one or another of these forms. The question asked here is, how would evidence be related to a theory so that the theory might be 'proven'?

II. *Explanation an ideal*

The point has been stressed that the objective of sociological theory is to 'explain' social events and trends. Of all the other uses that sociological theory might have, as an aid in social policy, or as material of academic interest only, it loses its justification to the sociologist if the objective of theory is not to explain something sociological. This objective is an ideal, and is, in absolute terms, out of reach. We can never completely explain everything, nor does it appear that we can explain anything without raising questions about procedure and adequacy. One hastens to point out that this is probably advantageous. If we did possess that final sociological theory which made all social actions scientifically understandable, life might be far more rational, but far less interesting.

41

But if a final theory explaining everything completely and adequately is out of reach, we can make significant advances, and it is precisely because we can formulate the idea of a complete explanation that we are able to advance. That is, the idea of a perfect explanation defines the areas in which we must work the hardest, and provides the criteria by which real achievement is judged.

III. *How explanations have been judged*

In general, the ideal of an explanation raises three distinctly different but related questions, and gives three different sets of criteria by which to judge an explanation.[1] In no particular order, the three are:

1   Which explanatory systems in sociology most closely approach the required logical purity of the particular form of explanation in use?

2   Which explanatory systems in sociology explain the most clearly and with the widest scope the most empirically observable or interpretable data on human affairs?

3   Which explanatory systems in sociology most completely bring our curiosity to rest?

It may appear, at first, that a theory particularly impressive on one of these criteria would automatically be good on all of them, but it is not so. For instance, in an earlier day, much social evil was explained by the supposed presence of witches. The theory of witches, for so we can call it, said in effect that certain people were possessed of the devil, and hence were in a particularly effective position to do evil. Such a system, in its day, was well suited to bringing curiosity to rest, and it did explain an amazing amount of otherwise unexplainable data. But witch theory does not stand up very well from a logical point of view, although the realization of this was a long time in coming.

Similarly, we can take the somewhat more subtle case of a theory which does rather better on empirical grounds, but which is not very satisfactory as an assuager of curiosity. Such a theory would be the 'opposites attract' thesis of Winch.[2] He argues that persons having complementary needs tend to marry each other, and that persons having strengths and weaknesses along parallel lines do not tend to marry. Winch has offered evidence to show that this is so, but the 'reasonableness' of the evidence is not demonstrated. Hence the theory does not satisfy us.

It might seem that logical minds would tend to be satisfied by logical theories, but this does not seem wholly true either. For example, one might consider individuals as 'satisfaction maximizers' who go about

---

[1] Nettler deals with how explanations are judged at some length in Gwynn Nettler, *Explanations* (New York: McGraw-Hill, 1970).

[2] Robert F. Winch, *The Modern Family*, 3rd ed. (New York: Holt, Rinehart and Winston, 1971).

trying to reduce their costs and maximize their rewards in social interaction. Many interesting deductions from this thesis are possible, some of which are supportable by evidence. But this theory does not satisfy us that it is a real explanation of human action, since we often feel something human is left out, although that something is hard to specify.

Clearly, then, while the ideal explanation is yet to be found, it is a great help in that it clarifies the purposes an explanation must fulfill. But one further point needs to be made. If a theory addresses one of the criteria alone, there is no reason why an explanation must also fulfill other criteria. A completely logical system like arithmetic need not refer empirically to anything. And indeed, pure mathematics does not empirically refer to anything. Neither does a curiosity-satisfying system require logic to perform its services. And in addition, there is no set of rules to follow which will yield an explanation which serves equally well in the three areas. Hence, when we actually do have a somewhat logical arrangement of ideas which satisfactorily explains empirical phenomena, it must be regarded as a creative product of man, and not the result of some kind of routine application of rules for explanation. We do have rules of logic and we do have rules for the arrangement of theoretical statements, but these rules ought not to be taken as the only criteria by which theory is judged.

IV. *Description and explanation*

What divides *description* from *explanation*, and how are the two related? These two questions are central to the study of any theoretical discipline, because they raise the question of the kinds of terms in which a phenomenon is described. They also point to some of the applications of models, the idea of which was introduced in Chapter 1.[3] We turn first to a discussion of the types of terms in theories, and then to a general statement of how description and explanation are related. Then we will be ready to discuss types of theory in sociology.

A. *Observational terms*

Obviously, a description of an event is not the same thing as the event itself, but a description has the ability to call forth images or understanding of that event.[4] This in itself may sound trite, but it points toward the

---

[3] A particularly good discussion of scientific terms and their relation to usage is found in Mae Brodbeck, 'Models, Meaning and Theories', in Mae Brodbeck, ed., *Readings in the Philosophy of the Social Sciences* (New York: Macmillan, 1968).

[4] It is impossible here to go into just how a symbol can do this, but an excellent treatment of the philosophical issues involved is found in Susanne K. Langer, *Philosophy in a New Key* (Cambridge, Mass.: Harvard University Press, 1951).

differences in types of terms found in descriptions and explanations. The most clearly understood terms in a description, from the standpoint of intuitive grasp, are *observational*.[5] These are the terms which label events and facts for conceptual use. They are names. For example, an observational term often used in sociological work is 'person', as in 'This person has $100,000.' Now, 'person' might have all kinds of theoretical and conceptual meanings to a psychologist or a theologian, but in the sense in which we mean it here, it simply labels the thing which possesses the $100,000. 'Person' can have all kinds of explanations, from various viewpoints and toward various ends, but when the term is used simply to designate something without further intent, it is observational. Sometimes such terms are called 'descriptive' as well.

B. *Constructs*

It is important to understand that many of the things we speak of as having observed, we really have not observed, and they cannot be designated by observational terms. Chapter 1 discussed the use of the word 'role' in another context, and the same word can serve to point out the difference between observational terms and other theoretical words. For example, it is common to speak of observing the role of someone. Usually what is meant is that we observe a series of specific behaviors over some extended time or in various situations. These specific behaviors could be labeled with observational terms, but in no sense could we say that we observed the role of a person in the same way as we observe Blossom the cat sitting on the window sill. 'Role' refers to the abstractly constructed coherence of all the specific activities we do observe. The word 'role' is in fact a *construct*. Constructs make reference to observable things and behaviors, but are not themselves the names of observational entities. Another example is the word 'government'. We are always speaking of 'government' as if it were something to be observed directly. This example is instructive because there is a difference between the traditional British and American understandings of the word. The American usually says, 'The government is . . .' He uses the term to designate almost an entity, or a monolithic structure which acts and has a state of being. But the British tradition is much more accurate. It says, 'The government are . . .', meaning that the collection of men in power are acting collectively in a certain way. The construct 'government' is intended to refer to the actions of men, but it does not name the actors or the actions directly. It names the mental construct of their collective action, taken from a given point of view.

---

[5] There is some variation in the words which name the kinds of terms used in scientific theory, but from context it is usually easy to tell which kinds of terms are meant. The usage here follows that of Abraham Kaplan in *The Conduct of Inquiry* (San Francisco: Chandler Publishing Co., 1964), pp. 56ff.

In a similar way, the foundation concept of all sociology, 'society', is a construct, and not an observational term. 'Society' may be real enough in that it is important in hundreds of ways to the lives of individuals. It may even have its own unique explanation and behave according to its own historical laws, as many theorists have suggested.[6] But it is a fact that 'society' does not refer directly to something we observe. The subject matter of sociology (society) is the collective representation of individually observable acts taken together as an abstract construct. It is this construct, and all the related ones that grow up around it, which are to be explained as the first job of sociological theory. Hence, in most sociological theory, explanations refer to constructs.

1. *Primitive terms and analogies*

Constructs in the social sciences may be divided for analysis in a way that brings out the important distinction between *primitive* terms and *analogous* terms. This distinction is at the basis of the use of models in sociological theory. A 'primitive' term is rooted in the observation of something which is directly germane to the construct itself. That is, the primitive term 'society' can be understood as a collective construct of individual behaviors, as we have seen.

But not all constructs in social science have this quality – in fact, a great many do not. Consider, for example, the idea of force. We often speak of 'social forces' as though there were stresses and strains in society working against each other, as if there were almost irresistible pressures directing the lives of persons. But speaking realistically, there is nothing we could observe to arrive at the mental construct 'social force' in the same way that we could observe individual action and conceive the idea of 'society'. While the term 'force', when used in social science, does seem intuitively to be descriptive of some kind of social experience, we could never observe an example of it directly, as we could observe an example of a given act of behavior. 'Force' is a term in use in social science which is not primitive to social science. The term is primitive to physics, where it has a specific physical definition and may be calculated quantitatively.

Terms like 'social force' which are in legitimate use in social science yet not primitive to it are called 'analogous' terms, or analogous constructs.[7] At times it may be unclear to which field a term is really primitive. For example, 'evolution' is an ambiguously primitive word. Commonly, it is

---

[6] What usually goes under the name of 'the philosophy of history' is the work done in philosophy relating general abstract principles to total societies.

[7] The meaning here is similar to that in a treatment of theories of social order in P. Meadows, 'The Metaphores of Order: Toward a Taxonomy of Organization Theory', in Llewellyn Gross, ed., *Sociological Theory: Inquiries and Paradigms* (New York: Harper and Row, 1967), pp. 77-103, but the categories and conclusions are different from Meadows'.

used to designate the biological process of changes in a living species by adaptation to its environment, but 'social evolution', or some other term which had the same intent, was in use two hundred years ago to designate the changing social order as it unfolded.[8] Biologists use 'evolution' today as though it were primitive to biology, but actually it might be a grand analogy to another usage which emerged to describe a human social process.

(a) *Types of analogous constructs in social theory.* The great utility in grasping the difference between primitive and analogous constructs in social theory is that it allows one to understand which kinds of constructs are actually descriptive of observational entities and which are not. Even more important, the basic processes hypothesized in some theories are analogies, and hence have their root meaning in some other science or branch of knowledge. In the history of sociology, many theories have grown up around analogous constructs. Consider, for example, Table 3.1, which locates types of theory under the analogy hypothesized for the main explanatory idea. Now consider each of the analogous constructs in order.

TABLE 3.1

Type of analogy	Main explanatory ideas
Mechanical	Force, equilibrium
Logical	Interests, rationality
Moral/ethical	Consensus
Biological	Species survival, vital principles

(1) *Mechanical analogy.* It was noted above that the term 'force' is an analogy to physical principles. When it comes into use in sociology as 'power' or 'coercion', the major dynamic ideas of such theory are actually analogies to what we mean when speaking of levers and pulleys, pressures and containers.[9] The dynamics of 'coercion' theory suggest that a 'force' exerted in some social fashion on some entity will cause that entity to 'move' in something like the physical sense of 'change position', but actually we do not mean this at all. We are not speaking of the physical movement of men, nor are we speaking of pitching them off their feet with levers, but we are conceptually using an analogy to these kinds of acts which mentally suggests the idea of force and movement, physics terms.

8 See J. W. Burrow, *Evolution and Society* (London: Cambridge University Press, 1966).
9 The terms 'power' or 'coercion' do not refer to specific working theories, but points of view. See P. Cohen's treatment of the typologies of theory in social science in his *Modern Social Theories* (New York: Basic Books, 1968), Ch. 2.

(2) *Logical analogy.* A more subtle but nonetheless important analogy in use daily in social science is the logical one, in which 'interests' and 'rationality' play a large part. Pure logic and mathematics have basically two sets of terms, those that designate the entities and those that designate the operations. Hence, '2 + 3 = 5' has no empirical meaning, since '2', '3', and '5' have no empirical referent. They are definable logically from within the mathematical system to which they are relevant. In this example the operations or connectives are the plus and equals signs. The expression tells that, without any empirical referent, when we do a certain logically defined operation called 'addition' on two abstract things called 'the numbers 2 and 3' we have a result which is called '5'. The reason we will automatically have the result is that two plus three is by definition in a state of 'equality' with five. Hence, '2 + 3 = 5' is 'true' not because it refers to anything in the world which is empirically true, but because it is true by definition.

Now consider the concepts of 'interests' and 'rationality.'[10] Interests may be called the things that individuals want, or what they would consider rewards, together with the things they wish to avoid. It would be in their interest to get what they want and avoid what they do not. 'Rationality' may be defined as the facility of mental insight or penetration which can be applied to one's interests. That is, before actually acting, if a man has rationality and uses it, he can see what quantities of rewards a certain action will bring him, or what he will avoid by acting in a certain way.[11] If he had perfect rationality, he could see precisely what to do in each situation which would maximize his gains and minimize his losses in it.

Now consider the concept of interests as analogous to the numbers in the example from arithmetic above, and consider rationality as analogous to the plus and equals signs. It is clear that if a given set of interests is combined in a certain way (by 'perfect' rationality), a given outcome is assured, in just the way that five is assured by the addition of two and three. That is, the outcome for the perfectly rational man is sure to be the best possible maximization of his pleasure by the maximizing of his rewards, and by the avoiding of all the things that it is in his interest to avoid. This is a true statement in just the same way that 'two plus three equals five' is true. It is true by definition, since interests are defined as the ingredients of human action and rationality as the connectives or relational terms between interests. Hence, the perfectly rational man can always be expected to behave in ways that will serve his interests in the best possible way.

---

10 Both of these terms, when applied to human behavior, are somewhat ambiguous. Part of the ambiguity is caused by their being used in a great many different ways by different writers, but to illustrate the point about logical analogies to sociological theory, this ambiguity need not detain us.

11 Defining 'rationality' with precision is beyond the scope of this chapter, and not of any great usefulness here.

This all becomes a very elegant sociological theory, putting aside the difficulties related to real rationality and real interests. All we need do is assume that persons have interests, which does not seem to be hard to do at first, and to assume that they behave in rational ways. Now, all that is needed from the theorist is that he reconstruct the rational process used by the individuals he is interested in, and reconstruct the influences of each action on each other action, always from the standpoint of the assumption that persons rationally serve their own interests. In this way, a full and complete explanation of all action and a complete prediction of future outcomes can be set down. However, it is only possible to theorize this way if persons have these kinds of interests and behave completely rationally. Unfortunately, they do not seem to do so, or at least not often enough and consistently enough to make this scheme work well.[12] Nevertheless, logic can be used as a conceptual analogy for social action and hence become the basis from which, by analogy, a stream of theory can be developed.

(3) *Moral/ethical analogy.* Perhaps the moral and ethical analogy is easier to grasp intuitively than is the logical analogy. It is sometimes a novelty to think of morality as having 'theory' connected with it, but so it has. Briefly, moral theories argue for certain duties we have to each other by virtue of our being bound together in some kind of common experience as men. Usually, these duties, like kindness, brotherhood, and the Golden Rule, are duties of such a nature that they cannot easily, if at all, be made laws of the state. Nevertheless, moral theory argues that we all depend on each other to some extent to behave in these ways, because life would be unlivable if we did not.

It is important to emphasize that these duties are not legal ones, and that they cannot be readily enforced on individuals. This is important because it is only through their being voluntarily accepted as proper, legitimate requirements of human life that they can have any influence over men's lives. Hence, it is the common acceptance of these moral prescriptions as being good and proper that gives them their utility as regulators of conduct.

The analogy to sociological theory should now be easy to see. If indeed something about the laws of conduct put all of them more or less outside the realm of enforceable strictures, then there must be some degree of acceptance of norms and rules as the basis of social organization in general. If we argue that social organization is too complex and vast to be accounted for in any other way than by saying that it is due partly or wholly to individual acceptance of defined prescriptions, then we are employing an analogy to moral theory. Such a sociological theory emphasizes acceptance and consensus just as moral theory does. In fact,

---

[12] Charles Dickens brought home this point in his novel *Hard Times* (London: J. M. Dent, 1907).

in an earlier era, the discipline we call sociology was often combined with something of modern economics and political science, as well as law, and called 'moral science'.

(4) *Biological analogy.* The world of biology has provided one of the richest analogies for sociologists. This is because there is a great similarity between the biologist's conception of his unit of study as one that forms a complex functioning whole and the sociological theorist's emphasis on interconnecting links of influence or outright determination among the various parts of his unit of study. There is some confusion, however, concerning what the unit of study ought to be when sociologists use the analogy to biological theory, and this has caused much confusion in sociological theory. Sometimes the body of the living animal is taken as the unit of biological study to which the analogy is made, as when we speak of 'the body politic', meaning the collection of 'political people' making up society. In this analogy the general idea of a body's being made up of parts which operate so as to service and complement each other is emphasized. This kind of theory asks questions specifically aimed at finding out these kinds of connections, and considers a thing explained when these connections are made clear. For example, it is obvious that the rest of the living body needs the stomach because of the important functions carried out there, and similarly the stomach and all the rest of the organs need the heart, and so on. It is a matter of some disagreement what the usefulness of the appendix is, and hence this organ remains unexplained in the body.

While the issue is no longer important to academic biology, we might point out that the principle of 'vitalism' still seems to appear in the sociological theories based on biological thinking. In an earlier time, biologists noted that the explanation of all the parts of a body in terms of all the other parts still did not yield them an explanation of 'life'. As with Frankenstein, it might be possible to hook up the proper connections among parts, but it did not seem possible to make this collection of parts 'live' as a body does. Hence the principle, which is no more than an assertion of what seemed obvious, that biological organisms operated on some 'vital' or living principle which was not explained simply in terms of the interconnections of parts.

The sociological use of this kind of thinking has somewhat declined in its bolder affirmation of biological principles, but much of the outline of the theory still exists in modern sociology. The analogy to the body suggests the functioning and specialization of function among the institutions of society. It is no surprise, from this point of view, that the educational and economic institutions of Western society are closely linked. It is precisely this that would be predicted from the biological analogy: as the organs of the body are linked in complementary function, so the institutions of society are similarly linked. This analogy suggests that if we were to examine closely and fully enough all the institutions of a society we would find a similar kind of connection among them all.

But what of the vital principle? Do societies live, as bodies live? Taken literally, it is absurd to suggest they do, but the suggestion has been made. When we say that a society 'grows' or 'develops' or 'adapts', we are saying something like this. We are saying that the organized collection of individuals and institutions called a society (not the individuals, but the organization of them) has the ability to perform functional tasks. When we say that the whole is greater than the sum of its parts, we are suggesting that the details of all the functional interconnections among institutions and persons in a society do not amount to a full explanation of the society. Something analogous to the 'vital principle' is left out of this. This something accounts for the difference between the sum of the parts and the whole.

Using the biological analogy in this way suggests a rather harmonious cohabitation of the parts which perform interdependent functions; but when we take not the body but the species as the level of biological analogy, this picture changes. It is among the first principles of evolution that a species is set in an environment which must sustain it. Hence, there is a certain natural antagonism among the individual members of a species with regard to the environment and other species. For the species to 'adapt' to the environment means simply that as time passes, individuals born into that species who cannot get along produce no offspring, and their characteristics are lost to the species. But this is for the good, since those who do get along (having natural characteristics useful or favorable to life in the environment) do tend to produce offspring and hence pass on these favorable characteristics. As a result, the species as a whole is strengthened and becomes 'adapted' to the environment.

Turning this kind of biological analogy to sociological description has produced quite a different picture from the one suggested above. The relations among individuals in a society are now ones of intense competition, since individuals are struggling for survival in their environment. It suggests that if persons were left to their own devices, there would be no concern for those who cannot survive, and indeed it is suggested by this analogy that to care for such persons is bad for the 'species', since it tends to perpetuate non-adapting types who would otherwise die out. In short, the sociological analogy drawn from this kind of biological thinking suggests that human society will as a whole tend to become strong insofar as it promotes competition and insofar as it rewards the winners and leaves the losers to suffer the consequences. Human societies tend to weaken the natural adaptiveness of the race to the extent that they extend helpfulness and kindness to the weak, support sick and foundering institutions, and so on, this argument suggests.

Put in these terms, analogy to human affairs sounds unbelievably harsh and inhumane, but the fact is that we use a form of this kind of biological analogy every day, and think it perfectly proper to do so. When it is suggested, for example, that the patterns of work and leisure or the standard expectations of sexual morality will 'have to change' to fit new conditions, what is meant is that the 'progress' of society (analogous to the species) depends on these old patterns' being thrown out and new ones put in their place. When we accept new technology as a 'more efficient' way of handling goods and services, we are suggesting that there is an 'efficiency' consideration in the ways in which we adapt to our environment, and that, for survival's sake, we must choose the more efficient. A recent example of this is the coming of container technology to the handling of seagoing shipping. Containers have put hundreds out of jobs in dock work throughout the world, but there has been no very serious opposition to this. There was recognition that those not using containers would be at a competitive disadvantage among the rest. While the species moved ahead, individuals competed and struggled.

2. *Primitive terms, analogies, and description*

We can now return briefly to the theme of types of descriptions used in sociology and draw some conclusions from the discussions of analogies. Descriptions of social phenomena may come in partially 'primitive' terms. These terms have their root meaning in sociology itself, and hence depend on sociological examples and sociological explanation for their descriptive denotation. But it is more common to attempt to describe social action by making use of analogies; this involves taking over the primitive terms of other fields and turning them into 'constructs' for sociological use. This is a kind of borrowing that goes on in the world of science all the time, but which has a built-in danger. The danger is that the description which emerges will also contain a hidden explanation of the thing described, and we might not wish to entertain this explanation at all. An example to which we can return briefly to illustrate this is one of the society's being like the animal body. It might be like the body in that certain identifiable parts are related in a complementary way, but it is another question whether or not this body 'lives' or carries out any of the other biological functions common to animal bodies. The fact that we have tended to carry the explanation over to sociological theory, not stopping at a descriptive analogy, shows the powerful influence the terms of a description have over the eventual explanation of a phenomenon. The terms of a description take on the richness of meaning in the context in which they formed and took root. Some of the connotation of this context must be retained for the terms themselves to have continued meaning for description. Hence, it is hard to use scientific or technical terms in analogous senses without having some of the implied explanations for these words come along.

It is for reasons like these that the language of the social sciences deserves so much attention and comes in for so much criticism. Attention to the precise meanings given to descriptive terms in sociology is a first step in stabilizing the meanings of these words, so that they may be analyzed and criticized. When these words come, as they often do, out of analogies to other studies, the denotations of constructs must be kept separate from the implied explanations of the constructs.

C. *Theoretical or explanatory terms*

In discussing the difference between observational terms and terms denoting constructs, we made use of the concept of 'reference'. The terms were divided according to the things they referred to, and we found that observational terms denoted things we could see, constructs denoted the things we could not see directly. To continue in this vein, theoretical or *explanatory* terms have yet another referent. It is the theory itself, or the constellation of concepts and processes which combines to form an explanation.

Two examples of explanatory terms will be discussed first, and then the more abstract job of placing these terms into the context of sociological description and explanation will be returned to. Consider, for example, the term 'the Protestant ethic'. Max Weber developed this term as part of his thesis on the rise of capitalism in Renaissance Europe.[13] Briefly, the term denotes a psychological turn of mind derived from Calvinist theological doctrines and applied to the worldly pursuit of economic enterprise. To Weber, it did not mean crude economic egoism, as we sometimes find the term degraded to mean today. It did denote a complex psychological orientation on the part of individuals. This orientation derived partly from the concepts of a 'calling' (being especially called by God to work in some specific way) and the related ideas of stewardship and election. 'Stewardship' is the term indicating that Calvinist theology asserted there could be no 'ownership' of goods in a permanent sense here on earth, since in the end all was owned by God who had originally made it. All that man did was become the caretaker, or steward, of certain goods during his brief time on earth. 'Election' refers to the theological tenet that God, being omniscient, already knows which persons will join him in Heaven, and all the rest are damned; this is beyond the control of individuals.

To Weber, the importance of this complicated theological doctrine was that it tended to foster a specific kind of orientation toward everyday work and leisure among those who believed in it. These persons took their 'calling' seriously. It was no light matter to be called by God to a specific task. It was natural to wish to perform in the task to the best of

---

[13] *The Protestant Ethic and the Spirit of Capitalism*, tr. Talcott Parsons (New York: Scribner's, 1958).

one's ability. It was not a haphazard business either, since to be a steward of the Lord's goods required careful attention and performance. Neither could one waste God's goods. Extravagance and self-glorification with God's goods would be a sin. It was equally important to recognize that one could not influence the Lord's choice of the elect by good works. Election and damnation were already set. Men could have no ulterior motive in behaving properly here on earth. Weber argues in *The Protestant Ethic and the Spirit of Capitalism* that this kind of orientation to the world could not help but foster economic abundance and the growth of capitalism, since it emphasized thrift, diligence, and thorough, rational achievement, and discouraged extravagance, wastefulness, self-glorification, and chaotic expenditure.

In examining the concept of the Protestant ethic as a theoretical term, it should now be obvious that the referent of the term itself is a complex set of ideas about man's relation to his world and to God. 'The Protestant ethic' does not refer to an observation directly, as an observational term would; neither does it apply to a construct which indirectly has its basis in observation. What it does refer to is something we might call a 'theory' of the relations between man and God, and the consequent implied psychological orientations. The term has as its only referent other ideas, so arranged and interconnected that the whole complex forms a meaningful constellation of thought.

Weber used 'the Protestant ethic', in the sense of its fullest meaning, as an explanatory term, and it is this function in an explanation that should be emphasized now. When he suggested that the requirements for the growth of capitalism were coincident with the tenets of the Protestant ethic, Weber was 'explaining' the growth of capitalism. He was giving the phenomenon of capitalism a theoretical treatment such that its growth was understandable and accounted for. Note that he was not 'describing' the growth of capitalism with the Protestant ethic. There is nothing descriptive of capitalism in the term's meaning. The referent is the understanding people had of their relationship to God, and the place this relationship had in their daily work. It is this relationship, argues Weber, which explains the related (but not identical) phenomenon of the rise of capitalism in Western Europe. Hence, the term 'Protestant ethic' refers to an explanatory set of ideas which gets its meaning in the explanatory context, and only attains its fullest meaning when used in that context.

An even more abstract example of theoretical terms having their meaning only in a theoretical context is provided by Freud. It seems legitimate to use this example, since so many people employ the terms 'ego', 'super-ego', 'id', 'projection', 'trauma', and so on in daily language. But the fact is that these terms 'mean' nothing, if what we are concerned with is a physical denotation. The id is not to be found inside the body or out. Neither is the ego, and a projection has nothing to do with physical or social events *per se*. The terms have their entire meaning locked up in the total conceptual context we might call 'Freudian theory'. It makes no sense to talk about the superego without describing it entirely in terms of its relations with the id and the ego, and so on. That is, there is no meaning associated with the theoretical term 'superego' that does not derive from the abstract theoretical conceptualization of superego in relation to other 'Freudian' concepts.

In what sense does Freudian theory 'explain'? It does not explain by making much use of observational terms, by relating observations to theory directly. Its mode of explanation is to suggest the proper interpretation that observed events deserve. Once one is familiar with 'Freud's theory' then it is possible to interpret actual events as though they fit into the pattern created in the mind of the observer by 'Freud's theory'.[14] The utility of this exercise is, of course, that an explanation of the interpreted events is the result.

The important thing to emphasize about truly theoretical terms is that they have *systemic* meaning. They derive their meaning from the system of concepts in which they are imbedded. A full definition of these terms using observables is impossible. Kaplan suggests that the relationship between observables and theoretical terms is that the observable 'marks the occasion' for the application of a theoretical term, and so it is.[15] When we know 'Freud's theory' sufficiently to apply it to something, the application consists in recognizing the occasions on which particular 'Freudian' concepts and processes are appropriate, as decided on the basis of 'Freud's theory' itself. Thus the terms of the theory have 'systemic meaning' relating them to the entire theoretical system in which they are found and defined.

V. Description and explanation: a summary

After having described the types of terms that appear in all theory, we are in a stronger position from which to sort out the differences between description and explanation. It ought to be obvious that an empirical discipline like sociology can not do without a firm basis in description. It is description which labels events with words and sentences; these create images of the events in the minds of those who use the descriptions. Description is thus the first step toward explanation. Constructs are the terms that help to organize observations and concepts about observations into a form that is applicable to more than the particular event in question, and which may be explained. Hence while we do not observe roles,

---

14 It should be noted that Freud's ideas developed as he grew older and there is, therefore, no single theory.
15 Kaplan, *Conduct of Inquiry*, p. 57.

but only actions, we may still employ the term 'role' in a constructed understanding of the coherence of certain actions as they relate together. It is at the theoretical level that we actually explain the relationships among the constructed and observed actions. Theoretical terms have systemic meaning, and impart this meaning to given explanations. They do this by pointing out the theoretical relatedness of observed behavior and constructed ideas. This pointing out can occur only in a systematically arranged array of concepts that make sense in terms of each other, and impart some of this sense to the events which have been described and conceptualized into constructs.

VI. *Types of theories*

We have just seen that theoretical explanations depend on the existence of theoretical terms with systemic meaning. The systemic meaning of a term is derived from its position and function in a system of ideas called a theory. We saw that the meanings of these kinds of terms could not be reduced to observations and constructs alone, but were dependent on the whole theoretical structure in which they fit. Now it is appropriate to ask the question, 'What kinds of theoretical structures are there?' What types of theories do we find in sociology? Note that the word 'types' here refers to the conceptual structure of the theory, the system in which a term gets its meaning and explanatory power.

In Chapter 1, a rough typology of theories was suggested, stemming from the kinds of 'packages' theories arrived in. The suggestion was that they varied from a rather loose grouping of theoretical ideas, with many of the systemic connections between the terms vague or undefined, on the one side, to a tightly organized and rigorous arrangement of concepts in a formal structure at the opposite pole. It is now time to improve this typology and divide it into three components. One word of caution. It has been emphasized that explanation, in a full and final sense, is an ideal not yet reached, and perhaps not reachable by any theory. Do not mistake the most thoroughly worked out theory in terms of clarity and precision for the one that explains the most. Neither should one take any single example of a theory as being entirely in one stage or another of precision. As we will see later, theories may have some of their parts less ambiguous than others, and we have to take systems of ideas as we find them.

We can easily identify three classes of theoretical types in sociology.[16]

16 This typology is adopted because it closely parallels the theories in use in modern sociology, but it is also based on the philosophical explication of theoretical forms. Cf. Kaplan, *Conduct of Inquiry*, Ch. 8; Quentin Gibson, *The Logic of Social Enquiry* (London: Routledge and Kegan Paul, 1960), Chs. 10, 11.

The first two types are better defined than the third and are differentiated on logical grounds from it. These types are:

the hypothetico-deductive, or simply deductive theories

the pattern or concatenated theories

perspectives

In terms of our continuum, the first two, while very different in logical structure, are far more toward the logical and rigorous end of the scale than is a perspective. In fact, perspectives are sometimes not considered theories at all, and the word may be used to differentiate a theory from a looser set of ideas or point of view. But since perspectives and theories are both employed for the purpose of trying to explain social events, perspectives will be considered here to be one type of theory.

A. *Hypothetico-deductive, or simply deductive theories*

Fairly recently in the long history of science, philosophers and scientists themselves have turned their attention partly away from their work and tried to reflect on the methods by which ideas are organized into theories, and the ways these theories produce statements to be tested and verified. By 'methods', the routine modes of calculation or ways of designing experiments are not meant, but the mental creative methods used by insightful and successful scientists and philosophers.[17] This attention to the theory of a discipline, taken as an area of study in itself, has given rise to the field called the philosophy of science.

The philosophy of social science has not yielded one standard account of the way social scientists go about their theorizing. There is disagreement among the philosophers on what scientists do, and there is also disagreement among the scientists. Nevertheless, the theoretical form which enjoys a position of 'near orthodoxy'[18] is the *hypothetico-deductive* type. This type relies on laws – general statements which eventually top a hierarchy.[19] Laws have the property of being more or less general, according to whether or not they can be deduced from other ones. The laws that cannot be deduced from any other laws are the most general ones, and occupy the highest level of generality. Laws are statements. They set down the relationships among aspects of their subject matter. Hence, it takes two or more concepts about the subject matter before one law can possibly be formed which gives a statement of a relationship. For example, economics contains what is often called the law of supply

17 In the social sciences, this kind of attention to the philosophical side of the subject is older than in the natural sciences, since part of sociology (if not all) has never been as far removed from metaphysics as the physical sciences became.

18 This is the way Alan Ryan puts it in *The Philosophy of the Social Sciences* (London: Macmillan, 1970), p. 46.

19 For an extended treatment of the logical status of laws, see Ernest Nagel, *The Structure of Science* (New York: Harcourt Brace and World, 1961), Chs. 4, 10.

and demand, which is actually two laws combined. It contains a law of supply and a law of demand. The law of supply states a general relationship between the market price of an item and the amount of that item which will be produced in a theoretically free market. The law of demand states the relationship between the market price and the amount of the item demanded. These two laws can be combined since they share the common term 'price'; this relates the two laws.

Laws must be general statements in theoretical work. A statement of a specific relationship (say between the supply and demand in a specific market for a specific item) is not a law, since the statement is intended to hold good only for that specific instance. Thus, laws cannot relate observational terms together into sentences. Only constructs can be used in making laws. 'Men like women' is in the form of a law; 'Oren likes Vesta' is not.

Several things have been suggested as the real relational meaning of laws – that is, the nature of the statement they make. The argument which seems to claim the most for laws says that the statements made by laws refer to causes: hence the name 'causal laws'. This argument is that if a law states a relationship which is always observed between two classes of events, the law is making a general assertion of cause and effect:

(events of type X) cause (events of type Y)

In this example, the cause and the direction of cause are both suggested by the statement, and it could be rewritten

(events of type X) $\rightarrow$ (events of type Y)

where the arrow indicates causation proceeding from X to Y. But we saw in Chapter 2 that 'cause' is highly problematical in the social sciences. This seems especially so, since the actual events of type X and type Y might be human ones taking place among persons who have the capacity to visualize the consequences of type X events and take steps to avoid or change these consequences. Thus, while the 'causal law' approach to the meaning of laws is relatively clear-cut philosophically speaking, it is the hardest to justify among social science approaches to deductive theory.

What else might the laws express? They might express a 'causal nexus', or a constant conjunction. The actual concepts that led to the proposition of a given law could not produce evidence for the causal article, since cause is not observable. But still, it is possible to envision laws as expressing, in general terms, the state of affairs between events of type X and type Y such that, in given conditions, these events would take the shape proposed by the law. We might write this as follows:

(events of type X) $\rightleftharpoons$ (events of type Y)

The arrows do not indicate that X and Y 'cause' each other, but rather that the complex relationship between these two types of events always takes a certain form.

Laws are not always used in connection with the idea of cause. A common alternative is the statistical law which is based on a very large number of observations of events (in this example, of type X and type Y). Used this way, the general form of the law states nothing directly about cause at all. Instead, the law says that in the presence of events of type X and certain conditions, events of type Y will be associated with a given probability. There is a certain statistical probability that these things will happen as they have been thought to happen in the past.

The use of the term 'law' making the weakest claim is in the 'lawlike proposition'. This argument asserts that, at best, it is a risky business formulating laws; we do not achieve one hundred per cent validity, nor do we achieve the highest level of generality. It is far better, says this argument, to make less of a distinction between laws and other general statements. Instead, we should rely on some statements performing a lawlike function in a theory, but we should not make the strong claims associated with cause.

We can see that there is variety in just what kind of statements to expect laws to make in deductive theory, but there is far less disagreement about the function of the laws in the theoretical system. The laws appear at the top of a deductive pyramid. They are the statements at the highest level of generality and have the widest scope; from them intermediate statements and hypotheses are deduced.

Deduction is reasoning from general statements at high levels of the theoretical pyramid to the specific statements, or hypotheses, at the very base of it. Hypotheses are about observables and actual events. When deduction is properly carried out, the statement of the hypotheses will be in the same logical form as the laws at the top of the pyramid, but the hypotheses will refer to specifics.

An abstract example and then a concrete one will help to make this clear. Let us say X represents events of a certain type. That is, X represents a category of events and is a construct. Y represents a construct applying to a second category of events. Since both X and Y are the names of categories or classes of events, any particular events of the general X and Y type should have exactly the same specific relationship as is suggested by the general relationship between the classes of events represented by X and Y. We can symbolize this by letting x represent a specific event of the X type, and y represent a specific event of the Y type. Now, having a general relationship symbolized by:

$$X \quad \text{general relationship} \quad Y$$

then

$$x \quad \text{specific relationship} \quad y$$

will follow – it will, because it follows deductively. Deduction is the method by which to get specific information for hypotheses and concrete tests out of general statements of relationships between categories of events. These relationships are stated in some way or another by laws.

A well-known proponent of this type of theory in sociology is George

Homans, about whose work more will be said in Chapter 4. As an example of the use of laws to explain specific events, examine one of his statements, which he prefers to call 'general propositions'. It reads, 'The more often within a given period of time a man's activity rewards the activity of another, the more often the other will emit the activity'.[20]

The statement is of the form: *X* relationship *Y*, given above. It says that in a situation of social interaction, where one person 'rewards' another, the rewarded activity will increase in frequency. We can symbolize the first part of the statement with *X*. Then, *X* represents the rewarding activity of one person, and *Y* the rewarded activity. Let r equal the relationship between these two general categories of action. In this case, r represents some direct function; as *X* increases, so does *Y*. Now, in symbols, the Homans general proposition reads as follows:

$$X \quad r \quad Y$$

Using the words for the symbols in this simple statement, read: The rewarding activity of one person is related to the rewarded activity of another person by some direct function.

This statement can be replaced in the deductive format as suggested above. We now have $(X \ r \ Y)$ as the symbolic form of the general statement made by Homans. In principle, it seems possible to look around now to see if there are instances of this happening. That is, we will search for $(x \ r \ y)$. We will look for instances of *X*, which we will symbolize by *x*, and instances of *Y*, symbolized by *y*, which have the hypothesized relationship between them, r.

Let's say that we notice a child brushing his dog, Pudgie, and receiving praise for it from his family, praise which the child regards as rewarding. Also imagine that this Pudgie-brushing behavior becomes more frequent and that it is continually rewarded. We have here an instance of $(x \ r \ y)$. We could now write symbolically:

$$X \quad r \quad Y \qquad \text{level of general proposition}$$
$$x \quad r \quad y \qquad \text{level of observation}$$

That is, the same relationship accrues at the observational level as is suggested at the general level.

Here it is necessary to make a point that is sometimes missed. When we already have the existence of the general statement $(X \ r \ Y)$, no matter for the moment from where it came, then we must, as a matter of logic, hypothesize $(x \ r \ y)$ as the deduced specific hypothesis relating the specific instances of *X* and *Y*. Deductive logic calls upon us to hypothesize the same quality of relationships between instances of *x* and *y* as is given in the general form $(X \ r \ Y)$.

But what if we do not find this? Apart from the implications about the usefulness of the theory, we still have a theory, we still have an hypothesis, and we still have an hypothesized relationship. There are several rea-

---

[20] George Homans, *Social Behavior: Its Elementary Forms* (New York: Harcourt Brace and World, 1961), p. 54.

sons why one might fail to find the hypothesized relationship; only one of these is that the general statement is 'wrong'. Hence, we can not simplistically argue that a theory which looks empirically wrong is no theory.

We can now summarize the points made in describing deductive theories, and draw some things together before going on. Deductive theories consist of statements, arranged in a hierarchical order, so that those at the top of the order are the most general. These are statements of relationships among constructs, in explanatory terms. Beneath these most general statements, or laws, are lower-level statements. Strictly speaking, one general statement or law and one very low-level specific statement, or hypothesis, would be considered a theory from the deductive point of view, if the hypothesis were derivable from the law by deductive logic. But in fact, theories which follow this type of hierarchical organization usually contain more than one law, and have a great many hypotheses. In fact, theories that are considered general enough to be given serious consideration as main organizing principles of a science implicitly contain all the hypotheses possible about the phenomenon to which the theory is addressed.

Up to this point, certain details have been neglected that must now be brought into line. In addition to the existence in deductive theories of statements and hypotheses, there must be statements of limiting conditions. Our hypothetical law stating $(X \, r \, Y)$ says in effect that 'All X have a specific relationship (r) with all Y.' Either stated or implied by this is the additional statement, 'This is so under certain conditions which are explicit and describable.' A commonly used phrase, 'other things being equal', is a way of saying that we expect our laws to produce empirically true hypotheses under conditions that gave rise to the formulation of the laws, but that we might not expect them to do so if one or more factors were constraining the behaviors of x or y so that they could not act in the manner suggested by r, their relationship. Hence, deductive theories must also contain a set of statements giving the conditions under which to expect the theory to produce true hypotheses.

To now draw upon another exposition of the function and operation of this kind of theory,[21] the following three points may be repeated:

1   All successful theoretical explanations must contain laws and statements of conditions which entail the hypothesis which is true, that is, the laws must lead as a matter of logical deduction to the specific statement of true fact.

2   The laws should be 'true' or at least have considerable evidence in their favor.

3   The hypotheses produced logically from the laws and statements

---

[21]   C. G. Hemphill and P. Oppenheim, 'Studies in the Logic of Explanation', *Philosophy of Science,* xv (1948), p. 156.

of conditions should be open to empirical test or, to put it another way, we must be able to find out empirically whether or not the hypotheses are true in fact.

The goal of explanation has not been forgotten in all of this. Puzzling observations are said to be explained when they fit an hypothesis as evidence and confirm it. It is then that facts become intelligible in terms of some comprehensive pattern of ideas. This pattern is the formal pattern (entailing the logic of deduction, and the hierarchical placement of statements) into which our observations are fitted. When this is successfully done, one could imagine other observations that would also be true, and thus see mentally the relationships between observations at hand and other possible ones. Consequently, a more comprehensive view of the subject matter is implied by a theory. Theories always go beyond specific cases.

Early in this chapter, three different criteria for judging theory were offered. The first of these was that the system must approach the ideal of logical purity appropriate to the form of explanation in use. We have now seen what the logical form is for a deductive explanation. The second criterion was that the theory must explain a number of observable phenomena. We have seen that one of the criteria for successful deductive explanation in science is that a theory must contain laws which have considerable support empirically and produce hypotheses which are found to fit the facts. The third criterion, that the explanation must be capable of bringing curiosity to rest, has no logic as such. To the extent that deductive theories can bring this about, they may be satisfying as explanations.

The emphasis on deduction has allowed, for the moment, the neglect of an important consideration about deductive theories that has nothing to do with deduction. This is the question of where the laws come from. We have taken as given the existence of general statements of the law type. The fact is that there are no formal rules for deriving laws from observations or constructs. There are rules for deduction, rules which when followed will always produce the logically 'true' conclusion from the given laws, but the laws themselves are harder to justify. This accounts in part for the controversy about just what types of statements the laws actually are. In fact, laws come from two main sources. One of these is from other disciplines, by analogy. Hence the previous discussion of analogies can now be seen for what it really is: a discussion of one source from which to draw by analogy general statements which might be transformed into sociological laws. These we can try to verify by experiment and observation. Hence the 'law of evolution' for the biologist can have not only a metaphorical meaning in sociology, but in principle it can have a scientific meaning too. The second source of laws is observation itself. When we, along with many others, see something occurring under specified conditions so often that it appears to be a very reliable regularity, we may cautiously suggest that occurrence under those conditions is a general rule. We can begin to treat the statement of it as a law from which to make specific predictions. When laws are generated in this way, we are likely to find the law couched in primitive terms rather than analogous ones.

Obviously, it is quite possible to be wrong about something or other's being a law. It is possible to start a deductive process with spurious statements at the highest level of generality – statements of a relationship which does not really exist. Hopefully, this error will show up in the testing of the hypotheses produced by such laws. These hypotheses ought to turn out to be empirically false. A more detailed discussion of this appears in the section on theory verification, but we ought now to be aware of the possibility of going on for some time in sociology with laws that are not laws at all, and with resultant hypotheses that are not adequately tested.

B. *Pattern or concatenated theories*

We have just seen that in deductive theories the systemic meanings of theoretical terms are derived logically from the formal deductive pyramid of statements of varying generality. In successful deductive theory, there is a smooth transition from high to low levels of generality when examining any phenomenon. This ease is produced by the deductive relationships among statements; statements could be said to display a 'vertical' relatedness. We are reminded of a pyramid, with specific hypotheses at the bottom, successively more general statements stacked on top of each other, and laws at the peak.

In *pattern* theories, by contrast, the vertical dimension is not as important, but what we might call 'lateral' logic is. The statements which compose the pattern and the constructs making up these statements are derivable from each other and are defined in terms of each other. When finally finished, theories of this kind form a system which contains in it logical referents and derivations of each concept, so that with reference to the system, each term or set of terms has an explanation. Hence, the system 'makes sense' as a set of ideas. The application of this system consists in 'seeing' the relationships between the theoretical terms and reality. This seeing has no clearly specified methodology, unlike deductive theory. Application of pattern theory is a more insightful exercise.

To give the sense of what is meant by this, compare a novel to a pattern theory. In a novel, there are no real people. The characters are all constructed in the author's imagination. Neither is there any real action reported. This again is invented. Nevertheless, novels have the power of invoking actual experience and illuminating the behaviors and feelings of real people in real situations. A novel does these things by giving the reader an insight into situations and patterns of action. The system of ideas, actions, and characters in the novel does not describe anything directly to be found in life. But novels contain systems of ideas and images that have the power to highlight, emphasize, and systematize real experiences so that we can feel that we have read of actual experience.

It is in this sense that 'Freud's theory' does its work. No one believes in the material existence of the 'ego'. Nevertheless, in Freud's story of the relations between this construct and other ones, the processes involving the ego form a pattern which has an internal coherence and contains a kind of sense. Application of pattern theory consists in knowing when and how to relate real experience to certain aspects of the pattern. The concepts in this kind of theory become appropriate on certain occasions in reality. When the concepts apply, it is appropriate to invoke the pattern as an explanation of reality.

Pattern theories have a natural tendency to become 'closed systems'. Since concepts gain their meaning from inside the pattern itself, the system gives full development to each of its component parts. In Chapter 1, it was shown that theories have a tendency to grow, attaining the status of general theory instead of remaining at the level which explains smaller portions of reality. It is this tendency that is now evident in pattern theories: insofar as they are able to achieve internal completeness and coherence by connecting all their concepts together in a system of related definitions, they become complete within themselves, or 'closed'. Parsons says of his theory that it

> 'is a body of logically interdependent generalized concepts of empirical reference. Such a system tends, ideally, to become logically closed, to reach such a state of logical integration that every logical implication of any combination of propositions in the system is explicitly stated in some other propostion in the same system.'[22]

Being logically closed, and yet intended for empirical use, it must thus be entirely general in its application.

Pattern theories, having this tendency to become logically closed as they develop within themselves the definitions of their concepts, contrast sharply with deductive theories, which are often called 'open'. At the bottom of deductive theory, there is room to accommodate new observations or to incorporate new hypotheses as these seem appropriate. Apart from the problem of selecting the terms to conceptualize these new hypotheses, deductive theory has little trouble in handling novelties. Similarly, at the top of deductive theory there is always room for another general principle which has the power to subsume all those below it. This is not so for pattern theories, because pattern theories are not so much concerned with the formalities of hierarchical deductive logic as they are

---

[22] Talcott Parsons, *Essays in Sociological Theory*, rev. ed. (New York: Free Press, 1954), p. 212.

with gaining an adequate theoretical description of a wide range of experience.

1. *Reductionism: changing forms of a given theory*

We know that theories tend to compete for territory and status. If there is more than one theory in a given area, all sorts of questions arise about the breadth, scope, and importance of each one in comparison to the others. This is quite natural, and in part has led to a debate in sociology known as the *reductionism* controversy.[23] Briefly, it has been argued that the theories of different branches and wings of science are, in principle, reducible to other more basic theories. Thus it is sometimes argued in sociology that 'sociological theory' (that which has as its focus of interest the behavior of collectivities) is reducible to 'psychological theory'. Psychology is the study which explains the individual, and since collectivities are composed of individuals, it is argued that we need no sociological theory at all. There should be only psychology. Of course, the biologist or geneticist could carry on this argument, saying that psychology is really reducible to his area; but the physicist might wish to argue that all of it is a matter of the physical mechanisms of atomic behavior – that these account in the end for biology, psychology, and sociology.

In an oblique way, each of these arguments would be right. Insofar as there are crucial dependencies among the social and biological sciences, the bases for reduction might be present. But if the theory of collectivities were reduced to terms of atomic mechanisms, it would be so unwieldy and cumbersome, and perhaps trite, that it would be of no use. Putting it formally, the levels on which theory operate are partly a matter of utility and convenience, and partly produced by observation and conceptualization.

This ties up nicely with the discussion of the difference between pattern-type and deductive-type theory in sociology. We noted that the pattern theories were concerned less with the hierarchies of deductive statements than with the internally defined and systematized arrangements of theoretical and explanatory terms. We also saw that the deductive theoretician regards something as 'explained' when it is deduced from a set of general principles. Now, it is possible to turn pattern theory into deductive theory simply by adding onto the top of a pattern theory a set of general statements which subsume the patterns described and allow one to 'deduce' the pattern from the added general statements.

There have been notable attempts to destroy sociology by reducing its

---

23 Although 'reductionism' is a general name for the reduction of any theory, in recent sociology the strongest claim for reductionism was made by Homans in 'Contemporary Theory in Sociology', in R. E. L. Faris, ed., *Handbook of Modern Sociology* (Chicago: Rand McNally, 1964), pp. 951ff.

theory to psychology in this way. The argument runs that if there is no truly sociological theory but only psychological theory, then there must not be any real subject matter for sociology, but only for psychology. In defense, sociologists have tended either to ignore the charge, or to derive uniquely sociological theories and generalizations. This has led to an interest in Durkheim's dictum that 'social facts' not reducible to individual facts are the subject matter of sociology. Similarly, social theorists have sought to use analogies related to biological and economic theory that give theoretical expression to phenomena which are not reducible to the behavior of the individuals participating, such as evolution, market, and so forth.

C. *Perspectives*

Perspectives are separated from pattern and deductive theories not by matters of kind so much as by matters of degree. Perspectives are collections of concepts which are important basically as 'sensitizing' agents. They point out important isolated aspects of reality. But perspectives are relatively less coherent and developed internally. In general, perspectives resemble pattern theory more than they do deductive theory.

For example, in sociology the school named 'symbolic interactionism', which is discussed in Chapter 6, is usually called a perspective. A perspective like this suggests and defines certain things which are of special importance when explaining social relations. In interactionism, we are asked to pay particular attention to the 'self' as it is formed, changed, and stabilized in interaction. There are several factors that, from this perspective, are important to the self-formation and -stabilization process. Some of these are the development of a particular self-definition and fortification of it against disconfirmatory or confusing evidence, utilization of symbolic communication to achieve social integration, and so on. A perspective provides a language in which to have discourse about a kind of reality, but it does not tell you specifically what to say in that language.[24]

There are several other 'theories' that might be called perspectives in sociology. Indeed, the term lacks precision partly because a body of ideas called a theory by one might be a perspective to another. If all we want to know is a theory's general suggestions and general explanations, we are taking it as a perspective. That is, theories can be considered perspectives; however, bodies of ideas lacking structural coherence and specificity can not be turned into theories without additional effort.

In addition to sensitizing us in certain ways to the social environment, and suggesting a language in which to describe experience, a perspective

---

[24] A. M. Rose's *Human Behavior and Social Process* (Boston: Houghton Mifflin, 1962) is a book based on interactionism. Although Rose attempts a 'systematic summary' of interactionism, the summary does not constitute a theory.

usually specifies certain general processes. When Marxism is taken as a perspective, the general process is conflict between naturally opposed groups. We need not ask too searching a question about the nature, origins, kinds, and conditions of conflict (that is, we need not have a theoretical treatment of it) in order to understand Marxism as a body of perspective based on conflict. However, Marxism might be used as a theory if the appropriate theoretical questions were answered.

VII. *Verification of theories*

Throughout this book the emphasis is on the types of schemes man uses to explain social experience. It is always a theory's explanatory value that is most important. Because this is the case, *verification* of theory is of central interest. Verification is the business of finding out which theories, or which aspects of a theory, are right. 'Right' means, broadly speaking, having the ability to produce theoretical descriptions or hypotheses which describe actual experience; 'right' theories come true. Hence, the verification problem is the problem of sorting out the theory which has some kind of truth value from the one which is 'false'. The question of verification is related to the question of the application of theory in actual research and interpretive work, and involves several problems soon to be discussed. As one might expect, the questions are different for the different kinds of theory. The problem of verification of deductive theory will be described below, then verification of pattern theory. Concerning deductive theory, the problem divides into two problems – a philosophical one and a methodological one. The philosophical aspect will be treated first.

A. *Verification of deductive theories*

When we have derived an hypothesis from a theory by deducing it, the hypothesis is logically 'true'. The hypothesis was implicitly contained in the general statements of the theory at a high level of generalization and, by deductive thinking, we simply applied the generalization to a specific case and produced a hypothesis. We added nothing, observed nothing, subtracted nothing in doing this – we simply deduced. Now the question is whether or not this logically true hypothesis is empirically true. Does the hypothesis, which states a logically derived relationship among ideas, state an actual relationship?

The obvious way to decide would simply be to go and look, and this is exactly what sociologists do. But what ought to be the conclusion if, on looking, the sociologist actually finds what he takes to be the hypothesized relationship? Would he regard the hypothesis as confirmed, and hence the theory as confirmed as well? Or is only the hypothesis confirmed? Or is even it confirmed?

He would tentatively conclude that the hypothesis had been confirmed, but he would bear in mind the following factors:

1 that the hypothesis could have been confirmed by 'chance'
   — that is, that it was a chance association he observed, and not one of regularity
2 that the hypothesis was true, but for different reasons than those suggested by the theory
   — that is, that while the hypothesis might be empirically true, the theory might still be wrong
3 that the hypothesis could have been found true because of its relation to unsuspected factors
   — that is, that it is a reliable but coincidental relationship he has hypothesized, and not a reliable and dependent one

Now imagine that the sociologist, hypothesis in hand, looks around and concludes that the hypothesis does not seem 'right'. Something logically 'true' appears empirically 'false'. What might his conclusions be? Again, it would appear that he should conclude the theory to be 'wrong', and so he should – but he ought to bear in mind that his observations might be inaccurate.

Note that when the sociologist is trying to decide what he should do on finding his hypothesis confirmed, he is in a deeper quandary than when deciding what to do if it is not confirmed by his observations. It is far easier and less risky to decide that a theory is 'wrong' when it produces empirically false hypotheses than to decide a theory is 'right' when it produces empirically true hypotheses. There are several reasons why an hypothesis might appear empirically true when it is in fact false. The spurious confirmations of the hypothesis result from the factors mentioned above, such as wrong observation, chance, intervening factors, and so on. On the other hand, when a theory produces an hypothesis which turns out to be empirically false, all the things that lead to the production of that hypothesis are logically 'in' the theory, and if that hypothesis is empirically false (and observation has been correct), then the theory must be 'wrong'. Hence it is far easier to say that a theory is 'wrong' than to say that one is 'right'.

This seems like an impasse. It seems that we can only come to final conclusions on the usefulness of deductive theories that are wrong. We can only come to a final conclusion when the theory is not good at producing empirically true hypotheses. It is not possible to come to a conclusion so final about a theory that consistently produces right hypotheses, because these might be right for reasons not contained in the theory.

Now, the topic being discussed is verification of theories, and we have demonstrated that it is not possible to 'verify' deductive theories in anything like a full and final positive sense, although it is possible to 'falsify' theories which produce wrong hypotheses. In fact, this is the way scientists tend to look at the verification problem for deductive theory. The whole program of verification in deductive theory is one of comparison among competing theories relating to the same phenomenon. The theories are narrowed down by falsification until there remain only the ones which are yet unfalsified. It is this residue of unfalsified theories that we work with until evidence builds up that they, too, are false. Hence, the theoretically minded sociologist does not take a theory as he would take a fact. A theory is always tentative, and the closest we can come to a final conclusion concerning an unfalsified theory is to say that it seems at the moment to be true.[25]

Decisions are not usually as clear-cut as this description suggests. Theories produce a whole range of hypotheses, not just one. Hence, it is probable that a given theory will produce by deductive logic some hypotheses that are better than others – some empirically true, some empirically false. Those that do turn out to be false can point out necessary alterations in the theoretical structure. Thus, the philosophical problem of verification is the problem of which decisions to make about a theory based on comparative falsification. These decisions and judgments remain tentative. If you have ever wondered why a science can carry on for a long time with false theory, this is part of the reason.

The methodological part of the verification–falsification problem with deductive theory concerns how theory actually 'contains' a prediction. The problem is whether the theory is really falsifiable at all. If it is not, then there could be no possible way of reaching the conclusion that the hypotheses are not empirically true. If there is no way, in principle, of coming to this conclusion, then we can never know the empirical usefulness of such a theory. An example of this will help to illustrate the meaning. Thorstein Veblen's idea of an 'instinct of workmanship' in *The Theory of the Leisure Class* provides an example.[26] If we wish to try to verify whether or not such an instinct exists, how would we go about it? Veblen says that it does, but that as affluence grows a person tends to waste money and leisure as a sign that he has 'arrived' socially and that work is no longer necessary for sumptuous maintenance. But we wish to try to verify Veblen's theory. On examination, we see many people working diligently, and some conspicuously consuming goods and engaging in wasteful pursuits. What do we conclude? That Veblen was right? How can we? People may work for many reasons, only one of which might have anything to do with Veblen's hypothesis of an instinct to do so. Also, if people are endowed with an instinct for workmanship and creative effort, how could they so easily abandon this instinct when they get money ahead? The fact is, Veblen has given two contradictory

25 See Karl R. Popper, *The Logic of Scientific Discovery* (New York: Harper and Row, 1959).
26 New York: Macmillan, 1899.

hypotheses about man's nature: that he (1) instinctively works and creates, and (2) wastes time and conspicuously destroys created materials. When we see someone doing one of these, Veblen appears right; when we see someone doing the opposite, Veblen again appears right. In fact, we cannot conceive of anyone doing anything that could not be given a Veblenesque interpretation. Hence there is no possible observation that could falsify Veblen's theory. We can never know, therefore, if his theory has any empirical truth or not.

A word of caution. Theories that are not falsifiable seem to cover a great deal of ground, as the above example shows, and do so with amazing facility. Sometimes these may seem to be the best theories. But the fact is that another theory, similarly lacking in falsifiability but different in every other respect, could be set against Veblen's. Then there would be two sets of unfalsifiable but opposite hypotheses, neither set of which could be judged according to its empirical value. Science would be no better off for having these two, just as it is no better off for having one or the other.

What things make a theory falsifiable? The answer is that it must refer to observables, either directly or indirectly. Generally speaking, a theory must yield hypotheses which are specific, and be clear about the conditions under which to expect its hypotheses to hold. Vagueness is the enemy of falsifiability. For example, Marx may have predicted that revolution will occur in capitalist societies, given certain general conditions. But what exactly is the revolutionary condition, and what exactly is a revolution? Can Marxian principles be applied to 'green revolutions' or revolutions in morals? Overgenerality and vagueness make Marxian theory hard to apply with precision, and therefore hard to logically falsify.

Concerning theory stated in non-observable terms, we see that we cannot falsify 'Freud's theory' because there are no observables related concretely or abstractly to the entities postulated in it. Hence we have interpretations, but not falsifiable hypotheses, even though we might speak of a 'Freudian hypothesis'. In short, if we are going to have hypotheses as a basis for adjudicating theories, then we must insist on falsifiability.

B. *Verification of pattern theories*

A key term related to verification of pattern theories is 'interpretation'. We saw that deductive theories were 'open' at the bottom. They produced by deductive logic hypotheses contained in the general statements or laws. Hence the form of the hypothetical statement did not change when the hypothesis was deduced, only the level of specificity. By contrast, in pattern theories we have no such convenient hypothesis-producing machine which turns out logically true hypotheses. Instead, we must interpret the theory in relation to situations we wish to have explained. To interpret it means simply this: to know the theory sufficiently well that one is confident the facts observed are similar in nature to those conceptualized in the theory – that they 'fit' it. To put it another way, we must use a theory of sufficient clarity and precision so that anyone familiar with it would, as a matter of common sense, see that the descriptive and explanatory content of the theory had an interpretive application to a real situation.

Of course, there are limits to this kind of interpretive understanding of a pattern, and again the analogy to the novel makes this clear. We do not expect children to read novels for the meaning, but they can understand the story. The difference between children and ourselves is that our experience with life makes episodes in the novel stand out as having particular meaning and significance. We see their application. We interpret the novel in experience, getting a level of meaning above that of the story and one which may be applicable to ourselves because it highlights aspects of reality we only dimly understood before. We interpret pattern theory in a similar way. We see the story. But beyond that, we see the implied or explicit reasoning and development which brought the story about. In novels we know the difference between fantasy and 'real life' simply because we realize one kind of book is not pertinent to what we experience, but that the other is.

A pattern theory is a kind of reconstructed picture of reality, which points out clearly the relationships among its part so that they can be grasped more easily and profoundly than without the theory. Application of this kind of theory is 'seeing' the reality on which the concepts and processes are based. By reference to such a theory, one can develop ideas about relationships and processes to be expected in reality.

We can seek these real relationships either entirely mentally, or mentally and empirically. If we do it mentally, we interpret what we actually see in terms of the theory, trying to cover every aspect. If it has seemed to give a reasonable and definitive picture of what is actually there, then we can consider this to be evidence of the usefulness of the theory. We can proceed more empirically, by interpreting what measures we might take and what observations we might expect to find. An example of this is found in the treatment of the concept of motivation in sociology and psychology. Motivation is something that no one will ever see, and hence it is entirely conceptual with respect to other ideas alongside it in a theory. Now when we seek correlations, for example, between kinds of motivation and achievement, we are seeking these correlations not because we have evidence suggesting they should be there, but because the pattern suggests they should be. In a real situation similar to our pattern of ideas we may have a piece of confirmatory evidence. This evidence confirms that part of the theory which suggested it. By implication, it confirms the whole pattern that gave rise to it.

As with the deductive model, it is much more sound to proceed on the basis of falsification than confirmation. We saw that the principle of falsification of a deductive theory added strictures of clarity and specificity. The same applies to pattern theory. But here the problem is compounded. Since we have constructed the whole pattern as a coherent picture of reality, it should contain an account of just about everything we might come upon in reality. Hence, by nature, pattern theories are less susceptible to falsification than are deductive ones. This is both a blessing and a curse. The blessing is that pattern theories are capable of extremes of internal coherence and meaningfulness which are intellectually very exciting. The curse is that they are less restricted in reaching these limits and can drift further and further away from any useful application.

VIII. *Conclusion*

In this chapter the types of terms and the styles of explanation now in use in social science have been surveyed briefly. It has been emphasized that explanation is more than just 'making clear'. It is an exercise contained by a more or less formal structure of concepts with specific relationships. These arrays of concepts have, to some degree, the power to bring our curiosity to rest, to do it logically and coherently, and to pertain to reality. We have noted that doing one or another of these things does not necessarily give a theory high status, but it is in doing them simultaneously that theories gain their staying power. It is worth noting again that explanation, while it must remain the prime goal of social science, is an ideal, probably never to be reached entirely. We do not have, and may never have, theories which maximize all the criteria of theoretical performance to the fullest. Thus, because of the need for accurate prediction and explanation, and the intellectual importance of coherent, reasonable thought, theoretical work is never complete and ought never to be regarded as a finished foundation on which to build. It is a changing and developing foundation, and it is worthy of particular attention for its own sake.

KEY CONCEPTS

observational term	systemic meaning
construct	deduction
theoretical term	hierarchical order
primitive term	concatenated theory
analogous term	deductive theory
true by definition	perspective
empirically true	laws
general proposition	'other things being equal'
falsifiability	reductionism
verification	interpretation

1 What is the difference between a pattern theory and a deductive theory? Could we have theories of both types pertaining to the same subject?

2 What is the difference between primitive terms and analogous terms?

3 What are some of the kinds of analogies in use in sociological theory?

4 How could a descriptive analogy disguise an explanation?

5 Describe how some hypothesis could be 'logically true' but 'empirically false'.

6 What are some of the things one might be referring to when one speaks of a 'law' in science?

7 What is the difference between verification and falsification?

8 What differentiates a pattern theory from a perspective?

9 How did the example of the 'spirit of capitalism' illustrate systemic meaning?

10 'Society' is said to be a construct. Why?

ESSAY QUESTIONS

How is a deductive theory verified?

Compare deductive- and pattern-type theories with specific attention to their internal logical structure.

If we deduce an hypothesis from a given theory and find it to appear 'true' empirically, what can we say about the theory from which it came?

Describe the ways in which the biological analogy has entered sociological description and explanation.

What does the phrase 'other things being equal' have to do with deductive theory?

What do we mean when we say we have observed a person's role?

Name some primitive terms from sociology and describe why you think they are primitive to it.

Discuss how a theory may be taken as a perspective, and tell what additional information and analysis are needed to transform the perspective into a theory.

FOR FURTHER READING AND STUDY

Brodbeck, Mae (ed.). *Readings in the Philosophy of the Social Sciences.* New York: Macmillan, 1968.

Gibson, Quentin. *The Logic of Social Enquiry.* London: Routledge and Kegan Paul, 1960.

Gross, Llewellyn (ed.). *Sociological Theory: Inquiries and Paradigms.* New York: Harper and Row, 1967.

Kaplan, Abraham. *The Conduct of Inquiry.* San Francisco: Chandler Publishing Co., 1964.

Langer, Susanne K. *Philosophy in a New Key.* Cambridge, Mass.: Harvard University Press, 1951.

Nagel, Ernest. *The Structure of Science: Problems in the Logic of Scientific Explanation.* New York: Harcourt Brace and World, 1961.

Popper, Karl R. *The Logic of Scientific Discovery.* New York: Harper and Row, 1959.

Ryan, Alan. *The Philosophy of the Social Sciences.* London: Macmillan, 1970.

4   Exchange theory

I. *Introduction*

In this chapter we begin to inspect a working theory in sociology –
exchange theory. A word about the name of this theory. As 'exchange'
theory implies, this theory concerns the trade or exchange among individuals of valued objects or sentiments as a basis for social order. The
exchange in question usually does not pertain to tangible things. Rather,
it commonly involves intangible commodities such as esteem, liking,
assistance, and approval. The idea of exchange also applies to the avoid-
ance of something such as pain, expense, embarrassment, and the like.
And sometimes exchange might involve opportunities, advantages, or
other comparative states between individuals. In general, the idea of
exchange is very broad and inclusive, not limited to the giving and
receiving of things which can be seen.

In the discussion of exchange theory, we encounter the *deductive*
approach to organizing sociological theory. Chapter 3 explained how a
theory could be built hierarchically according to lawlike principles, from
which hypotheses about actual observations could be deduced. One of
the modern founders of exchange theory in sociology, who is currently
its main proponent, George C. Homans, decided to organize his theory
this way. In studying exchange theory, there is an opportunity to see
deductive theory-building applied to sociological subject matter.

II. *Origins of the sociological use of the term 'exchange'*

As with most ideas, the idea of exchange in social science has a long and
varied history. Indeed, an idea as simple as giving and receiving is probably as old as man himself, but the review of it here will go back only as
far as the eighteenth century.[1] In the middle of that century, several
people were giving serious thought to finding a way to account for the
social order they saw around them. Others had thought about this, of
course, but previous theories were often judged unsatisfactory. For
example, several theories of social order had emerged using some varia-

---

[1] See Adam Smith, *An Inquiry into the Nature and Causes of the Wealth of
Nations* (Homewood, Ill.: Richard D. Irwin, 1963).

74

tion of the social contract concept which suggested that individuals of a given society had some collective arrangements with a sovereign power.[2] In some theories this sovereign power had unlimited authority once he was elevated to office, and in others he had power more or less at the pleasure of those making the contract. All of the contract theories employed the useful but highly artificial idea that persons composing the body politic actually made an agreement between themselves and the eventual governing authority. If this principle were extended to contracts between persons and an abstract government, matters became quite ambiguous.

The weakness in this kind of thinking for social science was not that it employed the concept of contract, but that it was clearly not empirically true that every person in a given society had such arrangements with his sovereign. Often peasants under the rule of great and famous kings did not even know the identity of their monarch, much less have any hand in his being powerful. Since this was true, it was hard to see how the theoretical justification of the political contract could extend to the actual social order discoverable in every town and village.

In the eighteenth century a new wave of critical thought about the nature of social order accompanied changing economic and social conditions. While there had been extensive commerce among European nations for some time, the mid-eighteenth century saw the reorganization of economic enterprise which was to culminate eventually in what is referred to as the Industrial Revolution.[3] This meant that trade and manufacturing, standards of value, organization of production and of markets, accounting procedures, wage labor, and so on, were important topics in the minds of thinking men of the time. It was bound to occur to somebody, sooner or later, that perhaps the forces which kept economic markets relatively stable and functioning were specific manifestations of the principles accounting for social order in general.

There was great advantage in this kind of theorizing. It seemed down to earth and, in principle, was based on observable activities. No more was it necessary to claim some kind of abstract contract between men. The idea of an economic market analogy to general social order was basically this: individual decisions about buying, selling, trading, and carrying, made in the course of commercial activities, were special cases of more general decisions about daily life, and these general decisions could be understood in the same way as economic decisions. The question, 'What am I going to get out of this?' took on a theoretical meaning. It seemed

---

2 Several thinkers contributed in various ways to the 'contract' school of social and political thinking, in particular, Thomas Hobbes, Jean-Jacques Rousseau and John Locke. For a secondary treatment of contract thought, see George H. Sabine, *A History of Political Theory*, 4th ed. (New York: Holt, Rinehart and Winston, 1973).

3 No date can be placed on the Industrial Revolution; historians are not agreed.

possible to apply the concepts of the economic theory of the time to all social transactions and emerge with a general theory of social order.

Some other occurrences about this time and on into the nineteenth century reinforced the emerging conceptual basis of exchange theory. As industrialization initially gained ground, the existing legal systems of Western Europe were not equipped to handle it and its consequences. At first, there was no body of regulatory law to control hours of work, minimum wages, conditions of employment, superannuation, benefits to families, and the like. Neither was there controlling law yet applied to monopolies, business practices, factory location, and so on. In general, until the reform movements caught up to the pace of the rapidly expanding industrial revolution, there was an era of free-for-all competition which emphasized extreme individualism. This individualism could be both good and bad. It allowed the free run of genius to build up capital for reinvestment, development of new techniques, and industrial practices. It also allowed a free hand to employers, employees, and competitors in exploiting and undercutting each other in irresponsible, even lethal ways.

It was primarily an interest in market economics, then, emphasizing the concept of exchange, which thrust the idea of an entirely free individual into the forefront of social thought. Later on, the theory of evolution, as popularized, emphasized a struggle among the individual members of a species in a limited and sometimes hostile environment. The theory of evolution added credence to the existing emphasis on the individualistic, freely competitive picture of social order then developing.[4]

It is this legacy of social history and theory which exchange theory carries with it today. Who exchanges what, in exchange theory? The answer is always that persons, individuals, exchange things. The unit of analysis is the person and not the collective, the society, the group. What does he exchange? He trades what is uniquely and privately his to give, whatever that might be. What does he get for it? He tries to get whatever he might personally happen to want. We do not need, in exchange theory, to imagine that a group of people must share common values to form a society. From exchange theory's point of view, persons of quite different tastes and propensities can live side by side in the same society if they can provide for each other the services and amenities each one happens to desire.

The period of extreme European and North American individualism as a way of life was actually rather short, although the political and social philosophy accompanying it lasts to this day. And extreme individualism engendered a reaction, a move toward collectivism, a banding together

---

[4] See Dorothy Marshall, *Industrial England, 1776-1851* (London: Routledge and Kegan Paul, 1973).

for the common good and mutual aid. This collective action was bound to need a philosophy and a series of theories to give depth and justification to it. These theories were forthcoming; a theoretical opposite to extreme individualism emerged in sociology with many variations.

We are the intellectual heirs to these exciting times of the eighteenth and nineteenth centuries. Sociology has gravitated, at one time or another, toward either the individualistic or the collectivistic pole of a theoretical continuum. The years from approximately 1937 to the late 1950s were dominated by sociological theory emphasizing structured relations, specification of roles, and perhaps a tendency toward collective determinism. (There is a great deal more about this in Chapter 5 on the theories of Parsons and the functionalists.) Exchange theory, in its present form, is actually a return to the spirit and principles of extreme individualism as a reaction to structuralism and functional theory of the 1940s and 1950s.[5] The emergence of exchange theory in the late 1950s and its development in the 1960s can be viewed as another chapter in the continuing debate about the proper theoretical way to picture the individual-in-society, a question first raised in a modern fashion by the coming of the industrial age.

Modern exchange theory also owes a deep debt to experimental psychology. As a well-defined position among the schools of psychology, experimental psychology bears remarkable similarity to the main features of individualistic social theory just described. It emphasizes the concrete behavior of specific individuals or, more often in this field, experimental animals. It takes this individualistic veiwpoint in combination with considerable emphasis on the concept of motivation – the apparent eagerness of individuals to act for reasons of their own. However, private motives may sometimes be manipulated experimentally. While not contradicting the individualistic assumption about motivation, it is possible to see how persons could come to exhibit orderly patterns of activity based on their individualistic natures. Experimental psychology is a branch of 'learning theory'. It suggests in general that persons' actions can be shaped, controlled, and therefore predicted by altering environments, especially the things that reward them and the things they wish to avoid. In experiments, it is possible to control these rewarding and punishing qualities fairly precisely, and in real life it seems possible to observe such things, applying the same principles of explanation outside the laboratory as inside it. Thus it is possible to observe a subject as he learns to cope with or master his environment and correspondingly con-

---

5 Modern exchange theory (from the 1950s onward) arose partly as a critique of sociological functionalism. See Alvin Gouldner, 'Reciprocity and Autonomy in Functional Theory', in Llewellyn Gross, ed., *Symposium on Sociological Theory* (Evanston, Ill.: Row, Peterson, 1959), pp. 241-70.

ceptualize this by suggesting that the subject is particularly responsive to the rewarding or punishing features of his environment.[6]

The experimental psychology tradition bears considerable similarity to a very old philosophical movement called hedonism. Not much detail is needed here, except to point out that experimental psychology is based on more than just experiments with animals. Hedonism as a philosophy affirms that individuals are capable of discriminating between pleasure and pain and that naturally they will always try to avoid pain and gain pleasure for themselves. As a philosophy, hedonism was largely applied to the problem of how to organize the world so that all could experience pleasure and minimize pain and so that one person's pleasure did not entail another's pain. It was thought that this pleasure-and-pain principle was a basic law of human affairs, and that it would be senseless to expect people to behave as if it were not. Experimental psychology makes somewhat the same assumption in postulating that we can always expect persons to discriminate among stimuli and act on the basis of whether they find them rewarding.

We have now built up a sketch of the intellectual background from which exchange theory draws. Briefly recall the objective of theory so that we can see more clearly what these intellectual foundations were bound to produce. The aim in sociological theory is to explain social order. Hence, exchange theory's simple purpose in sociology is to build upon a set of basic principles drawn from consistent and complementary lines of thought (economic individualism, experimental psychology, and hedonistic philosophy) and to erect a coherent and workable general explanation of social order.

III. *A general statement of the principles of sociological exchange theory*

As with all sociological theories, it is difficult to separate particular theoretical statements from the generalities of the theoretical model. Exchange theory is no exception to this. This chapter considers particularly the works of George Homans and Peter Blau. In addition, other contemporary contributions, comment, and critical material will be reviewed. But first, in order to highlight the main ideas, a generalized description of the elements of exchange theory is presented.

A. *The unit of analysis in exchange theory*

The unit of analysis, the thing to watch when observing, and the one which plays a main part in the explanation of order, is the *individual*.

---

[6] Of particular importance to this movement in psychology was B. F. Skinner, *The Behavior of Organisms* (New York: Appleton-Century-Crofts, 1938).

Exchange theory does not ask preliminary questions about things like institutions, public opinion, or cultural commitment. Nor is the group *per se* the main focus at first, although exchange theory usually ends up saying something about groups, institutions, sentiment, and so forth. Exchange theory does not remain focused on the individual. However, it begins there because it intends to examine the social interchanges persons have among themselves which eventually lead to order and change. By focusing primarily on individuals as a starting point, its practitioners hope to learn something about the nature of groups. In exchange theory, groups are understood as serving the ends of their members. Hence there is no justification for suggesting that groups begin with special identities of their own, have a nature not derived from their members, and so on.

B. *Motive in exchange theory*

It is assumed that persons have their own private desires and ends-in-view. Everyone may need certain things, but this does not make these things 'common goals'. We all need food, but food is not a common goal in the same sense that victory is the common goal of an army which organizes and disciplines itself toward that end. Assumed here is the premise that persons are egoistically motivated by their private and unique combinations of goals and wants (even though these may eventually be accounted for by 'culture'). The exchange theorist persists in viewing *motivation* as a private and individual matter, although he may see culture as having a hand in it. But no matter what, motivation is expected to be in the direction of gaining wanted commodities, pleasure, satisfaction and the like, and nothing else.

What about the altruist? How does exchange theory account for the person who gives away his money to charity, or risks his life to save a drowning man? Certainly these activities entail loss and risk, something seemingly contrary to the assumption. The usual way this kind of problem has been handled is to point out that giving away your goods to help others imparts a sense of deep emotional satisfaction, even if it does mean a money loss. Remember that the rewards involved in exchange theory can be of any type whatsoever, and it is said that emotional reward can offset money loss. Similarly, it might be worth the risk to dive in and save a drowning man. The payoff for such an act could be recognition and self-satisfaction, to say nothing of the enormous debt the saved man would owe his rescuer in gratitude or esteem. It is also worth remembering, if you are considering rejection of exchange theory right now, that the altruist is much in the minority in human affairs, and if exchange theorists simply wrote him off as unexplainable, there would be a very large amount of behavior left over.

C. *Profit*

We have assumed a person acts egoistically to gain himself pleasure or satisfaction. With all persons doing this, no one can act in a vacuum. All will have to give as well as get. They must, because to disregard the other person is to deny him his reward. In the absence of mutual satisfaction there would be no social interaction at all. Because of this give and take, as the exchange theorist sees it, there is always some cost involved in gaining reward. Cost is normally defined as the effort required to gain a satisfaction, plus the potential rewards that we might have had if we had done something else. This last point requires some attention.

We might be interested in explaining why Bill and Pat went to the movies instead of going out to eat. Of course, the date is going to cost them something, no matter what they do. But this simple example is complicated, if we really try to understand the concept of 'cost'. First, there is the relative price of eating and of watching a film. But it is perhaps also important to Bill to impress Pat, and taking her to a 'B' movie might be decidedly less effective than treating her to dinner in a good restaurant. Also, consider the fact that he cannot take her to eat in common clothes; he might have to spend more time and effort (not to mention money) dressing for this occasion than for a trip to the cinema. Without going any further, and without considering the viewpoint of Pat in any way, we see that an array of possible rewards and costs is set before Bill. The exchange theorist views Bill as being aware of these rewards and costs (in principle he is aware of all of them). Being so informed, Bill makes his choice.

Now, what are his costs? They are the actual costs of what he did – take Pat to the movie – plus the forgone rewards he would have got if he had taken her to dinner. Why does dinner come in again? It comes in because his efforts with Pat would have been advanced by taking her to dinner, but he chose not to do this. He lost the benefits of that activity, and he must count them in with the costs of doing what he chose to do. Bill did, however, get something out of his decision. He went out with Pat, which is bound to have been of some benefit to him, and he did not have to pay as much to do it, either. On his calculations, what he got for his pains was a good return on effort, and what he lost by not taking her to dinner would not have been worth that much more, anyway. If we can say the above is true for Bill, we might say that, all things considered, he made a *profit* in the movie date. In more formal language, he maximized his reward and minimized his cost. His profit is determined by comparing reward and cost; it is the difference between them. Profit accrues when reward is greater than cost. Bill might have had higher rewards from the dinner date, but he would have had higher cost, too. The difference, taken as profit, was not as great in the case of dining, and so he chose the films.

D. *Voluntarism*

It should be evident that exchange theory emphasizes the type of social action we might label *voluntary*. It views everyday behavior as responsive to individual desire and calculation; it assumes a large degree of freedom of choice for the actors. How could it do otherwise? If a person had no choice about action, it would make no sense to speak about comparing rewards and costs of alternatives. In sociology, we sometimes emphasize the constraints placed on persons by outside forces, but exchange theorists never overemphasize this since, for exchange theory, it leads to an absurdity. The absurdity lies in conceptually denying the individual powers of decision. There is considerable choice in human affairs, and no matter how dominant culture may appear, it is never so complete as to specify totally the actions of people.

E. *Social approval*

One more thing should be pointed out about human exchange systems – the apparent importance of approval as a general satisfier and motivator. Up to now, little has been said about the things which reward people. Reward is a cornerstone of the theory of social exchange, but no one has really specified what it is. In fact, exchange theorists are reluctant to be too specific about this, since to do so would be to construct a set of categories of reward which would then require justification. Why would such-and-such actually be rewarding? Exchange theory avoids this because of its emphasis on individuality and voluntarism. The things that reward people may be unique to them; hence categorization of rewards would violate a basic assumption about individuality.

But it does seem that we can discover generalized rewards, and the most powerful one is *social approval*. In everyday terms, this is the 'liking' people seem to seek and enjoy in social relations. Persons prefer others who like them and approve of them, and shun those who are disapproving or critical. Furthermore, this is not always a conscious, calculated matter. Experimental evidence suggests that persons will respond to approving aspects of their environment even when they are concentrating on something else and are completely unaware of the subtle approving nature of the environment. A warm, encouraging, pleasant interviewer generally gets more full and complete responses from subjects than one who seems disapproving or curt. We usually try to cultivate a 'neutral' attitude in interviews so that people will not manufacture responses just to prolong the pleasant conversation. As the term implies, social approval can take many concrete forms. It is the apparent regard of the approver that makes the encounter a rewarding one.

IV. *General theory of social order based on exchange fundamentals*

Thus far the subjects discussed have been individuals and the ways they are motivated, from the exchange theorist's point of view. But the sociological theorist's aim is to reach conclusions about the nature of groups. And examining individuals who exchange does imply a picture of group action and cohesion. Whom would we expect to associate regularly? Those who can substantially reward each other. Those who require rewards which can be gained in interaction with particular individuals will regularly associate with those individuals. How will they do it? They will establish 'rates of exchange' among the things they trade (tangible or not). Associated with these rates of exchange will be the relative costs of producing rewarding actions and the relative availability of them. Usually these dynamic forces lead to varying amounts of esteem becoming associated with the members of the group. Thus we might account for 'group structure', which consists of the predictable positions occupied by members and the relative importance and centrality of such positions. Group structure will be accounted for by the dynamic interplay of individually derived forces at work in the group.

Viewing social approval as a generalized reward, we can predict roughly that mutual social approval will be high among people who regularly associate freely together. And we can suppose that if social approval is all a person has to offer, it alone will be sufficient to attract at least some others and that, in a group, all persons will gain at least some approval. But there is one thing about social approval which makes it inadequate as an explanatory concept for much of what happens in groups. Social approval does not usually cost much to give and it is in never-ending supply. When we approve of someone, we do not thereby reduce our stockpile of approval, making it more costly to approve of him next time or to approve of someone else. From an exchange viewpoint, mere approval is exceedingly cheap as a commodity. This means that while social approval as a general reinforcer can explain some association, other rewarding qualities of persons, such as knowledge or skill, remain crucial. A general reward such as social approval, which costs little or nothing, will probably not elicit other scarce resources in the give-and-take imagined by exchange theorists.

A. *Ranking and value*

Imagine we wish to investigate the *ranking* schemes found in groups. We might observe a particular group in which there is a definite hierarchy of persons (there usually is). This 'pecking order' may be indicated by who defers to whom, whose word is least often questioned, who sits at the head of the table. All these aspects of ranking within the group are components of the general social order evident in the group. To explain ranking using exchange, we employ the ideas of value and scarcity introduced above. Social approval is not usually the only basis for high rank. It is too readily available to be highly valued. But many exchange commodities are rare; something may be highly sought after and be in short supply, perhaps hard to produce. This comparatively scarce yet wanted item will be *valuable* in the comparative sense in which we are using the term 'value'.

Regarding the rank ordering in a group, compare two men. Let us say that one is highly capable of rewarding the other with witty and intelligent conversation. He might possess wisdom, and his delivery might be easy and agreeable. The other person, however, is not so witty, and usually can think of the perfect comeback only after the opportunity to use it is long past. However, this latter one is able to give approval to the witty man. Now we will undoubtedly see that the wit and charm which seem to be a gift of the first will outrank the simple approval proffered by the second. It does so because it is a scarce commodity, not easily attained. It is worth something to have a man like that around, whereas the more simple-minded are 'a dime a dozen'. This outranking makes the supplier of the charm and wit of special significance for the enjoyment of all, and his presence will be sought ahead of that of the others. That is, he ranks high in that group.

B. *Value is comparative*

Obviously this is a very simple example. Groups are usually far more complex. There is often a wide array of valuable activities which cannot all be produced with equal facility by any one person. This array of rewards becomes the basis of the *comparative* ranking system in our sample group. How does one kind of reward come to outrank another? Those which are comparatively the most valuable, because they are of most service yet hardest to get, will 'cost' the most. This cost, perhaps in terms of social approval, goes to the providers of these valued things and becomes observable as their esteem within the group.

C. *'Explaining' the group*

What else would we like to know about the group we are now discussing? One of the stock-in-trade items that sociologists research is *conformity* to rules. How do standards apply? We might be tempted to say that group standards apply universally and that deviation is likely to be viewed in the same way, no matter who deviates. But alas, it is not so. Group standards apply differentially and, as we will see, this may be a good thing. It is important to keep in mind that we are not now studying another group, but the same one. We are extending our investigation into the theoretical account of group behavior. Hence, we must keep in mind the basis of the exchange theory account of rank ordering. We add to the analysis now by considering the dynamics of rank ordering, yielding a theoretical account of conformity to group norms.

First, recognize that conformity to group standards might be a source of satisfaction in its own right. Doing what others expect of us without being forced is what we usually mean when we talk about moral behavior or 'socialized' activity. But most exchange theorists would not stop at this as an explanation. We must explain, they say, why these commitments arise, and not just say that they do.

Note that we are not looking for just one reason to account for all the conformity among the group members. It is a basic principle of exchange theory that individuality implies private motives. Hence, the conclusion left to us is that conformity to norms gains individuals something. That something may vary from person to person. But whatever the happy results of belonging may be for a particular person, there is at least one way of obtaining them: by conforming to group standards. Conforming behavior is an outward sign of belonging, an advertisement to the other members and to outsiders that the benefits of group membership ought to be conferred on the conformer.

According to this, the person on the receiving end of group benefits would always be the most conformist-minded. If he is giving mostly social approval and getting something more scarce and harder to obtain in return, the balance at this juncture seems to be in his favor. We might expect those benefiting most in our group to be the most conformist. If a real situation were this simple, exchange theory would predict precisely this. But it might also be true that persons in the lower ranks are receiving less benefit from group membership than those of more importance. In relation to what they give they may be getting good measure, but compared to others giving more, they may be getting less. Hence their commitment to the success of the group might be less. And because of this lesser commitment, the standards of the group might be less important to those in the lower ranks. This would be especially true in the light of another of our basic starting points – that reward is calculated on a comparative basis. If another group were competing for the loyalty of our lower-ranking members, it would probably draw off some of their commitment to group expectations, lowering their willingness to conform to group standards.

Under conditions of least competition for group loyalty and best return for effort, we would expect the lower ranks of a group to be the most committed to it, but under changing conditions and competitive loyalties, we might have to modify our prediction. But what about those higher up? Do we expect them to be regularly conformist or eccentric? Here again, rank itself interacts with the tendency to conform to rules. Remember that when we started out analyzing this group, we thought that rank was roughly related to contribution to group satisfaction. But rank itself can become a kind of license to deviate. As many people suspect, activities which would be punished or disapproved of in ordinary group members are tolerated or even welcomed among 'higher ups'. This tolerance of deviance can be thought of as having been 'bought' as a privilege. It is part of the reward of high status, which, in turn, derives from contributions to the group. Of course, there will be limits. The deviation we are talking about now cannot be total, and it might be only trivial. Alternatively, extreme commitment to group practices often goes with high rank, and this rewarding commitment can form a counterweight to deviance, as in the case of the country landlord who is always prominently placed in the parish church on Sunday morning.

This sort of explanation of conformity to group standards implies a particularly interesting question for exchange theorists. How are the norms changed? How do certain ones fall into disuse and pass away, while other ones become prominent? We might regard this as a question about *innovation*. Everyone in this imagined group we have been talking about is in a position to innovate, but for different reasons. Those in the lower ranks might be less committed to norms, especially if they have alternative groups to belong to, because their rewards for membership are comparatively less. Also, their contribution to the group is probably less. These persons will have a certain freedom with respect to conformity, simply because less is at stake, both on the contribution and payoff sides. It might be easier for such persons to change the rule and make it stick simply because the removal of group rewards is not that crucial; hence they might be willing to take that risk. Similarly, there is a built-in freedom to innovate for those who contribute very heavily to group satisfaction, since their pleasure will often be considered by others as imperative to ensure their continued performance.

Now, in a perfunctory way, we have discovered some links between important aspects of group process and structure. We have considered ranking as it tends to grow up in groups, conformity to group standards, and norm change or innovation. We should review in formal terms how we have gone about discovering these things. They were found by starting with a set of assumptions and provisional ideas concerning the nature of individual motivations among persons who group together. It appeared that explanation of one thing immediately involved the possible explanation of another. In the example used, ranking was really inseparable from conformity and innovation. In this way, it appeared that group processes were mutually related, not separable, and that groups had characteristics not entirely reducible to the characteristics of individuals – but, as exchange theory sees it, the order we observed did derive from our beginning points in individuality and unique motivations. That is, a minimum of assumptions were made about groups themselves. But we made assumptions and did not reach our conclusions by observation only. Our assumptions were about individuals. Manipulation of these assumptions led to hypothetical ideas about the behavior and characteristics of groups. Explanation of groups was our objective, and it appears to have been our achievement.

V. *Deductive exchange theory – G. C. Homans' propositions*

So far, the background of exchange theory has been described, its viewpoint and some of its main ideas have been introduced, and the way exchange theory might be applied to some interesting aspects of groups has been considered. Something of the general 'explanatory' nature of the theory has been given. We will now sharpen our tools by looking at a statement of exchange theory made by one of its strong proponents and major contributors, George C. Homans. In particular we are concerned with the extent to which Homans explains social order by deductive theorizing and how he employs his exchange propositions to do so.[7]

Homans has been particularly explicit about exchange theory. He reasons as follows: we can only explain aspects of social order and change by referring to some small number of general propositions from which the particulars we wish to explain may be deduced. There is a specific form and sequence to ideas in a deductive theory. The general propositions are organized into statements of broad scope. Furthermore, Homans believes these statements ought to have as their subject the individual actor and ought to be propositions about motivation and the ways men respond to their environment.[8]

Homans has written widely, but it is useful to focus on two particular works and briefly consider their relationship. The books are *The Human*

---

[7] The following works contain Homans' theoretical contributions to exchange theory: 'Bringing Men Back In', *American Sociological Review,* XXIX (December 1964), pp. 809-19; 'Contemporary Theory in Sociology', in R. E. L. Faris, ed., *Handbook of Modern Sociology* (Chicago: Rand McNally, 1964), pp. 951-77; *The Nature of Social Science* (New York: Harcourt Brace and World, 1967); 'Social Behavior as Exchange', *American Journal of Sociology,* LXII (May, 1958), pp. 597-607; *Social Behavior: Its Elementary Forms,* (New York: Harcourt Brace and World, 1961; rev. ed. 1974); 'Theory of Social Interaction', *Transactions of the Fifth World Congress of Sociology,* IV (Louvain: International Sociological Association, 1964). pp. 113-25.

[8] Homans' work on this is *The Nature of Social Science.* He often cites as his mentor in this regard Richard B. Braithwaite, *Scientific Explanation* (New York: Harper and Row, 1953).

Group[9] and *Social Behavior. The Human Group* is a descriptive book. It is largely a review of research in social relations, and it contains a good deal of data, but the book is not particularly strong 'explanation'. It says a lot about 'what' but not much about 'why'. *Social Behavior*, on the other hand, contains more theory and correspondingly less description. It contains more 'why' and less 'what'. We might view *The Human Group* as the foundation material from which the inductive process sprang, and *Social Behavior* as the deductive link in the chain where the explanatory propositions are stated. Hence, *Social Behavior* is where one finds Homans' exchange theory most fully developed. The revised edition restates Homans' propositions in new wording, but the logic and substance of the theory remain essentially the same.

A. *The propositions*

The approach in this section is to give the propositions as Homans has done, with explanation and comment but not criticism. Critical material will be included later in this chapter, together with an assessment of the general success or failure of exchange theory.

Quoted from the first edition of *Social Behavior*, Homans' first proposition is:

'1. If in the past, the occurrence of a particular stimulus-situation has been the occasion on which a man's activity has been rewarded, then the more similar the present stimulus-situation is to the past one, the more likely he is to emit the activity, or some similar activity, now.'[10]

In the revised edition, Homans renames this the 'stimulus proposition' to emphasize his intention to link human behavior with environmental stimuli. It is restated thus:

'1. If in the past the occurrence of a particular stimulus, or set of stimuli, has been the occasion on which a person's action has been rewarded, then the more similar the present stimuli are to the past ones, the more likely the person is to perform the action, or some similar action, now.'[11]

Let us take these propositions apart. First, Homans' reference is to some person's past. As with experimental psychology's learning theory, a person's past is of particular importance to his present behavior. According to the proposition, the past is composed of situations in which the person was either rewarded or punished (or, rewarded or denied reward). Some aspects of the past have bearing on the probability of

[9] New York: Harcourt Brace Jovanovich, 1950. This book is actually functionalist in inspiration, although Homans has used its contents in another way.
[10] *Social Behavior*, p. 53.
[11] *Social Behavior*, rev. ed., pp. 22-23.

behaving in similar ways now. Homans expects that history is, at least in some gross way, repeatable. When one of the situations in which a person has been rewarded recurs, behavior of the kind displayed in the previous situation will be enacted. This is really no different from expecting Strong the dog to walk on his hind legs in response to rewards given by his master. Strong and master created the original situation, and now the master can control things by reminding Strong of the rewarding aspects of the previous situation. The emphasis in Homans' proposition is on the individual's response to pleasing circumstances and his willingness and ability to voluntarily emit behavior of this kind again.

> '2. The more often within a given period of time a man's activity
> rewards the activity of another, the more often the other will emit
> the activity.'[12]

The revised edition labels this the 'success proposition', and restates it as follows:

> '2. For all actions taken by persons, the more often a particular
> action of a person is rewarded, the more likely the person is to per-
> form that action.'[13]

Of special interest here is the fact that Homans has introduced the concept of frequency of activity. We more easily count frequencies of actions than infer strength of feeling or other more subjective aspects of behavior. The propositions say there is a direct relationship between frequency of rewarding behavior and frequency of response to the reward. This proposition combines two of the things Homans is especially interested in, reward and activity, and states the kind of relationship he expects between them. In form, this statement fulfills the requirements of a high-level general proposition for deductive theory.

> '3. The more valuable to a man a unit of the activity another gives
> him, the more often he will emit the activity rewarded by the activ-
> ity of another.'[14]

This proposition is called the 'value proposition' in the revised edition, and is rewritten as follows:

> '3. The more valuable to a person the result of his action, the more
> likely he is to perform the action.'[15]

These propositions give the expected relationship between value and activity. Individuals have their own ideas about what they value, and values are not the same to all individuals. Hence, the theory forecasts a direct relationship between frequency of activity achieving valued reward and the degree of value the reward carries. If it is extremely important that a person obtain the good will of his roommate at all times, he will be

---

12 *Social Behavior*, p. 54.
13 *Social Behavior*, rev. ed., p. 16.
14 *Social Behavior*, p. 55.
15 *Social Behavior*, rev. ed., p. 25.

at particular pains to behave so that this is forthcoming. Since the person cannot do everything at once, there may be times when he has to choose between pleasing his roommate and doing something else which might also be of benefit. In situations like that, the relative values of pleasing the roommate and the alternative must be weighed. If the value of pleasing the roommate is greater, then this is the activity our friend will choose. The greater the number of alternatives outweighed by pleasing the roommate, the more often roommate-pleasing activities will be attempted; hence, as the proposition says, the more often we can expect the behavior.

Here, exchange theory is being stated in terms of units that appear measurable or countable. While it is hard to measure value (this is something about which more will be said later), and it is not entirely clear how to measure units of activity, the proposition is still given in what might be called observational terms. It says there should be a direct relationship between strength of rewarding activity and frequency of activity gaining the reward.

In case it appears that propositions 2 and 3, the success proposition and the value proposition, are saying the same thing, note that proposition 2 gives a general relationship between reward and activity gaining the reward, whereas proposition 3 says something additional. It introduces the concept of value and says, in effect. 'Proposition 2 is true, and also, the more valuable the activity discussed in proposition 2, the more it will take precedence when there is an alternative.'

> '4. The more often a man has in the recent past received a rewarding activity from another, the less valuable any further unit of that activity becomes for him.'[16]

Proposition 4 is named the 'deprivation–satiation' proposition in the revised edition of *Social Behavior*, and appears thus:

> '4. The more often in the recent past a person has received a particular reward, the less valuable any further unit of that reward becomes for him.'[17]

This proposition might first appear to contradict some of the others, especially propositions 2 and 3, the success and value propositions. But it does not contradict them. Notice especially that Homans has limited himself to the recent past in these propositions and that he is giving a general statement about the extra amount of activity he expects once the rewarding exchange is in progress. That is what is called a marginal statement – it is describing the effects of additional units of activity. For example, suppose a student goes to talk with his professor and finds the encounter stimulating. He would, according to proposition 2, the success proposition, return to visit the professor again. But he does not come

16 *Social Behavior*, p. 55.
17 *Social Behavior*, rev. ed., pp. 28-9.

back in quite the same condition as on his first visit. He is probably somewhat more informed now and, also, the professor may already have presented his most striking insights during the first meeting. The student may find that the second visit, while probably still rewarding, is not as rewarding as the first. If 'visit to the professor' is the unit of activity, then unit two is of less value than unit one. Unit three will probably be even less rewarding, in comparison to the previous two. Proposition 4, the deprivation–satiation proposition, leads us to expect the value of these visits to continually decrease. Also, suppose proposition 3, the value proposition, is relevant. That is, as soon as the value of professor visits drops below whatever the competing alternative may be, the visits should stop, and the more valuable unit of activity should take over. Proposition 4, the deprivation–satiation proposition, is the sociological exchange equivalent of the 'law of diminishing returns' of economic theory.

> '5. The more to a man's disadvantage the rule of distributive justice fails of realization, the more likely he is to display the emotional behavior we call anger.'[18]

Homans argues that it is possible to establish a rate of exchange among traded behaviors and sentiments. In general, the investments a person makes in an exchange, calculated in effort, commitment, time, and the like, ought to be compensated by payoff in direct proportion. If we invest heavily, we feel entitled to considerable reward. Additionally, we do not expect those who have not invested heavily to receive a large measure of reward. Now, if we happen to entangle ourselves in an exchange with a person whose investments are small in comparison to his apparent rewards, especially at our expense, our sense of distributive justice is outraged, and we display anger.

Some interesting advances in exchange theory have been made through the introduction of the distributive justice idea. Remember the comparative nature of value. Exchange is a highly individualistic theory, true enough; but a person in an exchange relationship does not limit his calculations to the rewards and costs of only persons in that particular relationship. Going rates of exchange between other people become our own standards. And while we need not assume other people's values, they do influence our choices.

Also in connection with the idea of distributive justice is the time dimension. Without distributive justice, one might imagine that exchange theory took no notice of the continuing nature of interaction. Without it, it might seem that particular exchange situations make up little dramas unto themselves, which people play out for what they are worth, and then abandon. But the emphasis on investment suggests a time dimension in exchanges, and that the present may be payoff for past services. In times when the old, the hale, and the young huddled around the same

[18] *Social Behavior*, p. 75.

stove to keep warm, we usually found grandfather nearest the fire. This was probably not because he had worked the hardest that day, or earned the most for the family. Rather, grandfather 'deserved' to be made comfortable in his old age because he had in the past made sacrifices for all and had undergone hardship which benefited the family. In exchange theory terms, he made heavy investments in an extremely long series of exchanges with family members, and he is now in a position to expect distributive justice to come into play, giving him reward.

The first four propositions were cast in terms of Homans' basic theoretical ideas: units of activity, frequency of activity, rewards for activity, value of activity. With the fifth proposition he introduced distributive justice, but this always seemed more difficult than the other propositions, particularly because distributive justice was not obviously and immediately linked to the theoretical terms of the previous propositions. In the revised edition of *Social Behavior* Homans divided his distributive justice proposition into two and discarded the term itself. While the idea remains the same, the new propositions are in terms more similar to the others. These new propositions are called the 'aggression–approval' propositions. Part one says:

> 'When a person's action does not receive the reward he expected, or receives punishment he did not expect, he will be angry; he becomes more likely to perform aggressive behavior, and the results of such behavior become more valuable to him.'[19]

This proposition introduces an additional theoretical term, 'expectation', and suggests that expectations of reward must be consistent with actual reward or displeasure will follow. This seems simple enough. But additionally, if reward is not up to expectation, aggression results and such aggression, Homans says, is gratifying. In everyday terms, this seems Homans' way of writing the getting-even idea found in the original distributive justice proposition.

The second part of the aggression–approval proposition states the same ideas in positive form:

> 'When a person's action receives reward he expected, especially a greater reward than he expected, or does not receive punishment he expected, he will be pleased; he will become more likely to perform approving behavior, and the results of such behavior become more valuable to him.'[20]

B. *The deductions*

After Homans' introduction of the propositions and the deductive theoretical format, we would expect to find some examples of deductive theo-

[19] *Social Behavior*, rev. ed., p. 37.
[20] *Ibid.* p. 39.

rizing. Several deductions, resulting in an array of hypotheses, should follow at this point. Homans himself does not provide them. While he has been attentive to deductive theory and its logic, he has done little about derivations from his main propositions. His real concern is to illustrate the propositions thoroughly. But this does not mean that derivations are impossible. In fact, there are quite a number.

The deductive format encourages the production of hypotheses by logical inference from abstract starting points. Such inference can be the demonstration that a particular hypothesis follows directly from a general proposition in one step. This would indeed be logical inference, but it would also be rather trivial. The step would be immediately obvious to most people and the production of such an hypothesis would seem exceedingly easy. But intermediate steps performed on Homans' propositions can yield a greater number of hypotheses which, if the inferences are carried out properly, would not be obvious. If they were all followed up, these hypotheses could occupy any number of researchers for quite some time.

In *Social Behavior*, first edition, Homans gave at least twenty-three such hypotheses, although he did not formally deduce them. As an example of how the propositions may be employed to derive an implicit hypothesis, one of Homans' own theoretical statements will be examined. This statement is not directly derivable from any of the general propositions in one step; we must combine some propositions.

> 'When the costs of avoiding interaction are great enough, a man will go into interaction with another even though he finds Other's activity punishing; and far from liking him more, he will like him less.'[21]

Examine proposition 2, the success proposition. It says we should expect a direct relationship between activity which is rewarded and the frequency of that activity. The directness of the relationship implies that the less a man's activity is rewarded, the less frequently we should expect this activity. This suggests that even activity which would normally be considered punishing can still have some value. The proposition covers instances of small as well as great reward. There could be times when activities and rewards entail only relative punishments. This is the 'least of evils' condition. Homans' statement suggests that when this occurs, a man will enter such a relationship, even if it is punishing. This is so because he will be cutting his costs.

Now it is necessary to examine the relationship between 'liking' and the general propositions, since Homans is talking about liking in the

---

[21] *Social Behavior*, p. 187. This statement is also derived somewhat differently in a commentary on Homans' logic by Ronald Maris in 'The Logical Adequacy of Homans' Social Theory', *American Sociological Review*, xxxv (December 1970), p. 1074.

statement just quoted; but 'liking' is not a theoretical term found in his propositions. Consider proposition 3; Homans names it the value proposition. If an exchange ensues between persons in which liking, or 'social approval', is the currency being paid in exchange for some activity, these propositions tell us to expect a direct relationship between reward, liking in this case, and the activity which fetches it. As in proposition 2, the success proposition, this direct relationship suggests that in cases where activity leads to disliking, the expectation is that this relationship will entail less activity, eventually reaching zero and breaking off.

Combining these propositions, the derivation is that the unfortunate individual Homans describes makes a cost-cutting deal with the other because it is in his interest to do so (the success proposition), even though he is unhappy with the results. This interaction which allows him to avoid an even worse fate causes him to assume an interaction pattern which he dislikes. The value proposition (3) indicates that the more he participates in this activity, the more he will be motivated to break off the relationship because of his not liking it. But this is precisely what he cannot do. In fact, he is forced to maintain some level of participation in this relationship, enabling him to avoid the worse fate.

Now, why will he like this predicament less and less, instead of simply simmering away at a stable level of dislike? From proposition 4, the deprivation–satiation proposition, we see satiation entails an inverse relationship between activity and reward. The benfits derived from avoiding the worse fate will become less valuable as time goes on. The dislike built up in the relationship will eventually come to outweigh the benefits of avoiding greater costs, and 'liking' will continuously decrease.

The statement by Homans which we are trying to explain said we should expect less liking between parties to this interaction, not more, and that the amount of liking between them would fall. By combining the meanings of some of the propositions, which in themselves do not directly treat such situations, we can account for this statement. This is so despite the fact that the statement is not derived directly from any of the propositions in one step.

In principle, it is possible to examine the relationships suggested by the five propositions and, by substituting some equivalent terms or inverting the form of the statements, to derive many more hypotheses.[22] In fact, it would probably be possible to produce several hypotheses never before given. These would be logically 'true' if we made the correct inferences. It would be up to the researcher to discover if the statements were empirically true. If research indicated the hypotheses were empirically true, the theory would be supported (but not proven outright).

[22] Maris derived forty statements which were logically possible extensions of Homans' propositions and the corollaries accompanying them. *Ibid.* pp. 1069-80.

C. *The institutional and subinstitutional in Homans' theory*

It is now appropriate to leave the more technical and deductive properties of Homans' theory in order to consider its other aspects. Emphasis on the individual and the concepts of reward, cost, activity, and so on have kept the discussion focused directly on the individual, or on a two-person group. Homans spends considerable time talking about his hypothetical characters, Person and Other, and how they get on with each other. But sociological theory commonly addresses units of larger than two persons. And Homans does go beyond Person and Other to give an exchange account of institutional and subinstitutional levels of social life.

Homans says that institutions are based on the same principles of exchange as is interpersonal behavior, but that institutions are more complex networks of exchanges. The complexity is related to specialization of activity and indirectness of exchange relationships. By specialization, he means that tasks which once might have been done by one person are broken up and the components are performed by many different people. As a result of this, the beneficiaries of the performances are indebted to several persons, whereas before they might have been indebted to only one. Also, there may be many beneficiaries. Institutional arrangements stabilize these complex exchanges among the many persons related by their participation in divided tasks.

Moreover, basic activities of institutions cannot be random, according to Homans; they must fulfill certain 'needs' or desires which are common to all.[23] This point would seem to be a departure from Homans' previous meaning of 'rewards'. He had emphasized that rewards are entirely the private concern of the person rewarded. Indeed, Homans made quite a point of liberating individuals from commonly held value positions – it was a cornerstone of his emphasis on individuality. But in his explanation of institutions, he modifies this stand.

Concerning institutions, he says there must be a basic and common 'repertory of human nature' which causes certain emotions and needs to be rather constant. To support this view, he cites anthropological literature to show that there are various institutions in quite diverse societies which all fulfill similar needs. This appears to amount to the contention that 'human nature' and the everyday requirements of living are not so free-ranging as the extreme individualistic position suggests. Homans says,

> 'Cultures cannot pick up any old sorts of behavior and hope without more ado to carry them on generation after generation. What they pick up must be compatible with some fundamental repertory of

[23] *Social Behavior*, pp. 381ff.

human nature, though the compatibility may, of course, be complex.'[24]

These needed fundamentals of human nature Homans later categorizes as 'primary rewards'.

But, according to Homans, these cannot account for the growth of institutions by themselves. Because not everybody responds to these fundamental propensities,[25] persons sometimes apply secondary rewards to bring nonconformists into line with the rest. Here Homans is no longer thinking of primary rewards, but of generalized rewards such as social approval and money. In short, the argument is that the secondary reinforcers of behavior are employed in support of primary ones, where the primary ones alone are not capable of ensuring the collective commitment to institutional norms.

To illustrate his approach to institutions, Homans explains the norm of expressing grief.[26] He says that those who feel genuine and true grief on certain occasions do so not because of any outside inducement, but because of their 'nature'. But not all who 'should' feel grief do. Those who do not are induced to behave as if they did by the application of secondary reinforcers, such as the loss of esteem which would accompany a failure to express grief at appropriate times. For such people, the expression of grief is not motivated by feeling grief, but by the desire to gain the benefits of conformity. True grieving is a more basic sentiment than the wish to maximize gain, but this wish may be the explanation for the widespread acceptance of norms regulating the expression of grief.

And why, according to Homans, do institutions endure? It is because of the complexity of institutionalized exchanges, and because values are 'handed down' to younger generations.[27] Complexity means a series of exchanges which are all related and which are therefore not easily altered. The decision to change behavior with respect to one institutionalized role might entail alterations in one's relationships in several others. Receiving pay for a service is a useful example to illustrate this. If one is paid for working in a firm, he must attend to his relations with the paymaster, in addition to those with the foreman, the work group of which he is a part, the firm in general, and the industry as a whole, to say nothing of his own desire to maximize profit and minimize costs. This complicated situation hems in a person not because it is inflexible but simply because the exchanges all influence each other. This complexity gives any particular working social arrangement an inertia or staying power. It is important to recognize that Homans is not drawing a distinction in

---

24 *Ibid.* p. 381.
25 *Ibid.*
26 *Ibid.*
27 *Social Behavior,* rev. ed., p. 41.

kind between interpersonal and complex institutionalized exchanges, but only pointing out differences in degree.

VI. *Exchange and the social psychology of groups: Thibaut and Kelley*

J. Thibaut and H. Kelley in *The Social Psychology of Groups*[28] adjust the focus of exchange theory somewhat, but they do not depart from the general idea very much. Their interest is not so much in the individual and how he functions in a relationship as in the relationship itself. They wish to explain it as a set of predictable outcomes. These outcomes are understood very much along the lines of Homans' explanation of individuals. Note, too, that their interest is mainly to explain the *dyad*, the two-person group, discussion of which forms the bulk of *The Social Psychology of Groups*. Thibaut and Kelley explicitly assume what Homans only implies: exchange analysis of the dyad is the proper theoretical standpoint from which to understand the larger group. They assume that if they can theoretically portray the dyad, they can subsequently extend the theory to encompass the problems of larger and more complex social relationships.[29] When considering critical remarks on exchange theory, we will want to return to this assumption.

Thibaut and Kelley employ the idea of a behavior matrix as an analytical tool to clarify their idea of exchange. In the matrix, a two-dimensional space represents the possible behaviors of two persons. Along one dimension are placed descriptions of all the behaviors possible for one member of the interaction, and along the other dimension are placed those of the second person. By cross-tabulating the two dimensions, several cells are constructed as shown in Figure 4.1.[30] In each cell, it is possible to imagine the desirability of the behavior of each partner by examining the outcomes for each represented by that cell. Thibaut and Kelley assume that 'interaction is continued only if the experienced consequences are found to meet the standards of acceptability that both individuals develop by virtue of their experiences with other relationships'.[31] Hence, Thibaut and Kelley expect that the cell representing maximum desirability for both players is the one which predicts the type of behavior each will display, and that it predicts the type of relationship in which the two will engage.

In deciding the desirability of outcomes, a person necessarily has his own ideas about rewards and costs. Thibaut and Kelley divide these determinants into *exogenous* and *endogenous* factors. Exogenous ones

[28] New York: Wiley, 1959.
[29] *Ibid*. Introduction, pp. 1-9.
[30] After Thibaut and Kelley's figures, see *Ibid*. pp. 14-18 for the general description of such matrices.
[31] *Ibid*. p. 10.

are those brought to the relationship by the participants in the form of values, needs, skills, or any other qualities that may transcend the particular interaction. Endogenous determinants of rewards and costs are those intrinsic to the relationship itself. These two types of factors, taken from

FIGURE 4.1

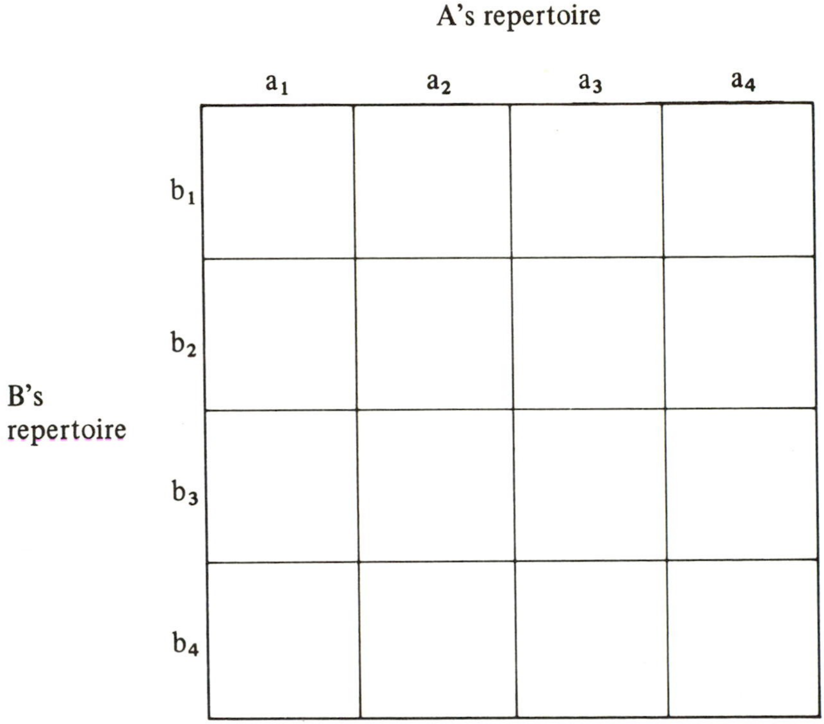

A's repertoire

B's repertoire

the points of view of both persons, are potentially paired. A good outcome for one could match a good outcome for the other. If it does, interaction of a type allowing this to happen ensues. In this way, Thibaut and Kelley predict the relationship and not individual actions.[32]

Similar to Homans' account is Thibaut and Kelley's idea that individuals evaluate their outcomes both according to the reward or cost involved in relating and according to the alternatives available. Using Thibaut and Kelley's terms, these comparisons are made according to *comparison levels*. The comparison level is an hypothetical internal measuring rod by

[32] *Ibid*. See Ch. 8, 'Norms and Rules', pp. 126-48.

which a participant decides whether or not his activity is getting him a just return for effort.[33] The *comparison level for alternatives* is the external measuring rod he uses to see if a similar amount of effort spent elsewhere might gain a better reward.[34] Remember there are two balls in the air at once. Enduring interaction will be that which satisfies two persons' comparison levels for alternatives, not just one person's.

Thibaut and Kelley construct an exchange-based theory of face-to-face interpersonal behavior, but they also claim that such a theory has wider implications. Relationships developed by maximization of outcome do eventually become stable. The things we expect people to do tend to be predictable by association with the situation, and not directly from an analysis in reward and cost terms. When the participants achieve such a stable relationship, Thibaut and Kelley believe it becomes normal for people to be less concerned with precise calculation and comparison of reward. Habits established in this fashion take the emphasis off calculation, and behavior becomes automatic. Thibaut and Kelley thus arrive at an explanation of stable exchange patterns in which cognitive calculation of reward is of decreasing importance. This kind of reasoning comes later to underlie some basic principles in Thibaut and Kelley's account of larger groups.

How do Thibaut and Kelley account for the third person; that is, how does the theory of the dyad become the theory of groups in the more ordinary sense? This is important. Sociology probably needs this level of analysis more than that of the dyad alone. For several reasons following from individualistic psychology, the third person is problematic. For instance, the group might break down into smaller units, eventually reaching the dyad again. Thibaut and Kelley realize there are cases like this – isolation of members, or cases in which only two members of a group really care to continue relating.[35] But their more interesting assertions, to which we turn now, are those about the benefits of group relations to all involved.

In this category Thibaut and Kelley include the notion that an 'economy of scale' may be obtained, in which it may be more profitable to produce one's favorable outcomes collectively, because for some reason it is cheaper to do so. Also expected are joint enjoyment of rewards and mutual facilitation of enjoyment. These points imply the notion that persons are motivated to help produce collective rewards, and that such rewards are in some measure easier to get collectively. (We shall return to such implications of exchange theory in the critical section of this chapter.) Then too, Thibaut and Kelley suggest that sequential patterns of dyadic exchange account for the attractiveness of some groups,

---

[33] *Ibid.* pp. 21-3.
[34] *Ibid.* See Ch. 4, 'Interference and Facilitation in Interaction', pp. 51-63.
[35] *Ibid.* p. 197.

although a series of dyadic exchanges is not usually what is meant by group action.

An important assertion is that there exist emergent properties of groups which do not appear with only two participants. An example of this might be found in a problem-solving team, in which each member adds his contribution, imperfect though it may be, with the result of a more impressive or better solution than could be had by one or two persons alone. Also, coalitions could be considered, in which the larger group breaks up into smaller factions. The guiding principle for this breakup is the matching of favorable outcomes among subgroups. If the whole group cannot achieve a mutual matching of favorable outcomes, perhaps some members can. Failure of total mutual matching leads to pairing off of some persons, or coalitions.

Thibaut and Kelley have contributed to the theory of social exchange, but their form of presentation differs from that of Homans. Thibaut and Kelley's work has been richer in concepts than in explicit formal deductions. Their work is indeed 'theoretical'. They give a set of general principles which seem to organize the data they present. Their principles 'seem to' because the logical procedures for deriving conclusions from starting points are often skipped. Remember what was said about having to take theoretical ideas as we find them, and not being too quick to reject something because it is incomplete. We have now seen two examples of how the work of the theoretician is indeed long and hard. Homans' propositions require considerable manipulation to achieve connective links between propositions and hypotheses. Thibaut and Kelley's work is valuable because it sets up a solid beginning in a particular mode of theory building, and it is up to the user to provide the finishing touches if he feels a need for them.

VII. *Exchange and power: Blau's use of exchange principles*

Of course, this discussion has not exhausted the interesting possibilities of exchange theory. Peter Blau's book *Exchange and Power in Social Life*,[36] is of special interest because his intention is to add more principles of economic theory to the social exchange viewpoint.

A. *Blau's interest in exchange*

In describing exchange theory, this chapter first emphasized individuality and the atomized view of social life which emerges when psychological determinants of exchange are stressed. In the works by Homans and Thibaut and Kelley, the major accomplishment was explanation of the dyad, although efforts at explaining larger groups were conscientiously made.

---

[36] New York: Wiley, 1964.

In Blau's work, the concentration is on social structures which grow out of exchange, and on accounts of order, legitimation, opposition, power, and the like. Blau maintains the view, similar to that of Homans and Thibaut and Kelley, that it is appropriate to approach social structure from the individualistic viewpoint, and that, in the main, we should run into no insurmountable problems if we do. He feels we do not need any assumptions about groups themselves in order to build a theoretical account of group action. This attitude, that explanation in sociology can run smoothly upward from the smallest to the largest unit of analysis, aptly characterizes the exchange position regarding social structure.

First, consider Blau's particular view of exchange. In general, he examines the same kind of mutual exchange interaction previously described, but he particularly notes the types of rewards and costs involved. He assumes that in exchange persons wish to maximize rewards and minimize costs, but that surely imbalances will arise. Some exchange deals will not equally reward both parties. To the one who is less fortunate, a cost is incurred to produce the other's pleasure which may not be recouped. This is an *imbalance*. The unbalanced nature of most exchanges impresses Blau, and he sees this as the key issue in understanding the emergence of group structure and social power.[37] To collapse the theme of his book into one statement, one might venture this: Blau is trying to work out the details of how social structures stabilize exchanges, while also depicting the ways these stabilizations engender opposing forces, eventually tending to alter stabilized exchanges.

B. *Unbalanced exchanges: some consequences*

Imbalance in an exchange can occur when one party is capable of rewarding the other more than the recipient is capable of reciprocating. Of course, there may be alternative associations available and the relationship may break off; but all such relationships do not break off. In fact, Blau suggests that the usual nature of social exchange is imbalance. The lesser party in unbalanced exchanges might compensate his benefactor by a species of general reinforcement Homans called social approval. Blau refers to this as subordination or compliance.[38] This means that in return for getting some benefit for which one cannot pay in full measure, one tends to give up some of his will to the other and become subordinate.

Subordination in unbalanced exchanges is a kind of 'credit' to the superior partner. It credits him in the sense that his position becomes well known, especially where exchanges are public. It is also credit in a

[37] *Exchange and Power in Social Life*, pp. 4-5.
[38] *Ibid.* pp. 170ff.

more 'economic' sense. His will can come to dominate, for he is allowed a kind of license to command others which ordinary persons do not have. This is likened to having command of other people's money when one receives a note of credit from a bank.

The upshot of unbalanced exchanges is not free license, of course, since complying persons always evaluate exchange according to the principles of cost and reward. They might take away their compliance. But several factors induce them to continue in subordinate positions. The great utility of having someone in command is that it promotes efficient task performance. Everyone knows that any task which is too much for one person must be divided, and this division requires a coordinator who recombines the divided parts to complete the whole. It isn't everyone who is capable of leadership, insight, and the like. Also, everyone knows the cliché about too many chiefs and not enough Indians; coordination of effort requires that both command and compliance be features of social systems which work toward a goal that all desire. Finally, compliance shifts responsibility to the one in authority. For all of these reasons, people may be willing to continue in a subordinate position.

Structural analysis in sociology is the investigation of arrangements for coordinated effort toward collective goals. Blau works his way toward explaining structure by way of exchange and power plus the concept of *legitimacy*. Legitimate social structure is one which has the general acceptance of participants. Where legitimacy obtains, structure may be refined and elaborated, and to the extent that it remains legitimate it will endure. To the extent that structures fail, become corrupt, exceed the control of their members, and so on, members will withdraw their view that structures are legitimate. Blau then sees forces arising which change the structure. Thus social structures founded on exchanges may develop, retain, or lose legitimacy, and this will either increase social stability or promote change.

But this picture is too simple. Surely exchanges which either directly or indirectly involve a number of people will be viewed differently by each. Legitimacy and illegitimacy of social structures are not absolute conditions, but only tendencies. There will certainly be simultaneous forces, some encouraging and entrenching social structures and others working in the opposite direction. A recurrent theme in Blau's work is to find a situation portrayed as having particularly happy results in one way, but very unhappy results when viewed another way. In such situations, it is impossible to maximize satisfaction according to the simplistic model suggested by the assumptions of exchange theory. We cannot eat the cake and have it, too. Blau suggests that when people face these situations they sit on the fence. When one kind of result starts to outweigh the other, they alter course to minimize the unpleasantness associated with a bad series of outcomes, perhaps knowing all the time that the change will entail other unpleasantness, as well as other kinds of benefits. This lack of clear, all-or-nothing alternatives is explored but not clearly formulated by Homans and Thibaut and Kelley. Blau makes it the keynote of his view of exchange.

C. *Kinds of reward and kinds of relationships*

There are parallels between Blau's work on exchange and the other exchange theories. For Homans and for Thibaut and Kelley, the concept of value implies comparisons between action at hand and other possible action. In Blau's work, this same theoretical idea turns up in the form of a typology of rewards: *intrinsic* and *extrinsic*. This typology corresponds to Thibaut and Kelley's endogenous and exogenous rewards. Associations based on 'intrinsic' rewards are their own reward; there may not be much of utilitarian value to be gained in them. Where intrinsic rewards are mutual, the relationship is one of 'mutual attraction', which amounts to giving a name to something that is considered 'natural'. Exchanges based on these kinds of bonds can, in the end, have all the earmarks of other kinds of exchanges. They stabilize associations, give rise to norms of conduct, give satisfaction; but they are not really exchange relationships in the economic sense, where something is given and something taken, and the give and take is the reason for the relationship. 'Extrinsic' relationships are those among exchange partners who participate in the relationship for some gain of their own choosing. 'Value' enters here as a theoretical term, since it is in pursuit of some valued item that persons participate. Comparisons among alternatives become possible in principle; we may visualize reciprocal extrinsic exchanges as the basic form of exchange.

But what if reciprocation is introduced as a variable? Considering that any given exchange can be either reciprocated or not, we see that unreciprocated intrinsic relationships will lead to the grief of only one partner, as his attentions will go unrequited. This may be unhappy, but perhaps not serious. However, if an extrinsic relationships goes unreciprocated – if one expects something or is led to expect something which is not forthcoming – then we have a more potent case. If the lack of reciprocation is caused by one partner's inability to repay, then the way is open for a power dependency of the poorer on the richer. If the lack of reciprocation is on the part of the stronger, then the weaker will see his compliance as fruitless and he may withdraw it. Hence, by introducing two variables (intrinsic–extrinsic and reciprocation and lack of it, or 'unreciprocation'), we can trace the types of possible outcomes of exchange relationships.

This may all seem obvious enough, but in Blau's hands it becomes quite insightful. For instance, what appears to be an intrinsic relationship must have started as an extrinsic one, since there would probably have previously been no basis for two persons' gaining reward simply by being together. Furthermore, if a relationship starts as extrinsic, there are hidden dangers in it for all parties. It is probably normal for persons getting to know one another to appear to be 'regular' types. Neither exposes anything that might repel the other, if they care anything about the relationship which is forming. But to be too much of a regular person might ruin everything, since the blandness caused by suppressing one's eccentric qualities might appear insufficiently comely to an exchange partner for him to select this exchange over competing extrinsic ones. It is for each to select some kind of strategy that introduces something of interest to the other without putting him off. But if this relatonship is potentially to result in one partner's having dominance over the other, superior qualities must be exposed. Braggarts are frowned upon, but obviously superior people are esteemed. A fine line distinguishes the two as people form exchange relationships.

In groups, similar problems beset social integration, making what might appear a simple case of mutual attraction a complex one in danger of collapse. Impressive and useful qualities are what draw people together in extrinsic reciprocal relationships. But dilemmas arise. To what extent ought the superior person be accorded esteem? Clearly if his services are not recompensed in some right relation to his worth, he will be lost, and the group will suffer. But too-willing compliance is outward evidence that the complier's status has been threatened or undermined completely. ('No matter how valuable you are, I cannot become dirt under your feet.') Hence there will be a tendency to protect status by underpaying the valued member, and consequently always a tendency to lose him.

Blau has also added light to the matter of the effects of competition. Surely competition for status occurs along more than one line. Nobody has everything and everyone else nothing. Thus, competition for the esteem of others has a tendency to break up the group, but the different dimensions of the competition, the different ways in which one may excel, tend to hold it together. If excellence is distributed in general according to the different requirements of the group, then status competition can be smoothed over while the various tasks get done. It should be emphasized here that Blau has again shown the utility of his structural focus on exchange. The possible dangers to relationships if personal competition is emphasized have been pointed out, but when Blau returns to the group's requirements, its tasks, and the various kinds of rewards its members want, he clearly shows that it is the structural relations among the members that lead to substantial integration. The fact that excellence is divided and spread among the members of the group leads to social integration, even where members are always competing. It is the resultant structure, coming out of preliminary exchanges, which endures despite the constant danger of collapse.

D. *Microstructures annd macrostructures*

It is Blau's contention that the same basic processes which characterize face-to-face relations are typical of larger units. Face-to-face interactions Blau calls *microstructures*.[39] They are 'structures' in the sense that regulatory rules, dominance, power, legitimate control, and task division are all supported, for some time at least, by the rewarding nature of the interactions based on them. They are 'micro' in that the interaction is at the level of person to person. But sooner or later size will get in the way. As the numbers to be accommodated increase, it becomes more sensible to talk about formal organizations, committees, bureaucracies, and the like. These larger collectivities may themselves be composed of microstructures. Blau's view of the whole of social organization in a society is one of the interconnections among these *macrostructures* by a variety of means.[40] To examine his account of social solidarity in exchange terms, we do not have to introduce many new ideas. We apply the old ones, since the principles of exchange apply to macrostructures as they do to microstructures.

1. *Values and social structure*

Studying exchange has shown that persons valuing rewards for their own reasons will congregate, by and large, in groups which can further individuals' ends. But attraction in interpersonal relationships assures that wildly differing or opposed values will be modified or ejected. Also, the common goals for which organization is undertaken will have an integrative effect. What is the consequence of this for social solidarity? Sharing group values will have two kinds of consequences, from Blau's viewpoint.[41] The first is that sharing becomes a mark of solidarity among those who share. But secondly, the same sharing that leads to integration and commitment will be a mark of dissimilarity with respect to other groups. Thus, by holding different values, groups are marked out as distinct from each other, and this can lead to hostility and disunity between them. More than this, values having such effects pose dilemmas for individuals. To be highly committed to the values held in one's group may be a method of gaining status in that group, as we have seen. But it would simultaneously earn particular dislike from one who does not share the values. Being a good 'citizen' and a good group member may

---

[39]　*Ibid.* pp. 253-4.
[40]　*Ibid.* Ch. 11, 'Dynamics of Substructures', pp. 283-311, esp. pp. 284ff.
[41]　*Ibid.* pp. 91ff.

conflict. This tendency is counteracted to some extent, says Blau, by the fact that all values do not have this double effect. For instance, commitment to financial success may have the effect of unifying society at the level of macrostructures, for it is something all may agree upon. Also, such general agreement will provide a dimension of comparability within microstructures, as financial success might become a point of comparison between individuals. To the extent that personal competition endangers microstructures and entrenches macrostructures, it again presents individuals with dilemmas of loyalty and self-interest. The fact that financial success is a widely accepted guide to social achievement gives some coherence to the social structure as a whole, and also ensures that it will become divided between those who do relatively well and those who do not. Hence Blau is suggesting that one consequence of having universal values may be the aggravation of associated divisive tendencies.

Again a simplified example has been invoked to make a point, and now things must be complicated slightly to better represent Blau's intent. Social structure has opposing tendencies latent in it which make social solidarity problematic. But over against this, we must see a mosaic of macrostructures, all side by side at the same time. Individuals belong to many at once, and this overlap gives a continuity through membership which does not usually allow divisive forces free rein. Also, macrostructures are themselves interpenetrating; there may be several with the same general goals, or with complementary ones. Such macrostructures may or may not get along well with each other. Movements toward ecumenism in modern religious circles can be seen as a case in point. Further, the boundaries between macrostructures may not be as clear as the theoretical description has suggested, and this fluidity (perhaps resulting from mobility of membership) will have its effect on solidarity. Since there are different kinds of macrostructures, we can expect the diversity to have a partially solidifying effect on the whole. For example, class consciousness crosscuts communities and bureaucracies, providing points of contact and agreement which could not be predicted from the knowledge of class or bureaucracy alone.

E. *Further analogies to economic theory used by Blau*

Obviously exchange theory borrows from economics when it employs ideas like cost, profit, and investments as theoretical terms. Blau has gone quite deeply into economic theory, seeking parallels in it to sociological explanation. His reasoning is that if we were to make preliminary assumptions about social exchange similar to those of economic theory, then, by following up these assumptions, we would be carried along toward specific theoretical insight about exchanges and how they may be described. Following this line of reasoning, Blau's discussion of the 'dynamics of change and adjustment in groups' is drawn from economic theory – specifically, from price theory. If the economists can explain the rise and fall of prices in relation to demand, supply, and economic markets, then exchange theory ought to attempt a similar analysis using sociological concepts. Hopefully, this exercise could yield specific predictions which would be obtained deductively from general ideas and assumptions. The deductive format of explanation would have been approximated.

Let us examine Blau's use of 'indifference curves'.[42] This will give an indication of the lengths to which the assumptions of exchange theory may be taken, and the kind of sophistication which Blau sees as possible. First, we must know what 'marginal analysis' is. When we speak of margins, we mean additional units. If we think only of totals, problems arise: how to measure the value of units of utility? Since we do not have the units in which to measure the utility of an action or a commodity for a person, marginal analysis does not try. Instead, it takes a comparative view. It says in effect that, rather than try to account for the value of an activity, one ought to compare the consequences of having additional units of it. Such comparison will show how one additional unit compares with the addition of the previous unit, and how added units of other commodities compare in value. Note that we do not know about a person's total satisfaction in the exchange; however, we seek to make inferences about that from observing how these additional units of action affect him.

1. *The law of diminishing marginal utility*

The law of diminishing marginal utility in economics is similar to Homans' proposition 4.[43] The law says that, as persons receive added increments of a given action or commodity, each additional unit will be of less value to them. This is easily seen in the case where we are down to our last dollar, or to our last unit of some social behavior. The problem is what to do with this last unit. The answer is: do that which gains the most. To know which act will gain the most, it is important to have a comparative perspective on the several things that might be done with the last unit, that is, to compare the marginal utilities of all possibilities.

Obviously, the decision about what to do with the last unit will change according to what we have been doing recently. Alternatives will be at different levels of satiation. That which is of less marginal utility will be rejected; that which is marginally more important will take precedence. There is a dynamic force at work here. While we always expect persons to do what gains them the most for their last unit of effort, we cannot

---

[42] The following discussion follows Blau's Ch. 7, *ibid*. pp. 168ff.
[43] See p. 89 for proposition 4.

always expect this to be the same thing. Hence, while there are ways in economic analysis of modeling a person's behavior in a market, the market is not seen to be static, but is fluctuating as individuals change their behaviors to maximize gain. This is why Blau picks marginal analysis to try to understand the dynamics of change and adjustment in groups. He is looking for theoretical principles to elucidate the change and adjustment process and to yield predictions of group behavior, just as the economist might predict the behavior of an economic market using similar principles.

Note that by using this kind of analysis, Blau is trying to take the theoretical step between explaining the individual and explaining the group structure. If he can derive out of such theory an account of stable social systems as emergent properties, while retaining the individualistic viewpoint, he will have advanced toward explaining the group.

2. *Indifference curves*

A productive method of using the law of diminishing marginal utility is to employ indifference curves. To use marginal analysis to understand a person faced with spending his last unit of resource, imagine the simplest case, one where he has only two alternatives. Does he wish to give his last unit for some of this or for some of that? Does he want ten candy bars or three magazines, both of which might be bought with his last dollar? If he is indifferent, we have discovered something about him. We have discovered that, at the moment, his value scheme gives ten candy bars equal value with three magazines. By comparing these two possible rewards, we have discovered something about the relative reward value of candy bars and magazines, too.

But there are other combinations. Perhaps the person would feel equally attracted to several combinations: seven candy bars and one magazine, or three candy bars and two magazines. He is indifferent between these choices. Theoretically extending this kind of approach, we can draw up an indifference map, a set of curves on a graph indicating all the choices between two alternatives which the person is indifferent about.

Note in Figure 4.2 that curve AB indicates the situation just described, but note that there are other lines on the graph, as well. The additional lines represent different combinations of candy bars and magazines that may be had for different amounts of outlay. Note line CD. This is what Blau calls the 'opportunity line', what economists call a budget restraint line. It represents the limit of a particular individual's resources to exchange, and has been placed arbitrarily in Figure 4.2. Moving out from the origin of the graph (point 0 on both scales) indicates expenditure. When we reach the budget restraint line we cannot go

FIGURE 4.2

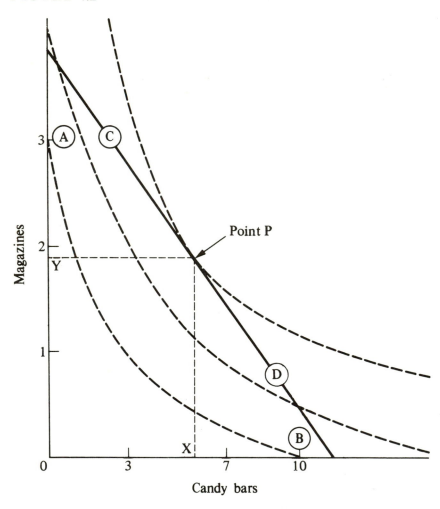

further because our hypothetical individual has no more resources. Movement upward, and to the right, indicates increased expenditure.

Theoretically speaking, how would the person in question do what we expect him to do, maximize his reward for a given level of effort (resources)? The prediction is that he will choose the combination of candy bars and magazines which gives him highest reward from both, but which is still within his means. This is indicated by the point where the 'opportunity line' just touches, or is tangent to, the highest possible indifference curve (point P). This is the prediction because it is this point where the opportunity line meets the highest indifference line. It is this point on the graph which portrays the maximum satisfaction obtainable from expending the limited amount of resources indicated by the opportunity line – other points are either above the opportunity line, and hence unobtainable, or below it and therefore on lower indifference curves. References to the horizontal and vertical axes of the diagram from point P indicate the numbers of candy bars and magazines which represent choices that maximize utility (points X and Y).

3. *Bilateral monopoly: the two-person exchange*

Follow now as Blau departs from economic theory somewhat, taking indifference curves with him. He uses them to describe the interaction between two persons acting in extrinsic exchange. Specifically, Blau applies his tool to predicting the exchanges between two workmates, one of superior knowledge and the other of less, who asks for and gets help from the superior. Here help is exchanged for compliance (this term is similar to Homans' 'approval'). The exchange is two-sided (bilateral) and the supplies of help and compliance are entirely controlled by the person who is giving it; hence the situation is monopolistic. Blau reasons that two sets of indifference curves, placed back-to-back graphically, can give a description of a bilateral exchange in which the commodities to be exchanged remain the same (see Figure 4.3). In his example, he considers problem-solving ability on one axis and resources for willing compliance on the other.

FIGURE 4.3

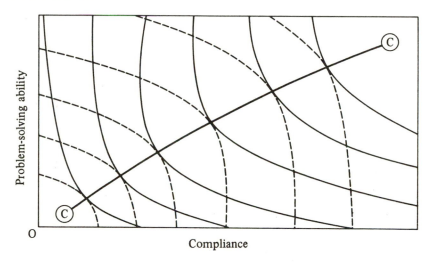

Problem-solving ability

O

Compliance

Simply stated, then, Blau has taken the assumptions used to explain one indifference map for one person and applied them to a two-person exchange. The assumptions are that each person will try to maximize utility by getting on the highest indifference line he can. Without introducing the opportunity line again (which does play some part in the development, however), Blau concludes that the optimum conditions for such an exchange are the points at which the two sets of indifference curves are tangent to each other. A line can be put through these points, which he calls the 'contract line' (line CC in Figure 4.3). It indicates that for any given level of effort on the part of either party, there is only one point on the contract line which represents the final point of adjustment to which the exchange will approximate. This point lies on the contract line where it crosses the tangential indifference line of the other party. The contract line Blau has derived marks off quantities of 'problem-solving ability' and quantities of 'compliance' which are represented on the vertical and horizontal axes of the graph.

Blau is now arriving at his objective. By economic analysis he is trying to give a general prediction about the amounts of compliance and problem-solving effort that will be thrown into an exchange at different levels of resources commanded by the two parties. His box diagram (Figure 4.3), the combination of indifference curves, summarizes information on problem-solving ability brought to the situation by each participant, amounts of willing compliance each has in store, the various combinations of these to which each is indifferent, and the theoretical points in terms of these at which the exchange will stabilize, if exchange partners act to maximize individual reward. Additionally, by assuming that receiving willing compliance from another raises status in the exchange (something not entirely clear), Blau can also derive a prediction about the relative levels of status with which each will emerge.

The scope of description does not permit further advances into economic theory analogies employed by Blau. The case of indifference curves and their applicability has demonstrated his approach. Notice that the discussion of analogies to economic theory has been in deductive form, but not in prose. In dealing with Homans' work, we considered an example of deductive theory mainly as a problem in interpreting given propositions to deduce a result. With Blau's economic theory analogies, we see deductive theory in new guise. Here it is applied in graphic form to indicate tendencies expected, and with predictions drawn from basic assumptions. Blau has been criticized for his application of economic theory to social science, on theoretical and logical grounds, and for other reasons. Some of the theoretical criticisms will be discussed presently, but it should be emphasized now that his work has demonstrated how far the deductive format can carry us and how, by conscious effort to maintain a small number of basic assumptions, theoretical accounts of social behavior are built up.

VIII. *Representative research arising out of exchange theory*

There is a symbiotic relationship between theory and research. Rather than the two being in separate universes, as is sometimes thought, they complement each other's well-being. In this section, selected research will be discussed which bears on the relationship between pure exchange theory and basic research. Such research shows the truth of the claim that to 'prove' a theory, or at least confirm it, is a very long job, carried out by many workers who do a variety of different tasks.

It should not be surprising that one would seek standardized measures for use with exchange theory in laboratory experiments and field observations. The basic questions are: what is exchanged, and how? Let us examine one example of a practical solution to the problems.

Longabaugh has tried to work out a set of standard categories as a guide to making observations of exchanges.[44] It is noteworthy that to the question of 'what is rewarding?' he can offer only an *ad hoc* answer. Remember, exchange theorists are loath to say anything too specific about what is rewarding for fear of transgressing their assumption about individual motivation. But this emphasis on individualism becomes troublesome. Longabaugh writes that rewarding things may be as narrowly defined as 'my Mother's smile' or as broadly as 'information', and that rewards ought to be defined so as to correspond to what is 'actually valued'. But surely there is no systematic way of doing this! As long as values can be anything, there can be no standard categorization of value, and hence standardized observation allowing comparison among instances of exchange are difficult indeed. We are left with the inference that what is observed must have been rewarding. We can know nothing for certain about which aspects of situations are rewarding, and, in part for that reason, it is hard to know why they were rewarding.

But concerning how exchanges occur, Longabaugh has come up with a set of categories or 'modalities' based heavily on common sense. The modalities are: seeking, offering, depriving, accepting, and not accepting. The point is that the exchange process may be thought of as a series of two-choice decisions; once one person seeks, the other has a choice of offering or depriving what is sought. Once the offer is made, the seeker has a choice of accepting or not accepting, and so on. The objective of this methodological exercise is to sensitize observers to instances of seeking, offering, depriving, accepting, and not accepting, and to

[44] Richard Longabaugh, 'A Category System for Coding Interpersonal Behavior as Social Exchange', *Sociometry*, XXVI, 3 (1963), pp. 319-44.

develop a standardized way to note these acts. When the observation session is over, the standardized notations may be analyzed to discover patterns which might correlate with other measures of satisfaction, satiation, and the like.

Note that the researcher is faced with problems of empirical application which run parallel to the theoretical problems of exchange. Where the concept of 'reward' or 'payoff' had to be justified theoretically, and derived mentally from general principles, so also the question of what is exchanged must be faced empirically. Similarly, when theoretical discussions turned to how an exchange would be carried out, we could expect the empirical application of exchange theory to require measures of the types of social acts there are. Insofar as exchange theorists refused to say specifically what they meant by 'value' and 'reward' they were being true to their theoretical principles. They wished to emphasize individualism and uniqueness, and that they did. But when it comes to the empirical importance of these theoretical terms, their meanings seem to vanish into thin air. If anything can be of value, the researcher has no guideline to follow in making observations. In this case, a good theoretical idea turns out to be a poor empirical one.

Considerable attention has been given in research to the standard example of exchange given in theoretical work – indebtedness and the 'flow' of deference and obligation from one to another as a result of it. One study has proceeded on the assumption that indebtedness was an 'aversive' state, and that it ought to be considered a motivator toward reduction or elimination of indebtedness.[45] In an experiment, Greenberg and Shapiro showed that feeling indebted does appear to be aversive, and that persons who do not expect to be able to repay a social debt are less likely than normal to engage in social exchanges where debts would be incurred. They are more likely to enter these relationships when the debt can be paid. Similar studies have arranged things so that the subjects experience 'weighted' exchanges, in which one person achieves most of a common goal for which two parties work together.[46] When self-esteem was measured independently it was found that high achievement in the experiment led to greater self-esteem, as predicted by the general exchange approach. Additionally, obligation among friends tended to show up as deference, while obligation among strangers tended to appear as greater effort in later trials of the experiment.

A more general problem in sociology is understanding the attractiveness of work for individuals. Specifically, why are persons satisfied with

[45] Martin Greenberg and Solomon Shapiro, 'Indebtedness: An Adverse Aspect of Asking for and Receiving Help', *Sociometry*, xxxiv, 2 (1971), pp. 290-301.

[46] Eugene Weinstein, William DeVaughan and Mary Wiley, 'Obligation and the Flow of Deference in Exchange', *Sociometry*, xxxii, 1 (1969), pp. 1-12.

and attracted to their jobs, and why are they dissatisfied? Might this be a function of the difficulty of the job itself, or the pleasantness or abrasiveness of it, or other factors which might affect the experience of reward? Suspecting that job satisfaction might be less related to difficulty of task and more related to the sociological setting, Yuchtman studied the officers and the workers in an Israeli kibbutz.[47] His finding from comparison of these two groups was that the officers experienced more intrinsic and extrinsic rewards from their work but liked it less than did the typical production worker. The explanation for this finding is drawn from exchange theory. Yuchtman compared the managers' experienced rewards with the apparent responsibility of the work, noting that the tasks they performed were in an especially egalitarian setting. Apparently, even though the tasks were rewarding to the managers both materially and psychologically, they were not rewarding enough. The lack was explained by the egalitarian ideology. Managers appeared to feel they were not allowed due reward, or their reward was not sufficiently different from the rewards of those whose jobs were less responsible. This is roughly the prediction that could be drawn from exchange theory, especially from Homans' distribute justice idea, or his 'aggression–approval' propositions. Blau's treatment of the relationships between esteem, unbalanced exchanges, and compliance also suggests such a finding.

Sociological field work has been done which bears in part on the extent to which the exchange hypothesis can be widely applied. Muir reports on investigations into the experience of social debt by members of various social classes.[48] He shows that social debt is unknown to no one, but that it is experienced in different ways. Generally, his findings are that the higher the class, the more cognitively the exchange process is mapped by the participants; the higher the class, the more concerned persons are with returning equal measure. Conversely, his lower-class respondents indicated indebtedness to each other, but were less concerned about getting or giving back in proportion, and they reported more willingness to give without expectation of reward. This kind of work is valuable since it brings to light effects not anticipated by the general theoretical approach, and it challenges the theory to explain the findings. Here is an example of the assertion made in Chapter 3 that research data derivable from a given theory can also exhibit unexpected results, which then call for interpretation. If successfully incorporated, the results of work like Muir's can improve exchange theory.

---

[47] Ephraim Yuchtman, 'Reward Distribution and Work-Role Attractiveness in the Kibbutz – Reflections on Equity Theory', *American Sociological Review,* XXXVII, 3 (October 1972), pp. 581-95.

[48] Donal Muir, 'The Social Debt: An Investigation of Lower-class and Middle-class Norms of Social Obligation', *American Sociological Review,* XXVII, 4 (August 1962), pp. 532-9.

IX. *Some critical remarks on exchange theory*

It is not enough for theorists to set out the main features of a theoretical system. Theories require analysis of their adequacy of explanation, appropriateness of concept formation, logical properties, and scope of coverage. Note that the object of this exercise is more than simply to find out how well the theory stands up to criticism. We must be able to use theory, if not always as a tool in direct research, then as an aid in straight thinking. Will exchange theory lead us astray?

A. *Is exchange theory falsifiable?*

Chapter 3 emphasizes that a theory ought to be falsifiable.[49] Briefly, this means it must say things that could be proven wrong if they were wrong, so that one could know whether the theory was 'telling the truth'. If there were no theoretical or practical way to check this, a theory would be much less valuable as an aid to research or straight thinking. Sadly, there are several reasons why we must conclude that exchange theory is largely unfalsifiable.

Consider reward, the cornerstone of exchange theory. From experimental psychology it enters Homans' propositions; it appears in Thibaut and Kelley's work and in Blau's. Similarly, it was used as an operative concept, by implication, in the research studies cited, for instance, in the case of the kibbutz managers' finding their jobs unsatisfying. But what, precisely, do people find rewarding?[50] Remember following Homans to the conclusion that we must not specify too narrowly what is rewarding to people, lest we violate our emphasis on individualism, human variability, and freedom to have particular values of one's own. Upon closer inspection, this decision to emphasize individual uniqueness shows some of its darker implications for exchange theory's logic. If man can value just anything, and if there must be no imposed scheme by which we understand categories of reward, or make additional assumptions about the rewarding nature of some acts, we can predict anything using reward as a key concept. For example, one critic has discovered that in some of Homans' recent writings on exchange, at one point or another it was rewarding to: husband one's resources and not husband one's resources; be an egoist and be an altruist; conform to group norms and deviate from group norms; pay a low price and pay a high price; be concerned with status and disregard status.[51] This criticism is related to Longabaugh's empirical problem with value, but it has additional theoretical

---

[49] See Ch. 3, pp. 67-70 for a discussion of falsifiability.

[50] W. Nevill Razak raises this point, among others, in 'Razak on Homans', letter to *American Sociological Review,* XXXI, 4 (August 1966), pp. 542-3.

[51] Bengt Abrahamsson, 'Homans on Exchange: Hedonism Revisited', *American Journal of Sociology,* LXXVI, 2 (September 1970), p. 281.

importance. 'Reward' and 'value' are indeed used as explanatory terms, but in every case they are used to explain something that has already happened, and they are used *ad hoc*. That is, we might observe a man doing something and, to explain his doing it, suggest that it must have been rewarding to him or else he would not have done it. Knowing nothing independently about the man's values or his state of previously being rewarded or punished, to add the concept of reward to the observation is really to add nothing. We could say, 'He did it; I saw him.' What more do we know, or what more can we predict, when we add, 'It must have been rewarding to him'? Whatever he might have done, the explanation could be the same. There is no way to prove the theory wrong if it is.

Additionally, reward is the basis of other strategic concepts in exchange theory. For example, the formula 'profit equals reward minus cost' is in part derived from the concept of reward, since 'cost' is itself a dimension of reward (that which is forgone by voluntary choice). If we cannot specify what is rewarding, neither can we specify what is costly. If this is true, the 'formula' has less explanatory power than it might appear to have. With unspecified reward and, because of that, unspecified cost, the difference between these two (profit) becomes a concept with little potential for rigorous use in social theory. It will suffer from the same deficiencies as reward and cost because it is derived from them.

B. *Can the 'supply' of value be quantified?*

Damaging as the above criticism is, it does not completely extinguish exchange theory. We could still suppose it might remain a guide to observation, or a 'sensitizing' theory to help us train our fire on certain kinds of acts. It appears to have been used largely this way in its research application. There are no complicated deductions in most studies. There is nothing as theoretically obtuse as this chapter's investigation of Homans' propositions or Blau's use of diminishing marginal utility. Nevertheless, such theoretical derivations remain to be evaluated mentally, awaiting the day they might be empirically useful.

It can be shown that borrowing from economic theory has been incorrectly done in certain cases. This could trip us up in our use of exchange principles if we are careless. The basic case of economic theory's being applied to sociological exchange involves trading valued items. In economic theory, value is comparative, just as it is in sociological exchange theory. The comparison is between competing items with their varying abilities to satisfy. But economic theory compares cost to the *supply* of the item at hand. This is very largely what 'price theory' is about – how economic markets ration goods and services by establishing their prices relative to supply and demand. Stating the case oversimply, but accurately from the theoretical standpoint, we expect the price required for an items to increase as the supply of it decreases if demand remains the same.[52]

It is this kind of argument that is implicit in the example of the intelligent, witty, and pleasant person used earlier. This fellow was in demand because his rewarding nature was scarce. The other side of scarcity is the ability to pay the price for the scarce good. The example suggests that a trade between this man and his friend might ensue in which his friend paid in deference and approval for what he got in intelligent conversation. The theoretical problem here is: in what sense is the supply of wit and intelligence decreased when it is 'traded' for approval and deference, and in what sense is the supply of deference and approval diminished as it is 'given'?[53] It would appear that a person having these qualities has them in infinite supply, and in fact giving them away might even increase their supply, since it would give one practice. Which is the true case – are qualities diminished when they are given, or not? This is a theoretical problem because if there is no diminishing of such commodities as wit and approval when they are given, then there is no justification for the thought that the 'price' of these should be responsive to 'demand' for them. In other words, the entire structure of the economic theory analogy could be undermined by this simple difficulty.

Exchange theorists are aware of this problem, and try to get around it in part by speaking in terms of time when they analyze exchanges. Thus, Blau asks a question about how much time the expert gives to the subordinate, and how much time this costs him in his own work. By using time, something measurable and constant for everybody, it might appear that the problem of economic supply is solved, since time spent doing something does diminish the time available to do something else. But alas, the problem remains. From noticing that a person spends one hour 'approving' of another, could we deduce that he has approved of him twice as much as if he had spent only half an hour approving? Surely, since we cannot draw up a rate for the value of 'approval per minute' or some such tool based on a constant time ratio, time is only a crude improvement. It is true to say that available time diminishes as it is used in an exchange, but it does not follow that the supply of whatever is given within that time diminishes in constant ratio to the amount of time spent.

Another aspect of this problem is found in Blau's work where he discusses problem-solving ability, depicting it and compliance in the box

---

[52] See James McGill Buchanan, *The Demand and Supply of Public Goods* (Chicago: Rand McNally, 1968).

[53] This and related issues are raised by Anthony Heath in two articles. One is 'Review Article: Exchange Theory', *British Journal of Political Science*, I, 1 (January 1971), pp. 91-119. The other is 'Economic Theory and Sociology: A Critique of P. M. Blau's *Exchange and Power in Social Life*', *Sociology*, II (1968), pp. 273-91.

diagram (see Figure 4.3).[54] One dimension of the diagram is labeled 'problem-solving ability', and when two persons are compared in the diagram, their abilities are added. But does it make sense to add up problem-solving ability? Can we conclude that two persons could solve problems together which neither of them could solve alone? If Einstein had had a hundred assistants of moron capability on his staff, could he have come up with a theory that was one hundred 'moron units' more ingenious than the one he arrived at alone? This sounds absurd, and it is. It is absurd because there is no evidence that problem-solving ability is additive; it does not diminish when it is used, and consequently theorizing about greater or lesser amounts of time spent 'giving' problem-solving ability to someone else makes little sense. Apart from the time constraints of analyzing the problem and simply saying what one has to offer, there is no reason to suppose that doing this twice, perhaps spending twice the time, is going to produce a solution twice as good, or call forth twice the approval as a result.

C. *Insensitivity of exchange theory to structural sociological explanation*

It might be possible to surmount the difficulties which have already been noted. There is no reason why, in principle, we could not adjust for the mistakes commonly made in exchange theory and arrive at a logically more adequate theory, retaining the intuitively appealing 'exchange' as a general idea. One way of going about this is to pay more attention to the influence on exchanges of existing social structure, or systematically structured values. Exchange theory has not done this, in part because it was born of a polemic argued between proponents of a somewhat rigid structuralism on the one hand, and its opponents on the other, who wished to demote structure and explain it individualistically. To some extent, Blau's work can be seen as an attempt to bridge over this polarization by deriving emergent structure from exchange. Structure then enters the picture as a more or less established fact bearing on subsequent exchanges.

An example of how exchange theorists have paid too little attention to social structure can be found by asking a simple question which momentarily returns to the matter of value. What must we conclude when we notice that value seems to appear systematically attached to certain things and not to others? Is it a coincidence that most persons of a given culture strive for certain ends while alternative goals never even occur to them? If such important systematic variation of value and reward is not to be passed over, it must be accommodated in sociological theory, either as basic principle or as derivation from other principles.

---

[54] This is Blau's name for his diagrams similar to Figure 4.3 in this chapter.

Recall how Homans made a stab at this problem in his discussion of the institutional and the subinstitutional.[55] He said that some persons innately have certain reactions which they influence others to emulate, others not having the innate reactions. His example was the expression of grief on specific occasions. Some felt it, and some did not. Those who did not were encouraged by secondary rewards to display grief anyway. But our question is about the ultimate explanation of structured value. Homans located this in the case of grief explanation in the innate emotions.

It should be made very clear that Homans had two alternatives when he emphasized innate feelings of grief. He could have said that grief expression was 'cultural'. This would have put the ultimate explanation of grief expression outside the person in some independent structured cultural system. Then the argument would have been that 'we feel grief on this occasion because it is part of our culture to do so'. But Homans chose his other alternative. He wishes to eventually explain culture, so he could not assume it in his explanation. Instead of going 'outside' the person to explain grief expression, he went deeper 'inside' him, concluding that there must be innate feelings (at least among some persons), that these innate feelings were the basis on which grief was felt and expressed, and that it was on these bases that grief expression was made a norm. Grief expression as a normative activity could have been structured outside the person as with a cultural argument, or it could have arisen from someplace deep within him, below his usual level of personality integration. In choosing the second alternative, Homans decided to emphasize atomized individuality. But in doing so, he posed the question of the extent to which all value can be explained on similar grounds. If we think it wrong to explain all valuing ultimately on innate feelings, then we simultaneously return to the question of social structure, culture, and its influence on value. To the extent that we accept a cultural hypothesis, we move away from the premises of individualized exchange theory. Of course, it is possible to 'go off the deep end' with cultural explanations too, simplistically giving culture the upper hand in explaining everything. Homans has pointed out this danger. But the opposite extreme appears to lead to an alley just as blind as cultural determinism.

D. *Exchange theory's model of man*

It has been argued that exchange theory appears to rob man of his humanity, portraying him as a calculating robot with no regard for anything but his own narrow desires and, apparently, no conscience either. Indeed, this is sometimes explicitly stated. And, to the extent that one takes the theoretical propositions literally, the critical claim is just. A lot

[55] See above, pp. 94-6, for Homans' way of dealing with the institutional and the subinstitutional.

is left out which reappears when we take a more humanistic view of our actor.[56]

But recall the intimate and intricate connections between description and explanation.[57] If we want a description, we must proceed somewhat differently than if we want an explanation, where explanation means a set of ideas and concepts shaped into propositional form which lead to logically true hypotheses. Taking exchange theory solely as an hypothesis-producing machine, it matters not at all what the propositions appear to describe. The important criterion is that they produce accurate hypotheses. Apart from the fact that exchange theory is not readily testable, its defenders would tell us that we have confused the objectives of explanation and description when we complain about exchange theory's model of man. Do we ask it for an explicit pattern, a satisfying description of actors, or for hypotheses? Exchange theory emphasizes its duties as a hypothesizer–predictor and leaves aside its duties as a describer and curiosity satisfier.

Does exchange theory assume rationality on the part of men? If you turn back to the point in Chapter 3 where the logical analogy is discussed, you will see the skeleton form of a theory which has only two operative terms: interests and rationality.[58] Interests are personal goals, and rationality is the mental facility required to reach these goals. In such theory, perfect rationality is absolutely necessary to make the system work properly as a theory.

The theorists discussed in this chapter have all faced the question of human rationality in their work and they have all tried to sugar-coat the pill by suggesting that they are not assuming rationality, at least in extreme form. This is to be expected. Assuming no rationality of any kind would cause exchange theory to come crashing down; assuming rigorous rationality would be absurd. Landing in the middle places only some very fuzzy limits on rationality. But we must conclude that some kind of rational man is assumed here. In this respect, exchange theory is not so far from the eighteenth century, with its doctrines of rational self-interest, self-evident truths, invisible hands, and the like.

E. *Explaining the group*

We have seen that exchange theory borrows heavily from economic theory. One area of economics that has always been particularly troublesome to economists is 'public goods', or those things that do not belong to anyone in particular but, rather, to the community in general. These

56 See William Skidmore, *Sociology's Models of Man* (New York: Gordon and Breach, forthcoming), Part I: 'Exchange Theory'.
57 The connections between description and explanation are examined above, pp. 43-55.
58 The logical analogy is discussed in Ch. 2, pp. 46-8.

things are owned collectively but they still cost something to provide. Such things are parks and bridges, fire and police protection, schools and roads.[59]

Note first that these things normally are provided by 'government', which has the legitimate power to coerce contribution toward the common good and can punish noncontribution with legal action. This is no accident. Exchange theory teaches that persons will attempt to minimize their costs and maximize their gains. Logically, the most profitable combination of rewards and cost is the situation where cost is reduced to zero, and someone else is persuaded to provide rewarding commodities free. If government had not the power to tax, who among us would contribute voluntarily to make the state run? According to assumptions in exchange theory, we should expect any voluntary contributions to be much lower than the value of actual benefits received, and the more 'rational' citizens not to contribute at all.[60]

Consider an example an exchange theorist might have thought up. Imagine two persons are exchanging help for approval. Adam is giving help to and receiving approval from Bob. Exchange theory generally predicts that the status difference in this dyad would have Adam on top and Bob on the bottom, a situation we might expect Adam to enjoy, but which Bob would regard as the inevitable price he must pay to gain the help he requires.

Now bring in Charlie, who is similar to Bob in that he is in need of help. We now have a true 'group' in the sense that emergent properties may be expected which did not appear in the dyad. Assume further that this group has free communications among all three of its members; it is not constrained in any unnatural way. What are the logical conclusions to be drawn from exchange theory about this situation? If Bob and Charlie both want the same thing from Adam, it will be in Adam's interest to give it to Bob and Charlie together, rather than to one at a time. This way, Adam can give his performance just once, saving him effort, and he can collect his approval from them both. We are led by exchange theory to expect that Adam will wish to minimize his costs and that he would naturally settle on this approach.

Considering Bob and Charlie, the picture becomes more complicated. They both know they must reward Adam in order to gain the needed help, and they both know that doing this will subordinate them to him. It must still be considered a fundamental rule of the game that both Bob and Charlie wish to cut costs. From this, the prediction based on exchange theory is that both Bob and Charlie will underpay Adam. Of course they will, because it will be in both their interests to minimize

---

[59]   See Buchanan, *Demand and Supply of Public Goods.*

[60]   An aspect of this problem with exchange theory has been discussed in William Skidmore, 'Social Behaviour and Competition', *Canadian Journal of Sociology and Anthropology,* VIII, 4 (November 1971), pp. 235-43.

costs. Also, to the extent that status in the group is related to the deference each pays to Adam, they will each wish to pay him less in order to
appear to need him less.[61]

All this comes down to an absurdity. We have been able to argue,
using exchange theory principles, to the following conclusion: in a group
containing three or more people, and in which there is a goal in common,
it will be in the interests of the members not to contribute to the achievement of the goal, but to try to take advantage of others who are contributing. Of course, when everybody sees through the game, then none will
contribute. To the extent that the participants all behave as exchange
theory suggests they will, the group is bound to achieve nothing. No help
from Adam, no deference or approval from Bob and Charlie, and no
status differential development among Adam, Bob, and Charlie.

We know that things somewhat similar to this do occur. For instance,
there is the classroom where the professor asks, 'Any questions?' and
everybody needs clarification but nobody wants to look more foolish than
the rest by asking, so no questions are asked, no clarification given. Yet
we also know there are myriad voluntary associations which keep going
on their own steam by willing contributions from members to the
common good. How ought we evaluate these contrary observations?

The fact is, given exchange theory as it stands, both these observations
could be predicted. Exchange theory can predict that groups are bound
to succeed and bound to fail, that they are bound to satisfy their members and bound not to satisfy them, that persons will be attracted to
groups for utilitarian reasons and that they will be repelled from them,
and so on. Therefore, at the very nub of sociological explanation (the
prediction of group action), exchange theory remains ambiguous, imprecise, and perhaps absurd. Here again, the prime difficulty derives from
the unspecified nature of reward, and the assumption of reward maximization. This difficulty comes down to us by deductive reasoning from the
basic principles. It shows the extent to which we must insist on precision
at every step in a deductive theory, if it is to be of real use.

X. *Conclusion*

The foregoing critical remarks have been rather hard on exchange
theory. Literally, exchange theory fails to do anything letter-perfect and
therefore, from a hard-line viewpoint, it ought to be tossed out. But this
is not the way sociological science is conducted, and tossing out
exchange theory is not recommended. However, recognition of its limitations and its weak points is definitely recommended. The idea of

---

[61] Extended discussion of this problem in the economic theory of social action is
found in Mancur Olson, Jr., *The Logic of Collective Action: Public Goods and
the Theory of Groups* (New York: Schocken Books, 1968) and Brian Barry,
Sociologists, Economists and Democracy (London: Macmillan, 1970).

exchange retains an intuitive appeal; it makes a certain kind of sense to think of social exchanges as vast trade-offs between numbers of persons who each have their own ends in view. Surely, this is a respectable point from which to begin. In addition, the organization of exchange theory into deductive form has obvious merit. The main benefit is the clarity this encourages. The journalistic accounts of social life, or partial stories we may tell each other under the name of 'theory', often do not have this clarity which comes from an attempt at rigor.

Exchange theory certainly has its troubles with regard to empirical test and measurement. Most of its important concepts do not permit anything like the observation necessary to confirm or falsify the processes proposed. Yet it is still possible to 'plug in' exchange theory with research. But such research has been almost entirely on the basic concept. Questions to the effect of 'Where and when are exchanges found?' and 'How do they work?' have been asked. Far too few empirical questions have been attempted which directly address derivative theorems. Partly because of empirical difficulties, we have not moved very far off dead center in research on exchange theory.

In case it seems curious to end a discussion of a theory by speaking of research, it should be pointed out again how much research and theory are interdependent. But more than this, the intent of this chapter has been to show how much mental 'research' there is in simply finding out what a theory says. Alongside efforts to find new data by empirical means, there must be theoretical research aimed at thorough and systematic appraisal of sociology's main organizing and summarizing content – its theory.

KEY CONCEPTS

exchange	intrinsic reward
value	endogenous reward
reward	indifference curves
investment	box diagram
profit	universal values
cost	rationality
comparison levels	bilateral monopoly
behavior matrix	microstructure
exogenous reward	macrostructure
extrinsic reward	propositions

TOPICS FOR DISCUSSION

1   In what ways is a non-falsifiable theory valuable in sociology?
2   Illustrate how exchange theory might 'explain' an event without being able to have also predicted it.

3　Which theoretical analogy is most similar to sociological exchange theory?

4　What is the model of man implied by exchange theory?

5　Describe some implications of allowing the concept of value to remain largely unclassified and undefined in sociological theory.

6　What are the uses and pitfalls of borrowing economic theory for sociological use?

7　Discuss the success with which exchange theory explains social structure and culture.

8　To what extent does Homans succeed with the deductive format of explanation?

9　Try to manipulate some propositions of exchange theory to derive hypotheses not discussed in this book. Do these hypotheses sound correct to you?

10　How might you test the hypotheses discovered by doing item 9 above?

ESSAY QUESTIONS

What are the consequences of exchange theory's not being highly falsifiable?

Compare Blau's theory with that of Homans and come to a conclusion about which theory provides the better explanation of institutionalization.

Try to improve on present knowledge about how to classify the concept 'value' so that it can become a more meaningful theoretical term.

Discuss the research findings reviewed in this chapter with a view to discovering the extent to which these research projects actually tested exchange theory.

Design an experiment in which you test whether or not a given person's status decreases if he has to ask for help from a friend. What are the implications of your findings?

Write an essay in which you combine salient points of Thibaut and Kelley's theory with those of Homans'.

Construct a behavior matrix for yourself and one other person, imagining you are job partners. What attributes of the matrix are useful in predicting the relationship between you?

FOR FURTHER READING AND STUDY

Abrahamsson, Bengt. 'Homans on Exchange: Hedonism Revisited', *American Journal of Sociology*, LXXVI, 2 (September 1970), pp. 273-85.

Altman, Irwin and William Haythorn. 'Interpersonal Exchange in Isolation', *Sociometry*, XXVIII, 4 (1965), pp. 411-26.

Barry, Brian. *Sociologists, Economists and Democracy*. London: Macmillan, 1970.

Blau, Peter M. *Exchange and Power in Social Life*. New York: Wiley, 1964
Buchanan, James McGill. *The Demand and Supply of Public Goods*. Chicago: Rand McNally, 1968.
Gergen, Kenneth. *The Psychology of Behavior Exchange*. London: Addison-Wesley, 1969.
Greenberg, Martin and Solomon Shapiro. 'Indebtedness: An Adverse Aspect of Asking for and Receiving Help', *Sociometry*, xxxiv, 2 (1971), pp. 290-301.
Hasenfeld, Yeheskel. 'People Processing Organizations: An Exchange Approach', *American Sociological Review*, xxxvii (June 1972), pp. 256-63.
Heath, Anthony. 'Economic Theory and Sociology: A Critique of P. M. Blau's *Exchange and Power in Social Life*', *Sociology*, ii (1968), pp. 273-91.
Homans, George C. 'Contemporary Theory in Sociology', in R. E. L. Faris (ed.), *Handbook of Modern Sociology*. Chicago: Rand McNally, 1964, pp. 951-77.
    'Social Behavior as Exchange', *American Journal of Sociology*, lxiii, 6 (May 1958), pp. 597-607.
    The Nature of Social Science. New York: Harcourt Brace and World, 1967.
'Reply to Razak', letter to *American Sociological Review*, xxxi (1966), pp. 543-4.
    Social Behavior: Its Elementary Forms. New York: Harcourt Brace and World, 1961.
    Social Behavior: Its Elementary Forms. Rev. ed. New York: Harcourt Brace Jovanovich, 1974.
Knox, John. 'The Concept of Exchange in Sociological Theory: 1884 and 1961', *Social Forces*, xxxxi, 4 (May 1963), pp. 341-6.
Longabaugh, Richard. 'A Category System for Coding Interpersonal Behavior as Social Exchange', *Sociometry*, xxvi, 3 (1963), pp. 319-44.
Louch, Alfred R. *Explanation and Human Action*. Berkeley: University of California Press, 1966.
Maris, Ronald. 'The Logical Adequacy of Homans' Social Theory', *American Sociological Review*, xxxv (December 1970), pp. 1069-81.
Muir, Donal. 'The Social Debt: An Investigation of Lower-class and Middle-class Norms of Social Obligation', *American Sociological Review*, xxvii, 4 (August 1962), pp. 532-9.
Mulkay, Michael J. *Functionalism, Exchange and Theoretical Strategy*. New York: Schocken Books, 1971.
Ofshe, Lynne and Richard. *Utility and Choice in Social Interaction*. Englewood Cliffs, N.J.: Prentice-Hall, 1970.
Olson, Mancur Jr. *The Logic of Collective Action: Public Goods and the Theory of Groups*. New York: Schocken Books, 1968.
Razak, W. Nevill. 'Razak on Homans', letter to *American Sociological Review*, xxxi, 4 (August 1966), pp. 542-3.
Thibaut, John and Harold Kelley. *The Social Psychology of Groups*. New York: Wiley, 1959.
Weinstein, Eugene, William DeVaughan and Mary Wiley. 'Obligation and the Flow of Deference in Exchange', *Sociometry*, xxxii, 1 (1969), pp. 1-12.
Yuchtman, Ephraim. 'Reward Distribution and Work-role Attractiveness in the Kibbutz – Reflections on Equity Theory', *American Sociological Review*, xxxvii, 3 (October 1972), pp. 581-95.

5   Functionalism

I. *Introduction*

In sociology, *functionalism* has probably aroused more controversy than any other theoretical point of view. In fact, there is so much critical comment concerning functionalism one can almost be assured that someone somewhere has already contradicted what others have considered too well established to deserve notice. Nevertheless, for the majority of serious critics, functionalism does have distinguishing features. These features recur in the writings of several prominent sociologists called 'functionalists'.

'Functionalism' is something of a generic term. There have been several ways of using the word to clarify what is meant in a specific application. While the most common approach is to use functionalism as the name of a theory, several hybrids have grown up. Parsons, for example, is sometimes referred to as a 'structural-functionalist' rather than simply a functionalist. Commentators apply the hyphenated label because sometimes Parsons talks about social structures almost to the exclusion of anything else and his ideas suggest that these structures do something we understand to be their 'function'.

At this level of generality, most sociologists agree that they are structural-functionalists if they are any kind of functionalists at all; but some have used the term in other ways. It has been turned around to read 'functional-structuralism' on occasion, to stress that the interest of the writer is to elaborate exactly what it is that is structured, and that only secondarily is he concerned with function.

Alternatively, some sociologists have been included with the functionalist group who do not actually call their own work by this name. In this category are persons essentially interested in describing social structure; they are sometimes called 'structuralists'. Usually, structuralists' writing can be turned into more directly functionalist theory if it is used as supporting evidence for a theoretical argument along functionalist lines.

Lately, sociologists who had been comfortable with the term 'functionalist' have developed newer approaches to theory, often by incorporating ideas from cybernetics or information theory. While not abandoning their previous viewpoints entirely, they find it convenient to use the abstract concept 'system', rather than the more empirical conventional term 'society'. *Systems theory* is the label often applied to this branch of theoretical work. In fact, there may be a great deal of older functionalism in systems theory, or none at all, depending on the theoretician. With the fuzzy boundaries existing around it at this time, it is hard for anybody to tell just what is meant when a person is described as a systems theorist in sociology.

Of course what sociological theorists are called is not very important. The important thing, as far as theory is concerned, is the extent to which functionalism is a theory at all, and the kind of theory it is. There is some debate about these points; they deserve attention now, before we delve into functionalism. Functionalism as a theory in sociology contains generalized statements about the nature of things social, in quite the same way as any theory says things in general about its subject matter. It would appear, then, without going further, that functionalism qualifies as a theory. But – and here is the main point – does functionalism make these general statements because they are true empirically, or because they appear true analytically, by extension from some model? There is opinion on both sides, and evidence, too. When functionalists attempt explanations based on empirical generalizations, they perform a theoretical role, just as any other theorists do. But if functionalists emphasize the derivation of concepts, the internal logic of related ideas, the formal properties of the theory, their work is better called an interpretive scheme or a viewpoint, or even an ideology. Of course, other theories contain these additional properties. It is just that functionalists have at times departed so much from explanation that they seem to have abandoned sociological theory. Also, there are those who would deny functionalism much of an explanatory role, saying instead that it constitutes only a methodological position. These critics argue that functionalism is more or less a set of 'truths' which might lead to certain discoveries.

II. *Functional model*

It is remarkable that a theory which has been criticized as vigorously as functionalism still retains an identifiable core of unifying ideas that could be called a model. The fact is that functionalists retain a considerable amount in common, and this common ground is very rich in theoretical resources. In this section, a model of functionalism is reconstructed which is not unique to any one practitioner, but which summarizes the main features of the theory. Later it will be necessary to note how some theoreticians have departed from this model. But with the model in mind, understanding individual functionalists will be that much easier.

A. *Function*

We do not have to go very far to run into trouble. What is 'function'? The most common way to understand this term has been to think of it as an effect.[1] The function of the light switch is to control the lights in the room; the light switch has the effect of controlling the lights. This example is apt. A social form, for example a particular gift-giving ritual, might have an effect on a society, such as solidifying or dramatizing social solidarity. The effect of gift-giving is some influence on the society resulting from the presence of the social form. The function of any action, then, is the effect. It is only a slight mistake to say that a form of social action 'leads to' an effect, but it is a mistake. This is because the effect is the important factor. For example, to say that the function of a particular government policy was to create new jobs, but that the policy failed to do so, would be to use the term 'function' to indicate intent. It must be emphasized that we are not talking about the intent associated with a given social form, ritual, institution, or the like. It could be that no one involved in performing an action has any idea of the effect it is having on society. But nevertheless the effect occurs. In the first place, then, functionalists try to identify the effects of given social action. This in itself raises problems.

B. *Structure*

What things function? Structures function. Remember, one of the names sometimes given to functionalism is 'structural-functionalism'. In the above paragraph on function, the terms 'social form', 'action', and 'institution' were used naïvely to indicate that something was acting. We must now sharpen up our language to see what that something is.

It must be borne in mind that the subject matter of functionalism is not individuals *per se*. The statement 'His function is to serve' makes no sense given the idea of function as an effect; attaching the service to the person involved is misleading. But functionalists could legitimately ask about the function of 'service'. They would be asking questions related to the effect of service as a form of social action. An example might be the service commonly required of indigenous populations of small feudal holdings by their European overlords. If such service were an important part of the society, then service to masters could be understood as a 'structure'.

To clearly understand service as something apart from the person who does it, we must know the activities associated with the performance of service. That is, service is to be identified in a systematic way by discov-

---

1 See Ernest Nagel, 'A Formalization of Functionalism', in Nagel, *Logic without Metaphysics* (New York: Free Press, 1956), pp. 247-83.

ery of the more or less invariant ways in which it is rendered by all those who serve. If these are known, then we say that we know some details about the structure of the relations between servant and master. It is not that we know the master and servant; we know about the relations between them.

In this example, a pattern of interrelated roles was described as structured relations. But this is, indeed, only part of the story. In addition to particular roles, it is possible to build up descriptions of more complicated multi-role relations. For instance, an institution is usually thought of in functionalist theory as a structured set of interconnected roles organized together because they are all contributing something toward some goal. An example would be education as an institution, in which it would be argued that all who participate in it have some effect on the institution as a consequence of their performance of specific tasks. The institution in turn has an effect on society – the institution functions.

1. *Levels of structure*

Note that abstracting institutions for special attention yields two *levels* in identifying functions of structures. One level is exactly parallel to the example involving service. The question here is, 'What are the functions of roles of individuals?' Another question, related but far from the same thing, is 'What is the function of the institution in society?' The first question asks, 'What is the effect of a role on its relevant structured environment?' and the second question is, 'What is the effect of the institution on *its* relevant structured environment?' In the first case, the level of structure in question is below the level in the second case. While it is possible to make a functional analysis in both instances, the entities which are said to function are quite different. In the first case, the entity is the role (strictly speaking, not the actor, but the role), and in the second it is the institution. The institution is a collection of related roles, which may involve still more intermediate levels of subinstitutional structures.

On the scale of levels of structure, the 'highest' level is the total society, in which structures doing the functioning are commonly institutionalized procedures, rituals, and the like. The lowest limit is the single individual role and its structured effects on its immediate environment. Intermediate levels of structured analysis are possible, and often useful. The thing to keep in mind is that no matter what the level of analysis, with functionalism similar questions about structure and the effects of structure are being asked.

2. *Systems*

The concept of *system* suggests relatedness. When several functioning entities mutually affect each other, it can be said that they form a system, which itself might take on its own characteristics as a result of all the functions of the units making it up. To understand a structure's functions we must know its specific kinds of effects, and the exact extent of these effects. We need to know in what ways the effects of a social structure will be felt; we need to know what things to consider in the search for a given structure's function. The concept of system speaks to these problems.

In the example of service as a structured relation, the logical question to ask in functionalist terms is, 'What is the function of service?' Asking this question raises the implicit problem of where to look for the effects of a structure. What should be considered particularly relevant, and what things are unimportant? Relevant and important things are the structured social relations of which service is a part. Service as a structure exists in an environment composed of social structures. The structure in question and its environment compose a system.

Recalling the discussion of levels of analysis, it is obvious that the consideration of a given role was made with reference to the institutional framework in which the role was found. But the search for the function of the institution itself was made with respect to the whole society. In a distant sense, the framework for considering the function of any single role is the whole society, but the more relevant consideration is the immediate impact the one role might be making.

(a) *Environment of a structure.* The realm of interconnectedness, so to speak, surrounding a given structure is the *environment* of the structure. Now, sets of related structures may be marked off for analysis, more or less arbitrarily, and discussed as if they were a system; whatever structures are left out form the environment. We can do this knowing all the while that there may be relationships between system and environment. But our problem has been to somehow designate the territory in which we expect to observe the effect of some structure or other. Using the concept of system, we can do this. If the system is properly described, with particular attention to how aspects of it are related to the structure under investigation, we will be better able to produce a functional account of a given social structure.

An example will help to clarify this. A well-known paper by Merton describes the phenomenon of bossism found in an earlier era of American big city political life.[2] In brief, Merton says that political bosses (persons who by legitimate and illegitimate means remained in formal positions of power) often engaged in vote buying and other less obvious forms of trading favors for political support. These favors were most effective when offered to persons in the greatest need, since such people were perhaps most easily won over. Also, ethnicity played some part, since many of those whose political support was bought were recent

---

[2] Robert K. Merton, *Social Theory and Social Structure* (New York: Free Press, 1957), pp. 72-6.

immigrants, perhaps ignorant of the duties of good citizens. Of course, the favors given in return for votes were real enough. Bosses put food on the table and boots under it.

Merton pursues the implications of this. He says a certain kind of structured relationship came to exist, in which what we might call 'institutionalized bossism' had the effect of providing welfare relief for people who had tenuous means of support. The favors strengthened their hold on life in the cities. Structured bossism had several systematic effects: keeping families together, promoting loyalty, breaking down immigrants' isolation from their new country, and introducing people to ranges of social acquaintance they might otherwise have missed. Conversely, this structure kept the bosses in power. Bossism's good health could be explained by the systematic effects of giving favors and receiving votes.

Bossism formed part of the political environment in which poor and immigrant people lived. With respect to the system, the effects of their political activity were particularly relevant. If the system of bossism were taken as a unit, it would be possible to ask a functionalist question regarding the effects of the system on other institutions in American life at that time. By shifting the idea of system higher (from the system of mutual benefit to the political system as a whole), it becomes clear that bossism was relevant to a more encompassing environment of legal constraints and moral institutions.

(b) *System boundaries.* A crucial stage in the description of the functionalist model has been reached. In the discussion of the environment of a structure, a case was made for considering the systematic effects of structures on neighboring structures. Exactly where to stop looking for these systematic effects must be specified clearly, and to do this functionalists have introduced the idea of boundary. Boundaries are partly convenient fictions. If we say openly that the boundary will be a certain place because it is impossible to observe beyond that place, we have defined the system of relevance for a given structure partly by conveniently forgetting whatever is outside the boundary. However, it might be possible to theoretically identify the extent to which a structure has functional relevance. This limit is the theoretical boundary within which the mutually influencing structures are contained – the *system boundary*.

Anthropologists who employ functionalist theory have often benefited from a certain vagueness about the concept of boundaries around social systems. In the bush, or on an island, when it is fairly obvious where the territory of a given people ends, the boundary around the system in consideration is no problem. In such empirical cases one can conveniently think of the system as a functioning unit without having to thoroughly consider the extent of the system. There is nothing so obvious about the extent of modern societies. If we wish to draw a boundary around 'Canadian society', for example, what do we do with the North? Do we include the Eskimos or not? Considering the extent of functional consequences of social structures, it might make more sense to draw the boundary to include the United States and exclude the Eskimos. Obviously, political boundaries are not what is meant by system-relevance of a social structure. In fact, a variety of indicators demarcate a boundary around a social system. Some of these are language, custom, ceremonial or ritualistic rites indicating membership in a given society, and the like.

But what about the boundary problem within a society? Here the empirical problem the anthropologists ignored becomes an analytical problem of convenience and logical necessity. We make the boundary where we want it, for purposes of logical necessity – to which we turn now.

(1) *The logical status of the bounded social system.* Explanation is what we seek. Functional explanation is the elaboration of a structure's effects on the environment in which that structure is imbedded. A complete explanation of a given structure must therefore include all the effects on all parts of the environment. All the ground inside the boundary must be covered, and it must be shown that the designated effects do not come from a structure other than the one under analysis. When these rather rigid criteria are met, it can be said that a functionalist account of a structure in a bounded social system has been given. If the boundary is ambiguous, or if it is penetrated at crucial points by intruding factors, the functionalist program of explanation is upset. Therefore, a rigid boundary (analytically speaking) is entirely necessary; the logic of functionalism requires that it be present.

C. *Integration*

In examining a social structure in this way, noticing its effect on some whole in which it is found, we have simplified the case. The fact is that functionalists view social structures as being environments for other social structures, and the whole to which they are all related consists precisely of all these others. Furthermore, this whole is generally seen as having a quality called *integration.* An integrated whole is one in which all the structural aspects, the parts, fit together with at least some minimal amount of unity or mutual compatibility. This unity comes about through the effects of one structure on another. Structures which endure in social systems have effects which, in general, help other structures to perform or contribute to the maintenance of these other structures. Taken together, the extent to which there is mutual compatibility among structures in a social system is considered to be the state of its integration. The concept of integration normally does not imply a state of perfection. Rather, it is a state toward which social systems tend. In a mechanistic sense, this is predicted simply by extending the concept of

function as an effect. Over time, it is expected that social structures existing together will shape their environment so that mutual compatibility
comes to exist among the structures.

1. *Social evolution*

The idea of *social evolution* in its more blatant biological form is out of
fashion in sociology now. But, as noted in Chapter 3, it is still around in
other guises. Some functionalists say a social system has tendencies by
which, over time, integration will come to exist. This means that in the
time between when we start observing a society and when we stop, some
kind of orderly social change will occur. The changes will be functionally
important, for they will enhance integration. Such change might be rapid
or imperceptibly slow. But the idea of a functionally integrated whole
does suggest evolutionary change.

The crucial point about the evolutionary metaphor applied to societies
is that the society as a whole is reaching some state of its own, which
must be understood in holistic terms and not by reference to individual
activities. Integration refers to the state of the system, not to persons 'in'
the system. To better appreciate this, we require additional detail on the
functionalist model.

(a) *Manifest and latent functions.* Surely social structures are constructed and maintained by persons. To say otherwise is to reify social
structures, making them the masters of men. Just the same, structures
men create have effects, some of them long-term, some not, which are
unintended or unnoticed by persons involved in their creation.
Furthermore, persons can be mistaken about the effects of their actions.
Where they intended one outcome, another may actually appear. Merton
developed the concept *manifest function* to denote the observed or
expected consequences of some social usage. *Latent function* indicates
the unanticipated or unseen consequences of social usage. Note that both
kinds of function are real, in that they are both effects.[3]

Consider latent functions. They are of particular importance for
explaining social evolution in the functionalist model. A difficulty arises
with the separation of manifest from latent functions. Latent functioning
implies that social evolution and integration are to some extent at least
unplanned, uncontrolled, and unexpected. This is so because whenever
evolutionary integration depends on latent functions, it is produced as an
unrecognized or unplanned effect. Evolution and integration, in other
words, occur irrespective of the motivations of people who create social
structures. Something about the system itself, unknown or misunderstood
by the participants, causes systems to evolve the forms they do.

[3] *Ibid.* pp. 60-6.

An example from Durkheim at this point should clarify latent function. In the *Division of Labor*, Durkheim is interested in explaining the effects, and the cause, of the division of labor into increasingly specialized tasks.[4] The cause of the division of labor he identifies as increased population density and the consequent 'moral density' accompanying it. He says that when these densities increase, a crisis arises in which men find themselves in unbridled competition, a threat to everyone and therefore to the social order. The point about a threat's arising from unrestricted competition is an old one, addressed notably by Thomas Hobbes and other contract theorists. But the Hobbesian solution to this problem was the appeal to reason, an individual characteristic, and to reasoned personal motivation. Hobbes saw the alleviation of uncontrolled antagonism in the rationally elevated ruler who had power to regulate society; and he saw society's members as being sensible enough to accept regulation, since not to do so would cause the situation to revert to its original state.

In contrast to Hobbes, Durkheim adopted an alternative point of view which employs functional thinking. He thought it was more realistic to expect men to adopt solutions that were less abstract and required less vision and political understanding. He saw that one characteristic way of accommodating to increased population density was to take economic advantage of the division of labor. Rather than try to remain self-sufficient in the face of increasing economic demand and increasing competition, men would adopt the idea of divided labor, in which specialization would make it possible for people to concentrate on specific tasks and do them more efficiently. The ultimate result of this specialization was unexpected by the persons taking part in it. Specialization created the need to combine and exchange specialities so that all would have a wide range of goods and services. And this combination lessened the strain placed on the social system by the original threatening increase in population and moral density.

What has emerged, in Durkheim's analysis, is a new kind of social integration, born of population increase and the accompanying threat to society. Men, in accommodating to the threat, created a system of mutual dependencies which called for a different kind of social integration. But new integration was not their aim. Survival was the aim. The latent functions of the division of labor adopted were the reduction of the threat and the establishment of a new social integration.

Durkheim displays the latent function of the division of labor. He saw that its cause, population density increases, constituted a threat, which the system itself seemed to respond to by evolving social arrangements that reduced or eliminated the threat to social integration. The survival

[4] See Emile Durkheim, *The Division of Labor in Society*, tr. George Simpson (New York: Free Press, 1964).

of individuals came to depend upon functional integration of society.[5] Indeed, it does seem from Durkheim's analysis that in some way the system of social relations acted on its own to protect itself and that the participants were the willing accomplices, even though they did not know it.

2. *Functional requisites*

Durkheim's discussion of the division of labor in society, together with the concept of integration, leads in a particular theoretical direction. The idea is that social systems require at least a minimum level of social integration or unity to function as wholes, and that this level must be constantly maintained. By definition, a social system is integrated – no integration, no system. A system must retain certain structural effects to remain minimally integrated.

What are the crucial functions which must be performed for a social system to be sufficiently integrated? In other words, what are the *functional requisites,* the functions that are absolutely necessary for a social system's survival? Could this question be decided by examining several societies to see what key factors they exhibit? This is too simple. There are no examples of societies which are not apparently minimally integrated. There are only examples of existing social systems, ones which by definition have the necessary ingredients. Hence, we have to make a choice concerning how to think about a social system's necessary functions. Let us explore the possible approaches:

1   We could say, 'The question of necessary functions cannot be answered; therefore, we ought to forget it.' In fact, after giving the problem a passing nod of recognition, this is often what happens in functionalist literature.

2   Another way of facing the question would be to compare a wide variety of societies to see what institutional arrangements they appear to have in common in order to get an empirical approximation to the answer. This has been tried; but it has yielded a bewildering array of institutional arrangements. Comparative studies have not provided a satisfactory answer.

3   Also, a plain *ad hoc* tactic could be used, in which necessary functions are delineated for a particular social system. In fact, some argue that this is the only acceptable method. Here, no attempt would be made to generalize from one social system to another.

4   Finally, sets of functional requisites could be deduced from the abstract concept of social system. This approach searches theoretically for differing requirements placed on the social system by its

---

5   But Durkheim did not use 'system' terminology.

environment. This is the method used by Parsons; details of his scheme will be reserved until later in this chapter.[6]

(a) *System needs and personal needs.* Related directly to the question of functional requisites is the idea of *needs.* Reasoning about functional social systems has led us to envision a system which must fulfill certain requirements as a minimal basis for survival as a system. These survival requirements have been called functional requisites. But in what sense could a social system have requirements? Is not the idea of social system an abstraction? So it would seem, from one angle; but remember the Durkheimian analysis of the division of labor, and the theoretical autonomy of social systems. The idea of a social system's having needs of its own has sometimes bothered functionalists and has fostered differing accounts of needs.

One approach is to derive the needs social systems exhibit from the needs of persons. Representative here is the theorizing of Bronislaw Malinowski, who derived a theory of culture and social organization from an analysis of what he called 'human nature'.[7] The basic reasoning is that, if men have continuing needs as a consequence of their biology and psychic composition, then these basic needs will call for social arrangements which consistently fill such needs. These arrangements will become the bases from which social systems develop. It may appear that social systems are organized according to their own principles, disregarding individuals; but for Malinowski at least, this is never really true. Instead, he would say that beneath any form of human social system, there exists a basic human need.

Does Malinowski solve the problem? Remember that the question of social system needs developed out of the discussion of functional requisites – what must social systems accomplish to survive? And remember that this problem is, in turn, derived from the observation that social systems seem to evolve independently of the motivated action of persons. Malinowski has tried to re-establish the linkage between men's motivated conduct and their social systems. His theory of needs suggests that it is because of motivated individual action that social systems are built up.

We now have two choices. We could accept Malinowski's hypothesis about needs. If we did but also believed Durkheim (that social systems seem to act on their own), we would have to conclude that persons are motivated by their needs but that such needs are largely unrecognized. This would put us in the position of saying that unconscious or subconscious desires for social integration must exist. But if we reject Malinowski's personal needs hypothesis, we are left with the needs of social

6 See D. F. Aberle *et al.*, 'The Functional Prerequisites of a Society', *Ethics*, LX (January 1950), pp. 100-11.

7 See Bronislaw Malinowski, *A Scientific Theory of Culture* (New York: Oxford University Press, 1960).

systems somehow existing on their own, not directly coupled to the needs or actions of men. The fact is, in functionalist theory now, there is no agreement on this.

D. *Equilibrium*

Functional theory employs the idea that needs are associated with the system itself. Bypassing the debate about the source of these needs, it is still legitimate to examine the idea. Then there re-emerges the picture of a system which undergoes changes with some end in view. Thus the idea of system needs links up with the concept of social evolution.

The end toward which a system is sometimes said to move is *equilibrium*. This concept is basically a mechanistic one, rather like the idea of a ruler balanced on the tip of your finger. Once it is in place, the tendency of the ruler is to remain there. It remains because the immediate environment of the ruler (your finger) and the ruler itself work together toward the 'end' of the ruler's balancing.

Social equilibrium is thought to be something like that. We have noted that social systems exist in environments – other social systems, or physical and cultural environments – and that the relationship between the system and the environment is determined by the functioning of the parts of the system itself. We could see this in Durkheim's discussion of the division of labor. Because of population increase, some changes internal to the system had the effect of enabling the social system to cope with the increase. Theoretically speaking, we could say that the population increase was an aspect of the environment. An environmental crisis set off mechanisms in a social system toward the end of maintaining the integrity of the system. Moreover, the change toward more highly differentiated labor had profound consequences for institutions other than those directly associated with work. Settlement patterns changed, family organization and lifestyles were altered, relations between the sexes became more sharply defined in terms of tasks and less by ascribed status. These readjustments were made necessary by the one fundamental alteration in modes of coping with the environment: division of labor.

Again we arrive at a point on which functionalists do not all agree. It could be argued that the successive alteration of social institutions is headed toward some final state of social relations. We have named this pattern *social evolution*. In a curious way, the final state itself exerts some kind of pull on the system, draws it ever nearer to the end configuration. But if the end state is de-emphasized yet the idea of a shifting equilibrium is retained, social evolution loses its directedness and the emergent picture is not one of straight-line progress or development, but rather one of simple adjustment, wandering, and alternation.

For functionalists not particularly concerned with social evolution, the focus is shifted to the interplay of functions internal to the system. Without emphasis on the end state or environment, the idea of equilibrium usually takes one of two forms. One emphasizes the adjustment process itself. The other emphasizes the states of the system at any one time, tracing out the lines of functional relatedness without paying serious attention to the shifting nature of the social bonds involved.

1. *Equilibrium, social evolution, and social change*

Critics have said that functionalism is unable, or does not try, to explain social change. This charge will be considered more fully later. At this point, it should be noted that the general model of functionalism outlined above can accommodate a particular kind of change. It can handle the change which results from the system's adjustments made to cope with its environment. About this kind of change there should be little argument. It is almost the first principle of evolutionary thinking that changes occur as responses to environment.[8]

One additional refinement of the functionalist model will be introduced now to show how complicated the argument about change and equilibrium can get. Remember the concept of levels of systems. One social system may contain several lower-level systems, perhaps called institutions. Similarly, these are composed of even lower levels. What level of social system we consider depends upon interest and convenience; various aspects of social life may be regarded as 'in' or 'out' of the system when we discuss a given set of functional relations.

All those aspects of a system outside its borders are, by definition, aspects of the environment of the system we are trying to explain with functional analysis. We explain the change in one level of system by reference to more inclusive levels. But the whole of the social system is what we are interested in knowing about. What do we do? If we shift up to the highest level of abstraction, considering the whole society the functioning system, we have no environment from which to draw explanations. This problem has led some mild critics of functionalism to observe that the model draws attention away from social change, even though functionalism can, theoretically, 'explain' it.

E. *Values*

Sometimes functionalists are said to have a 'value' perspective on theory. Of course, functionalists are not the only theorists to use the idea of values. For example, exchange theory relies on one version of it. But exchange theorists use value differently from the way functionalists do.

---

8 See Ch. 2 above, pp. 46, 49-51.

For the exchange theorist, values are personal, private, and wholly individual. In fact, one of the claims of exchange theory is that we need not assume integrated or collective values; they can be anything at all for each person. But for most of functionalism, the situation is just the reverse. Values usually appear in functionalist literature as *value systems,* shared by participants in structured social action and giving coherence, form, and shape to the action. This does not say that people have to think alike to accomplish social coordination. It does say that people must share in a coherent and stable pattern of values so that one person can have reasonable expectations about the other person's behavior.

Notice that the discussion is now about value patterns. The exchange theorist might still agree at this point on values, although he would chafe a bit about the systems of values' becoming too rigid. However, the exchange theorist and the functionalist would definitely part company when the functionalist talks about the values appropriate to a given social position. The functionalist is saying there is a set of expectations which are inherently necessary to the performance of a structured role. Similarly, inherent in the position opposite these performances is a set of structured expectations appropriate to receiving the action and properly reacting to it. Notice that what is structured is expectations. The structure does not dictate what to do, *per se,* as in 'Open the door, take five steps to the chair, sit down, question the patient, examine the patient, write a prescription', and so on. The value pattern gives, in general terms, appropriate ways of acting in specific situations. For example, in the doctor's office it is appropriate to remove one's clothes on command, but on the street this is hardly a normal action.

Values, which the functionalist sees as attaching to structured patterns of actions, are the bases on which everyday judgments of appropriateness and reasonableness, of right and wrong, good and bad, are made. The functionalist says that values cannot be individual or unique to individuals. They must bridge the distance between the private world of the individual and the external, social, and public aspects of his actions. The individual will know what activities are expected by referring to the patterns of values appropriate to his role behavior. He will refer to a value system. Value systems show the same coherence, unity, and appropriateness of implied action as the role systems to which they are attached.

1. *Socialization and motivation*

From the discussion of values, we can understand the importance of the concept *socialization* for most functionalists.[9] In broad terms, socialization refers to the inculcation of values and skills so that persons occupy-

---

[9] See Talcott Parsons and Robert F. Bales, *Family, Socialization and Interaction Process* (New York: Free Press, 1955).

ing roles have a required and sufficient knowledge of what to expect and how to act, plus the desire to expect and act in given ways. If these objectives of socialization are accomplished, then it is reasonable to view action-in-role as being motivated activity of valuing persons, whose acts are consistent with other persons' behavior in structured situations. This consistency and appropriateness has not been imposed (although, in a distant sense, anything taught has been 'imposed'). Rather, the actions are self-generated by the actors, once they have acquired and become committed to the basic value patterns attaching systematically to the social system.

This kind of thinking is based on the supposition that persons can be brought to embrace almost any kind of value system. Indeed, there is some evidence for this in the wide variety of value systems found in different societies. But is there a limit? It does not seem we have successfully implanted wholesale altruism; for all the preaching which has been done, the Golden Rule seems far from being established. Nevertheless, a value perspective implies activity motivated by value patterns indigenous to social systems. Such systems are, in turn, responsive to their environments as a matter of survival. Hence, functionalism needs to assume that the current value system associated with a social system is a sufficient and effective basis for the *motivation* of persons.

F. *What kind of an explanation does functionalism give?*

We now have an outline of functional explanation used by sociologists. There are some additional points to raise before passing on to a discussion of some functionalist-inspired literature. These points are not part of the functional model. They are, rather, comments on it – notes to keep in mind in understanding and criticizing functionalism.

1. *Pattern theory, categorical thinking, and reality*

What we have is a set of theoretical categories. The ideas of structure and function are the main defining points in functionalism. They are, as it were, class names for the things that are discussed by functionalists. Is something a structure? How does that structure produce some effect on other structures, or the system made up of several structures? Functionalism provides a class of questions to ask when researching some particular institution or society. In a similar way, the concept of 'system' is a general name for the interrelated structures we often look for. If we see the world in system terms, it makes sense to ask a functional question. It makes sense because the idea of system is bound up with the idea of parts and wholes – the parts fitting together to enhance survival value, integration, stability, or some other property of the system. The development in functionalism of other more narrow concepts, such as manifest and latent functions, can be seen as variation on this same theme. Such ideas are further specifications of the main categories of which functional theory is made.

The whole of functionalism, then, may be regarded as being a conceptual pattern of theoretical categories which can be made to do duty as explanatory theory. The idea of system is entirely abstract, and the boundary around a system can be arbitrary for theoretical purposes. It does not matter, with respect to the theory, where we draw the boundary, or what we call the system. These ideas are portable and can be moved about as the occasion requires. The important thing is that the arrangement of ideas, taken together, be understandable and internally consistent. It must also be at least partially descriptive. The categories must be understood to be 'about' the world so that we sense the appropriateness of saying that something or other functions since it has observable consequences for other structures in the neighborhood.

In the description of the functional model, we did not trouble ourselves with questions of whether or not we were describing anything real. We were describing our model, which is abstract and a product of the mind. But if we are to use this model to analyze real social action, then we must keep one thing clearly in mind: the model is not intended to be a literal description of society. It is intended to be a meaningful mental apparatus by which we can make sense of what we actually observe in society. The model and the society are not the same thing.

But the model is derived from serious attempts to understand human social organization, and it is useful in further attempts. There is a sense in which the model of society is also descriptive of it. To the extent that observations suggest that the model is useful in understanding a society, the conditions and processes hypothesized in the model may have their counterpart in the real world. That means, in other words, that the real world processes are analogous to the model. More correctly, the model is analogous to the reality, since it is the model that is contrived, and not the situation to which it is applied. In the end, theories are made up for a purpose. They should not be taken literally. Functionalism does enough things badly to prevent its verbatim use as a description, but it certainly provides useful concepts and categories into which we can fit our thoughts to make sense of them.

2. *Functionalism as ideology*

Functionalism could be used as an ideology, just as other sociological theory could. Theory becomes dogma whenever a thinker adopts a theory in order to turn its abstract theoretical constructs into assertions, instead of allowing them to remain ideas of possible use. A theory using the concepts 'function' and 'structure' could be said to emphasize these things. The idea of structure can easily slip over the bounds of its definition to take on additional meanings, such as 'constriction', 'limitation', or 'regimentation'. And if the idea of structure is thought to be more concretely descriptive than it is, then a picture of a limited, bounded, narrow field of action emerges in which people are imprisoned in structures. Because these additional meanings are obnoxious to our moral or political sentiments, the idea of structure might come into bad repute as a concept.

If 'function' is understood to mean effects, all is well. But somehow function can subtly turn into 'purpose'. Durkheim separated the causes of the division of labor from its functions, as we have seen. But he also indicated that the effect of the exaggerated division of labor was the reintegration of society. Yet for those involved, the 'purpose' of the division of labor was not the promotion of integration. Purpose implies motive rather than effect. One way out of this problem has been to suggest that someone somewhere knows how to manipulate social structures, and that structures are being run to someone's particular benefit. Where is the person who does not sometimes think himself caught up in a system knowingly operated by others? And here is how functionalist thinking can be turned to polemical use. Making the mistakes of imputing purpose to social structures and supposing that individuals have too much power and cunning wisdom, too much knowledge of future outcomes of interrelated social structures, can turn functionalism into an indictment of any society. Because society can be thought of as a system, it can also be critized as too much of a system, too well run, perhaps by the wrong people.

The idea of interrelated functions leading to social integration does not necessarily imply approval or disapproval of those functions or that integration. Moral judgments are not appropriate to serious analysis employing the functionalist model. The model's only legitimate use is explanation. If a functionalist personally approves of the structures and functions he seeks to understand, his responsibility is still to report the ways in which functionalist theory explains these structures and functions. If he does not approve of them, he is no less obliged to employ functionalism dispassionately, constructing an explanation of the system under examination.

III. *Robert Merton and functionalism*

In this section some of the important features of Robert Merton's work as a functionalist will be reconstructed. From the title 'Social Structure and Anomie', it might seem that Merton's paper is more about deviant behavior than about social structure.[10] It might appear that Merton

10 In *Social Theory and Social Structure*, pp. 131-60.

wanted to construct a typology of ways of behaving. Actually, the typology and the discussion of social deviance following it are derived from a functional model of society. It is this general scheme to which we now turn.

A. *Structures*

As we would expect with functionalist literature, Merton begins with a description of his idea of social structures and what they do. He also considers it important to refute explanations of deviance resting particularly on individualistic or psychological hypotheses about individuals. (mental health and illness, and the like). His purpose is to show that the state of social structure makes available to people a variety of modes of adaptation, and that it is this structural condition which is the root cause of social deviance. He is not interested in deviants or crime as such. He is interested in the social structural sources of the tendency to act in unorthodox ways. In fact, he thinks that action of this kind, under the circumstances he describes, is really normal behavior rather than deviance.[11] Persons who deviate are not especially odd or psychologically deficient. They are doing what could be expected of them, given the circumstances. Merton regards this 'doing what could be expected' as the crux of the explanatory power in his argument. He is showing how normal and predictable it is for certain types of action to arise in certain social conditions.

Merton understands social structure basically in the way described in the general introduction to this chapter. It is social regulation of acceptable means by which to achieve goals. The regulations (the norms, the mores) are constraints which persons face when they contemplate action. Not that these regulations are necessarily considered impediments. Usually, persons accept rules as giving guidance, comfort, predictability, and some coherence in situations which would otherwise be unmanageably complex. But the idea of structure must not be made too concrete. Structures are not things. They are standardized ways of acting to achieve ends, ways which give form and shape to action without directing it in every detail. To Merton the salient feature of structures is that they have effects on the social system of which they are a part. Because he is a functionalist, we expect Merton to describe the structures in which he is interested, and tell how these structures have these effects. He does just this.

1. *Goals and means to success*

Of specific interest to Merton are, first, institutionalized, structured

11 *Ibid.* p. 131

guidelines for action.[12] In addition, he notes, there are institutionalized guidelines for deciding what to try to achieve. It is natural for a functionalist to pay equal attention to both of these. The argument is that what people do is only half the story; the other half is finding out why they do it. There are institutional conventions centered on both.

Merton is particularly intent on documenting the 'success goal' in America. His original paper was published in 1938, during an era when personal striving appeared to be of crucial importance to survival. His purpose in documenting this theme is to show that institutionalized definitions of what to value and seek are equally important with institutionalized regulatory norms about how to pursue these goals. Merton's view is that a particularly strong emphasis on material success had been institutionalized in America. Money and things are easy to measure, and they may be the basis of other forms of judging.

Merton's second major point is to show the social regulation of the means by which persons achieve success. There are, of course, legal rules governing what one must not do. But there are also rules of ethics and etiquette in business and the professions, rules one understands implicitly about how to treat his neighbor, his lodge brother, or his community colleague. These regulations form the rules of the game of success. Of course, the rules do not tell us exactly how to play; there is room for considerable individuality. Merton theorizes that when extreme individuality becomes paramount and winning is the only consideration, then a subtle but important change takes place. The rules lose their force to regulate the game, and the whole idea of rules is devalued and debased. Institutionalized sanctions as a means to social order become inoperative, and all persons are thrown onto their own ingenuity and resources. This result may be put into sociological language as a destruction of 'integration', a term we encountered in the general introduction to functionalism.[13]

B. *Integration*

In focusing on institutionalized goals, means to achievement, and specification of the terms in which success ought to be measured, Merton sets up what might be called a system. *Integration* is a name for the state of the relationships between parts of the system. Merton places his boundary for analysis around only some features of American society. The integration of particular interest, the system-relevant integration, is that which describes the relationship between the institutionalized goals on the one hand, and the institutionalized means on the other. The mutually

---

[12] *Ibid.* pp. 132-9.
[13] In doing this, Merton groups extreme individuality and social disintegration together and opposes them to well-regulated social integration.

influential tendencies of institutionalized goals and institutionalized means create the functional relationship obtaining between these structures. Note that we want to emphasize a condition of the system. What is the state of integration of the system containing the two functioning elements under analysis? It is in this sense that Merton is not directly interested in deviance, but rather in explaining the system. He wishes to inspect the systematic effects of overemphasis on structured success goals.

Merton builds up a picture of a malintegrated social system, in which the malintegration is the overemphasis on the socially defined goal of success and a corresponding underemphasis on means to reach it. The malintegration persists because most people discover that such success is not available to them, at least not within the confines of social regulation. Finding this, people turn to deviant ways to succeed. This has the functional result of further debasing social regulation. Structural imbalance causes rules to sink in importance, while the goal of success by almost any means remains. Logically, the extreme case of this situation would be no rules, no integration, and a free-for-all of individuality.

C. *The typology of modes of individual adaptation*

Of course Merton is not talking about a free-for-all. He is still talking about a social system, which varies in its degree of integration. The system he sees is not moribund, but is strained by the overemphasis on goals and corresponding underemphasis on means. His view of equilibrium is of the balance which might obtain between emphases on these two structured aspects of the social system. Overstress on achievement is an open invitation to some form of the extreme individuality implied by poorly integrated goals and means. It is at the point where integration breaks down that the *modes of individual adaptation* enter the picture.

Merton's typology of the modes of individual adaptation is clear enough.[14] Mainly, the idea is that collective acceptance of both the goals and the means to achievement constitutes a balanced harmony between these two structured aspects of life, and this mode is labeled 'conformity'. But rejecting either the goal, or the means, or both, leads to one of four modes (characteristic ways) for the individual to cope with malintegration. These are:

innovation	–in which the goal is accepted but the means are not
ritualism	–in which the means are accepted but the goal is not
retreatism	–in which neither is accepted
rebellion	–in which the goals and means are altered, and a new type of integration between new goals and new means may be set up

In making up this typology, Merton's intent is to show that one may

[14] *Social Theory and Social Structure*, pp. 140-57.

expect systematic effects on social behavior if one or both structural features of social systems break down. Merton is trying to foresee in which direction heightened individuality will be carried by predicting it according to the expected effects of structural integration.

D. *Function and dysfunction*

Another contribution to the language and literature of functionalism was made by Merton in his 'Manifest and Latent Functions', which contains a full interpretation of functionalism as well as of the two concepts in its title.[15] Merton consistently retains interest in states of social integration. The concepts *function* and *dysfunction* assist in thinking about the effects of structural features of society on its integration.

By itself, 'function' means something quite simple – an effect. But imbedded in the pattern of concepts making up functionalism, functions tend to be particularly those effects which result in maintenance or enhancement of integration. This is especially so if an evolutionary view is taken, in which it is presumed that badly integrated structures will naturally pass away. Merton, in his treatment of the structural sources of disintegration leading to deviant acts, has actually given an instance of the need for another concept, 'dysfunction'.[16] This expresses the idea that a structure may have ill effects on the system, effects leading not to better integration, but to poor integration.

This might seem obvious to us. We have become accustomed to thinking about social structures as arenas for competing forces. But to persons who envisioned societies as tightly bound, mutually supportive bundles of institutions, the concept of dysfunction opened up functionalism. It gave the functionalists a way to talk about social systems as functioning orders without the inherent error of considering every structure something leading to functional integration. Merton maintains that we can still talk about equilibrium, about functional integration, and about social systems, without implying harmony in an ossified skeleton of social convention.

IV. *M. J. Levy and structural-functional requisite analysis*

No direct analysis of structural or functional *requisites* is given in Merton's paper on social structure and anomie. Recall that this concept expresses the tendency of social systems to perform required tasks to protect their existence. Existence is thought of as being continually under some degree of threat; hence the need to perform requisite functions. Merton did suggest, indirectly, that a social system too poorly integrated was in danger. He implied that some minimum level of integration of the

15 *Ibid*. pp. 19-84.
16 *Ibid*. pp. 5, 53.

system was necessary for social system survival. Levy makes the elaboration of such requisites and related structures the main focus of his theoretical work.[17]

A. *Levy's empirical emphasis*

Levy's specification of what these requisites are, however, should not be taken as final. He cautions that a complete list of the requisites for any society is found only with reference to the specific setting (environment) of that society. This position emphasizes Levy's empirical intent. He would consider it a mistake to draw up an entirely theoretical list of functional or structural requisites. It would be another mistake, in his view, to derive these from some abstract definition of society not based on actual circumstances. Levy takes this approach in order to maintain the close connection between sociological theory and actual societies. He does not speak in terms of 'social systems' as much as he does of 'societies'. He would think the term 'system' too abstract, although he applies a great deal of system thinking in explaining societies.

B. *What is required?*

As we saw in the general introduction, in functionalism the idea of requisites in social systems is always close at hand. To go on existing, social systems appear to make systematic demands – to have 'needs'. Supposing that a given society is a fairly stable ordering of social action among its diverse members, the functionalist question is: what effects of these structures does the system require? Levy has actually turned this question around, but he means the same thing. His question is: what are the things that would directly entail the termination of a society if they (or any one of them) were not there?

By a 'society', Levy means 'a group of human beings sharing a self-sufficient system of action which is capable of existence longer than the life-span of an individual, and which is recruited at least in part by the sexual reproduction of the members'.[18] From this, it is obvious that several kinds of things commonly called societies do not really qualify. The Society of Practicing Gurus is not the kind of group Levy is talking about. The United Kingdom or the Hutterites would come under his definition. Also, note that Levy is talking about a system of action and not directly about the people who do the acting.

---

[17] Marion J. Levy, *The Structure of Society* (Princeton, N.J.: Princeton University Press, 1952).
[18] This definition is derived from Levy's more elaborate one. *Ibid*. pp. 111ff, 'The Concept of Society'.

Levy suggests that four things could lead to the termination of societies.[19] These are:

1 biological extinction or dispersion of the members;
2 apathy of the members;
3 war of all against all;
4 absorption of the society into another society.

Biological extinction seems like a common-sense idea – no people, no system of action to regulate their conduct. On these grounds Levy combines in one requisite the regulation of sexual activity and the regulation of the relationships between the society and its environment. It is imperative for survival that a society provide personnel and keep them physically capable of action. Hence, we expect structural regulations of conduct directly addressed to personnel definition and recruitment, and to relations between society and physical environment.

The concept of apathy implies a danger to societies should members fail to maintain their social system through lack of effort. It is possible that persons might lose sufficient motivation to do the right thing, or enough of it, to keep essential services in action. These would include cultural and mental sustenance as well as more directly material matters. Some of the functional requisites are justified in terms of the need to control apathy.

The war of all against all is somewhat more complicated. This notion, taken from Hobbes, implies that, lacking constraints, there is a natural tendency for individuals to be self-seeking and unlikely to form collectively beneficial social conventions. This is thought of as a tendency of any society. Even if it were obvious to an outside observer that cooperation was required, involved individuals might still decide that yet further competition would win them big gains. Of course this would lead to the destruction of society as such. Levy puts it thus: if instrumental efficiency were the only consideration in social action, we could expect no society at all to result.[20]

Finally, the concept of absorption of a society by another does not necessarily mean political takeover or physical movements of persons or loss of territory. It means, rather, that a loss of identity is possible by which the uniqueness of the action system at hand disappears into a more general action system of the society into which it is absorbed.

C. *Functional requisites*

These four points are Levy's rationale for the following list of functional

---

[19] *Ibid.* pp. 137-40.
[20] It should be noted that this is a point of view divergent from that taken by exchange theorists, who would be more likely to argue that an unfettered individual is the best guarantee of well-ordered society.

requisites which he offers as the main organizing principles for a functionalist-inspired account of any society.[21] A society must have:

1   provision for relationship to the environment and for sexual recruit-
     ment
2   role differentiation and role assignment
3   communication
4   shared cognitive orientation
5   shared articulated set of goals
6   the normative regulation of means
7   the regulation of affective expression
8   socialization
9   the effective control of disruptive forms of behavior
10   adequate institutionalization

A typical chapter from Levy's book on functional theory describes the
action specific to a given institution or social convention by making reference to these functional requisites. Not all the requisites would be
appropriate to a given structure, but always Levy's intent is to show that
the structural features of societies can be accounted for in terms of the
ways in which they function in the areas listed above.

D. *Functional requisites and role differentiation*

As an example, Levy's chapter on role differentiation will be summarized
briefly.[22] This is the distribution of positions in a social system according to the specific tasks associated with each, and the various duties and
obligations accompanying them.

How might we expect role differentiation to take place? What would
be the salient categories in which to find social roles differentiated?
Levy's answer is that societies are differentiated in general according to
the following empirical criteria:

> age
> generation
> sex
> economic allocation
> political power
> religion
> cognition (thoughtways)
> non-human environment
> solidarity

Each one of these categories of differentiation and role allocation is given
a theoretical justification by reference to a functional requisite. Levy
works out a reason for differentiation on the basis that it satisfies one of

---

[21]   *The Structure of Society*, pp. 151-97.
[22]   This description follows Levy's Ch. 7, pp. 299-348.

the requisites. In other words, the methods of differentiating roles can be explained by the needs, or requirements, of the system (except for the final two types of differentiation in the list, which are handled somewhat differently). These parallel justifications, in order of the categories of differentiation, deserve our attention now.

Age differentiation is divided into absolute and relative age, and the former category is further divided into the familiar categories of infancy, childhood, adulthood, and old age. These are simply convenient ways of breaking down the concept of age. The progression from young to old, however, emphasizes that at each particular stage the individual's physiological relationship to the environment changes, and his ability to perform tasks relative to the environment also changes. It is necessary for society to define the performances expected of persons at each stage of life, and as a consequence of this, an arrangement of social differentiation we call age structure results.

The *generational* structure of role differentiation is somewhat similar, but it is relevant to another aspect of the requisite: the requirement to provide persons via sexual recruitment. This requirement highlights the fact that all societies regulate sexual activity and specify family and parenthood obligations. Societies make plain the role differentiation occurring between generations – the generational structure. Additionally, role differentiation on the basis of *sex* is derived from the first functional requirement.

Role differentiation based on *economic allocation* is derived from the requisite of relating adequately to the environment, and also from the idea of the war of all against all. Levy notes that no one can be self-sufficient. Hence it is inevitable that structural specification of economic goals, the means by which they are reached, and the distribution of economic resources would occur.

Differentiation based on *political power* is derived from the requisite of controlling disruptive action. In general, Levy theorizes, society is organized so that functioning structures will not be significantly hindered, since what they are accomplishing is necessary for the society's survival. Overly disruptive action is, therefore, a strike against the very existence of society, and there must be an institutional basis for social control, i.e. political power. Thus it is to be expected that social roles will differ in power in such a way that disruptive action will be minimized and controlled.

Differentiation on the basis of *religion* derives from the requisite of shared cognitive orientations and the regulation of affective expression. It appears that Levy views religion as a regulator of goals, since religious activity is considered that which is not a means to some end, but an end in itself. Hence role differentiation regulating religious practice and evaluation contributes to fulfilling a continuing need.

Socialization is the requisite on which differentiation by *cognition* is based. But it goes further than this. Persons in control of key ideas, or expert knowledge, hold a particularly crucial position respecting the survival of the whole society. Hence a system of institutionalized differentiation develops devoted to the regulation of this kind of power.[23]

Levy extends the functionalist work done by Merton. The Mertonian ideas of manifest and latent functions are included by Levy, as are the ideas of function and dysfunction. Levy uses these ideas as Merton did, but Levy is far more explicit about the nature of societies. Merton did not actually try to account for all, or even most, structural features of societies, preferring instead to concentrate on a smaller number of structural themes. Levy, by contrast, set himself the task of deriving a functional explanation of a total society from his preliminary thinking on the nature of functional requisites. If societies had to perform several crucial tasks to survive, then each structural development in any society could surely be accounted for by reference to the contribution it made to collective survival. Hence, Levy's functionalist writing, as the example of role differentiation shows, is devoted to showing how significantly regulated social action can be seen as contributing something of survival value to societies.

V. *Functionalism's treatment of stratification*

Note that in describing Merton's and Levy's ideas about functional sociological theory, little has been said about the individual and what he does. As one critic put it, functionalism seems to contain a lot about 'systems of action' but not very much about 'action'. Even Merton's typology of modes of individual adaptation to goals and means is not directly about action; it is a list of possibilities derived from a structural argument, but not a statement of the principles of motivation which might be the root cause for selection of alternatives. This is not to find fault with this approach taken by functionalism – describing systems of action. There is nothing especially wrong with this, even if some people are not convinced it is the right place to start. But inherent in this approach to theoretical explanation of social systems is the possibility that the concept of individual motivation will be overlooked or underemphasized. Levy noted the need to recognize motivation in his theory under the general topic of the problem of apathy. Since social systems are formed around certain continuous threats to order, the institutional structures designed to address these functional problems must operate effectively. Failure would lead, in the last analysis, to the termination of the society.

---

[23] In conclusion Levy notes three kinds of additional differentiation, but these are not directly based on the requisite analysis of the previous kinds of differentiation.

Hence it is an imperative not only that persons understand the rules of the game, but that they actually play by them. Why persons play by the rules is what functionalist theories address under the heading *motivation*. The idea of motivation in such theories is linked to the notion of the inevitability of the functional requisites. There are certain things that must be done to retain society. It is this necessity which puts the 'action' in the 'system of action', and lays functionalism open to the criticism that it is really a grand comment on what must remain a psychological theory.

A. *Stratification*

Motivation has been accounted for in part by *stratification*. K. Davis and W. Moore, in a classic paper on this topic,[24] attempt a functionalist treatment which has the following as its main objectives:

> to show that a set of stratified positions exists;
> to show that this stratified set of positions is needed;
> to show that the action required by these positions implies motivated persons to perform it;
> to show that a scheme of differential rewards provides the motivation required.

The functionalist theory of stratification is not really concerned with the essential contributions of all tasks, but rather with the means of getting them performed. Davis and Moore would not deny that garbage collectors are important, but they would argue in principle that it is easy to get people who are qualified to collect garbage.[25] More precisely, it is not a task which requires high wages or great prestige to attract sufficient applicants. There is an abundance of persons capable and available for the job. Davis and Moore would say that the means to collect garbage are almost everywhere at hand, whereas the means to fulfill other functions are very scarce in relation to the demand for them. In these latter cases, there is a need to attach relatively greater rewards to the positions as inducements to attract persons.

---

[24] 'Some Principles of Stratification', *American Sociological Review*, x, 2 (1945), pp. 242-9. This paper and some of the ensuing debate is reprinted in Rinehard Bendix and Seymour M. Lipset, eds., *Class, Status and Power: A Reader in Social Stratification*, rev. ed. (New York: Free Press, 1966), pp. 47-72.

[25] There has been continuing confusion about the functionalists' theory of stratified positions. Critics have noted that *all* positions in an integrated social system are crucial, since the removal of any of them would be a disruption to the differentiated system of interdependent roles which is a society. This is true. In fact, the more differentiated and interdependent a system becomes, the truer this is. Big-city garbage collectors demonstrate this when they strike; instantly it is clear that their 'lowly' occupation is indeed crucial. But Davis and Moore do not debate this point. Their intent is to show that scarcity of talent and interest accompany positions of high rank, not that only positions of high rank are important.

Davis and Moore formulate a theory of social stratification that is about positions and the relationship of these positions to each other in a social system containing them all. The fact is, they argue, that some of these positions will be more difficult to fill than others. It is because of this difficulty that the more demanding positions will have greater reward in the form of material sustenance, pleasure, or prestige. It is not that certain positions carry greater rewards which make them higher in rank, but just the reverse: some positions are necessary, yet hard to fill; these must carry sufficient rewards to induce persons to fill them.

We can now see how Davis and Moore have tied together the ideas of social system, position, and individual action in their discussion of stratification. The general theme is that individuals must be placed and motivated in roles derived from the functional necessities, and that this placement process must be sensitive to the relative supply and demand of persons who will fill the roles. The final scheme of stratified positions Davis and Moore regard as having evolved naturally over time according to the particular needs of social systems. Of course, there is no one stratification order, but as many as there are societies. The point about evolution serves to emphasize the dependence of the stratification hierarchy on the social system itself. And since stratification has evolved, naturally it cannot be explained by reference to rationally arranged schemes of power dependencies, or oppressive measures taken by elites. The explanation of stratification must be rooted in a society's need to motivate individuals to perform tasks relevant to the functional requisites of that society.

Davis and Moore analyze the relationship between stratification and some institutional areas.[26] Like Levy, they try to show that one can expect a social system to be highly regulated in those institutions which are most directly related to the survival of that social system. They point out, for example, that religious institutions are highly stratified and that priests have historically been accorded high rank because it was believed that priests stood in some particularly significant relationship to the deity who ensured society's survival.

Davis and Moore note that it is in the realm of legitimate monopolies over force and the setting of goals for society that another highly stratified order exists – that of government. Additionally, while technologists have lately been accorded high rank, they are usually not ranked with the leaders of religion, government, or business. Davis and Moore believe this is so because the technologist is engaged in finding efficient means to ends which are specified elsewhere. It is the definition of appropriate ends, and not the means to them, which is the greater functional problem

---

[26] This discussion is similar in inspiration to Levy's chapter on differentiation summarized above.

for societies; this relationship between goals and means explains the relative ranking of technologists.

B. *Stratification and values*

In the discussion of value systems as found in functional theory, we saw that *values* are the appropriate goals and evaluations of actions that go with a given social situation. Perhaps this implied that functionalists feel values cause persons to be content with their lot in life. But the idea of appropriateness in a situation must be kept separate from the idea of better and worse situations. Functionalists do not mean that an on-going system will be manned by happy, contented people, living in harmony due to their acceptance of a world order somehow created by themselves, but running according to its own laws and requiring persons to 'fit in'. Merton, and Davis and Moore, do not reach this conclusion. Their functionalist views do not suggest natural harmony. The picture one gets from them is that values do indeed form up into systems, with overriding goals perhaps as the keystones of these systems (as when Merton views the success goal as important). These goals and values attach themselves to roles in the systems organized to pursue them. But, as shown especially by Davis and Moore, there is within this structure considerable flexibility and competition. In fact, there would be no striving to fill positions of high responsibility and rank if there were not competition, individual desire to achieve, and willingness to take risks. Functionalist thinking on stratification is quit explict on this. The temptation to view ordered role systems and attached value systems as harmoniously functioning units must be resisted.

Functionalism remains, however, somewhat ambiguous about the ideas of value, socialization, and individuality. On the one hand, if the processes leading to complete socialization are emphasized, a rather passive picture of social action as role-acting emerges. This does not fit well with Davis and Moore's view of stratification, or with Merton's hypothesis that people will become uncomfortable if their rewards in life do not come up to their expectations. On the other hand, if the competitive aspects of social life are emphasized, as in the functionalist view of stratification, then the image of value systems spelling out the appropriateness of actions and their consequences appears inadequate. This point will be discussed again later in this chapter.

VI. *Talcott Parsons*

Talcott Parsons has contributed a great deal to sociological theory. Even his critics agree on that; and his critics are legion. Parsons has made what is perhaps the most debated statement about the nature of social systems in all of modern functionalism. In this section, some of his ideas will be examined.[27] A discussion of Parsons' work should begin by recognizing it as a synthesis.[28] Parsons did not develop his ideas within any one theoretical framework or perspective. While it is legitimate to label his work almost wholly functionalist in inspiration, he was not always to be found within this tradition, nor was he trying to be identified with any tradition at all. His earlier training was in the arts and in economics. His use of Weber's theory shows an interest in economic history. And Parsons has also dabbled in psychology.

Yet the Parsonian theory emerging over the last forty years has not been simply eclectic. One by one his works have appeared, each a substantial contribution, while a scheme of unification for them all was developing concurrently. It is usually this unifying scheme which is called the 'Parsonian system'; and it will be mainly this conceptual scheme, this pattern theory, which is discussed here.

A. *The objective*

The objective of all theory is to explain. Parsons' overall objective is identical to the objectives of all social theorists. His guiding problem is

---

[27] Some of Parsons' theoretical works used in preparation of this chapter are: *Essays in Sociological Theory* (New York: Free Press, 1949); 'Pareto's Central Analytical Scheme', in J. H. Meisel, ed., *Pareto and Mosca* (Englewood Cliffs, N.J.: Prentice-Hall, 1965), pp. 71-88; 'The Pattern Variables Revisited: A Response to Robert Dubin', in Talcott Parsons, ed., *Sociological Theory and Modern Society* (New York: Free Press, 1967), pp. 192-219; 'The Place of Ultimate Values in Sociological Theory', *International Journal of Ethics*, XLV (1934-5), pp. 282-316; 'The Point of View of the Author', in Max Black, ed., *The Social Theories of Talcott Parsons* (Englewood Cliffs, N.J.: Prentice-Hall, 1961), pp. 311-63; 'The Present Position and Prospects of Systematic Theory in Sociology', in Parsons, *Essays in Sociological Theory*, rev. ed. (New York: Free Press, 1954), pp. 212-37; *Social Structure and Personality* (New York: Free Press, 1964); *The Social System* (New York: Free Press, 1951); *Societies: Evolutionary and Comparative Perspectives* (Englewood Cliffs, N.J.: Prentice-Hall, 1966); 'Some Comments on the State of the General Theory of Action', in M. L. Barron, ed., *Contemporary Sociology* (New York: Dodd, Mead, 1964), pp. 572-89; *Structure and Process in Modern Societies* (New York: Free Press, 1965); *The Structure of Social Action* (New York: Free Press, 1949); 'The System of Modern Societies' (mimeographed, n.d., n.p.); Parsons and Robert F. Bales, 'The Dimensions of Action-space', in T. Parsons, R. F. Bales, and E. Shils, *Working Papers in the Theory of Action* (New York: Free Press, 1953), pp. 63-110; Parsons and Bales, *Family, Socialization and Interaction Process*; 'Phase Movement in Relation to Motivation, Symbol Formation, and Role Structure', in *Working Papers*, pp. 163-269; Parsons and E. A. Shils, eds., *Toward A General Theory of Action* (New York: Harper, 1951); Parsons and Neil J. Smelser, *Economy and Society: A Study in the Integration of Economic and Social Theory* (London: Routledge and Kegan Paul, 1957).

[28] *The Structure of Social Action* details Parsons' understandings of some previous sociological and economic theory and concludes by noting that several central ideas found in these works converge on common themes.

the 'problem of order'.[29] There is social order, and Parsons is trying to explain why. Parsons felt that his early works in this direction were empirical. But he had a curious way of using this term. His 'empirical' method was to search previously published works to see how these accounted for order. Parsons knew that many of these writers were on the right track. According to Parsons, while all of them had missed at least some of the truth, there was much of value in the competing theories. Parsons' 'synthesis' was an attempt to unite the portions of other theoreticians' works which he considered to be convergent (i.e. similar, although stated in different terms) so that a more complete theory of social order would result. For this program to be carried out, he needed the works of these men, which might be called the content of Parsons' theory; a language; and a conceptual scheme in which to unite them. Parsons may be seen, then, to have been pursuing his career as a theorist by continually elaborating his conceptual scheme, enhancing the contents of it, and extending both to a wide variety of topics in sociology. Parsons has never been much of a data gatherer. Rather, his strength has been as a conceptualizer, an interpreter of events, and an organizer of ideas. This emphasis followed from his original intent to unify various views on social order, and contribute his own.

B. *Early ingredients of the Parsonian system*

1. *Voluntarism*

Parsons knew what mistakes he wished to avoid. In the first place, theory should be *voluntaristic*. The theory should not picture individuals as subservient automatons but should state that persons, by their own cognitive and emotional mentalities, come to conclusions about how to act. Parsons wished to avoid the absurdities associated with too strong an emphasis on 'group will', 'collective determination', and the like. He rejected pictures of mechanical or organistic societies in which there was no room for individuality.

Yet Parsons wished to avoid the opposite extreme. Suggesting that social life was composed wholly of privately contrived and individually evaluated actions would lead to a picture of chaos rather than order. Surely empirical evidence indicated that persons do not make their decisions independently of the values and decisions of others. Parsons' objective was to arrive at a starting point for theory which would avoid both extreme individualism and extreme determinism.[30]

2. *Rationality*

Other pitfalls were to be avoided. One of these was *rationality*. Parsons

---

[29] See *The Social System*, pp. 30-3 for one of the several discussions of this point.
[30] *The Structure of Social Action*, Part II.

thought it would be absurd to suggest that persons behave rationally, if by that one meant that persons always knew all their alternatives and always understood precisely what the outcome of each alternative would be and always made a choice of action consistent with the most efficient alternative. Clearly, rationality of that kind was out. But what alternative is there? Parsons did not reject the whole idea of persons' behaving with ends in view or doing what they thought would result in a predictable outcome. The means–ends scheme was retained, but without the rigorous implications of rationality.[31]

3. *Value-attitudes*

Rejecting a thoroughgoing rationality left a grand problem. If we deny that persons perform in a rigorously rational way, where do we look for the mechanisms which grossly regulate choices, order alternative modes of action, and so forth? The answer came in the form of 'institutionalism' in economics.[32]

Parsons' training in economics informed him that attempts to apply classical economic theory failed in many cases because the assumption of a randomness of desires was not justified. Wants do not spring up in isolation, as if in a vacuum. Obviously some influence of the group as a whole constrains individual wants into more coherent patterns; these patterns might be called culturally determined *value-attitudes*. Parsons knew that the institutional economists in theory were assuming voluntaristic and somewhat rational behavior on the part of individuals, but they also equipped these individuals with communally validated and restricted sets of alternatives. Thus they added a qualifying condition to classical economics. It is the restriction of alternatives that Parsons accepted. He added the basic idea of 'value-attitudes' to his scheme.

Some further notes remain as enlargements on the point of value-attitudes. It is one thing to suggest that the community restricts or defines, over time, what its members will consider valuable. It is another question to ask from where these restrictions come, and what sort of restrictions they are. Should they be considered cognitive restrictions, intellectualized and accepted knowingly by all the community? There is good reason to believe not. For one thing, collective restrictions of that kind would be easily circumvented, and they would probably be arrived at by more clearly defined procedures than are evident in human society. Also, there is much evidence that persons are deeply attached emotionally to their judgments of value and right and wrong actions, and usually these opinions cannot be accounted for intellectually or rationally. It was Parsons'

---

[31] A cogent critique of the means–ends scheme implied by this is found in R. Bierstedt, 'The Means–Ends Schema in Sociological Theory', *American Sociological Review*, III, 5 (October 1938), pp. 665-71.

[32] *The Structure of Social Action*, p. 702.

tentative conclusion, then, that value-attitudes ought to be thought of as expressions of sentiment which went deep into the collective life of the community. They were not always easily available to intellect and reason alone.[33]

Furthermore, the communally derived value-attitudes were a property of the collective life and not directly attributable to individuals. There was something about the generation of these attitudes and modes of evaluation that could not be removed from their social context. This collective property made them appear to each member of the community to be something outside himself. Each person realized that the value attitudes were not due to his own thinking; rather, they were in his experience as an external property of his world – something in which he participated, yet something which was external.[34]

4. *Preliminary synthesis*

Parsons' synthesis of various viewpoints about social action now begins to appear. His hope was to account for action which was not controlled and determined, but which was volunteered for by individuals. This action occurred in a community which had an abstract power to define, in a general way, the appropriateness of actions and how they were to be evaluated. But the ultimate ends of action were not determined rationally or cognitively. Still, persons did not act superstitiously or impulsively. Emotional and non-logical choosing of alternatives and defining of ends and means was to be expected. It was also accurate, Parsons said, to regard the influence of communally derived value-attitudes as a property of the community. In that sense the 'spirit' of the community, or what we might call its culture, had a unity and coherence of its own which impressed itself on individuals as being exterior to their private consciousness.

C. *Systems and environments*

We can now apply some of the general scheme of functionalism to Parsons' ideas. In voluntaristic social activities which form up into coherent units as a result of the communal power to define and limit action in an integrative process, Parsons had the makings of a 'system' view of social action. It was clear that the acts themselves were not random. They were regulated, normative. Furthermore, they were regulated in a systematic way; similar behavior in similar situations tended to be reacted to in similar and predictable ways. This Parsons knew from everyday sociological

---

[33] *The Social System*, p. 44; *The Structure of Social Action*, Part II.
[34] Parsons discusses Durkheim in this context. See particularly his 'The Present Position and Prospects of Theory in Sociology', in T. Parsons, *Essays in Sociological Theory*, Ch. 8.

data. In itself, this is only a trivial idea. But Parsons applied the idea of system to this fact.

When Parsons viewed action as a system, it followed that there would appear certain uniformities about the action system itself. These uniformities attributable to the action system would be inherently abstract, since they would not be constraints on action itself, but on types of action and types of situations. The action system did not limit or constrain action *per se*, but types of action. For example, we should expect that there would be uniform ways in which persons behaved and evaluated others in buying something from a stranger in a shop. These uniformities would be systematically different from those of action appropriate to intimate social relations among members of a family. The system of action prescribed uniformities of orientation, evaluation, and thought appropriate to situations, characteristically leading people to perform actions that would be similar and done in a similar spirit, but these actions were in no direct way predetermined because they were systematic.[35]

Functionalism argues that a system as such makes certain requirements on its components' behaviors in order that the system may survive. This is the idea of system requisites.[36] To derive these features of human social action systems as Parsons did, we must think commonsensically about what human social action really is, and build from there. A social act entails a series of choices on the part of the actor. Actions are directed toward social objects, which may be other people or groups of people. Hence, among the first choices is how the actor will regard the object. The general problem of how to regard objects Parsons calls the question of the actor's 'system of *orientations*'. Is the object wanted, or not? What is the significance of the object to the actor? And so on. Parsons has outlined problems of orientation of the actor with reference to both motivation and value.[37]

These orientation choices made by actors appear to Parsons to be standardized. There are basically two kinds, and each of the two is subdivided into two parts. First, in making decisions about social objects in order to act toward them, the actor faces dilemmas about his own attitudes toward the objects. Secondly, he must decide what motivational orientation to take up towards them.[38]

Considering an actor's *attitude* toward an object first, there are two choices to make:

1   Shall the actor be gratified by the object and expressive toward it, or withhold this?

---

[35]   See *The Social System*, Ch. 2.
[36]   *Ibid.* pp. 26-38.
[37]   *Toward a General Theory of Action*, Introduction; *The Social System*, pp. 3-24.
[38]   *Toward a General Theory of Action*, pp. 76-84.

2   Does the actor orient to the object no matter what the gratificational interest, or in relation only to some specific gratificational
objective?

Remember, Parsons is talking about how an actor takes up an attitude
toward an object. All we have said is that he decides either to be gratified by it or to withhold gratification, and he decides whether to be gratified by it in its entirety or only with respect to some specific thing it is or
does.

Concerning the choices of *motivation* toward objects, actors face
another set of dilemmas. These dilemmas are concerned with how the
objects are related to the actor, or to each other.

1   An object may be important because it is of particular relevance to
the actor himself. It may be of no value to anyone else. Alternatively,
it may be valued for its general properties, independent of the actor.
2   The object may be important because of what the object is inherently, or because of what it does. The first is an intrinsic quality;
the second is an extrinsic performance it makes.

1. *The pattern variables*

Parsons calls these pairs of dilemmas of choice in forming social acts the
pattern variables.[39] To give them their Parsonian names now, in the
order of their introduction, they are:

affectivity versus affective neutrality	the dilemma of whether to feel gratification or with- hold gratification
specificity versus diffuseness	the dilemma of whether to orient to the whole ob- ject, or to some part of it
universalism versus particularism	the dilemma of whether to act toward the object in the light of its particular relation to the actor or because of its general attributes
quality versus performance	the dilemma of whether to be concerned about an object because of what it is or what it does

[39] Considerable critical comment has been made about the pattern variables. See
Max Black, 'Some Questions about Parsons' Theories', in Max Black, ed., *The
Social Theories of Talcott Parsons*, pp. 268-88; Robert Dubin, 'Parsons' Actor:
Continuities in Sociological Theory', in T. Parsons, ed., *Sociological Theory
and Modern Society*, pp. 521-36; T. Parsons, 'The Pattern Variables Revisited:
A Response to Robert Dubin', in *Sociological Theory and Modern Society*, pp.
192-219.

It is risky to introduce examples too soon, but consider the way Parsons might characterize the love relationship between a man and a woman. Certainly the relationship proceeds in terms of *affectivity* and *diffuseness* (one is gratified, and by the whole partner) and via *particularism* and *quality* (special aspects of the object's relation to the actor alone define the relationship, and the gratification coming from the relationship is due to what the object is and not what the object does). These general concepts, pattern variables, are directly related to Parsons' theory of the systems in which they occur, as we see in the next section.[40]

2. *System problems*

We are now in search of a reconstruction of Parsons' view of the invariant problems social systems must solve in order to survive. A social system is composed of the acts persons and groups perform in a society. Since we wish to view action as voluntaristic and not determined in any fixed way, yet as a problem-solving aggregate called a system, we must find a method of conceptualizing the social system which allows for individual freedom within a context of constraint. Also remember that the system is imbedded in an environment. Hence, aspects of the system such as other people as well as physical environment will bear on how the system problems are solved.

If the action system we are considering contains two persons in a railway station, then the actions of these persons which are mutually oriented constitute this action system, and all the others in the building and the building itself constitute the environment. Now if this system wishes to accomplish something in its environment it must expend energy.[41] Of course, the energy is derived from the individual participants, but the goal toward which the energy is directed is another question; it is agreed upon by some process of interaction. This example suggests two general system problems: the *adaptation* problem (existing and acting in a given environment) and the *goal attainment* problem (deriving a goal toward which to expend energy in order to adapt the action system to its environment). If the two persons in the railway station wish to converse, how loudly they must talk is determined by how noisy the environment is, and they may solve the noise problem by going to a quiet corner.

If a system has a problem of adaptation which it must solve by expending energy in order to accomplish goal attainment, the system will inevitably experience internal consequences. The expended energy will be gone, but something new may have been incorporated into the system in solving the problem. In general, the social system will be different in

40 See *The Social System*, pp. 58-67, 'The Pattern Alternatives (Variables) of Value-orientation as Definitions of Relational Role-expectation Patterns'.
41 Parsons, *Societies*, pp. 28-9.

some way after solving the adaptation problem than before. Such differences pose a problem of internal system readjustment which Parsons has
called *integration*. Finally, if the new, reintegrated system is to continue
in action, it must have some ability to maintain itself. This Parsons calls
the problem of *pattern maintenance*. Parsons means that in the absence
of activities designed to maintain patterns of action, the social system
would lose its coherence. He also suggests that pattern maintenance is a
state of readiness to address new adaptive problems as they arise.[42]

We have now seen that social systems face the general problems of
adaptation, goal attainment, integration, and pattern maintenance, no
matter what the specific system, how large or small, significant or insig-
nificant. These are general problems, parts of Parsons' scheme for unifying diverse ideas. In addition, Parsons has presented a separate argument
to the effect that all systems (more accurately, all abstract systems) face
similar problems. Anything considered a system faces these – cultural
systems and personality systems are analyzed by Parsons using this
scheme.[43]

Now we may return to the pattern variables to discover how these
dilemmas of voluntaristic action are linked with the general system problems. The guiding principle is still rather simple, although many new
terms will be used. The pattern variables are general statements about
universal aspects of human social action. Parsons has tried to make the
case that the pattern variables state fundamental regularities about the
ways persons orient toward and evaluate objects. These activities are
preliminary and indispensable to enacting social conduct toward objects.
Now the task for Parsons is to bring together the pattern variables with
the universal system problems. Of course, he has to do so to succeed in
showing that social systems are bounded and directed systematic aggre-
gated social interactions. Parsons must (1) give an account of the social
system in terms of personal action and (2) give an account of personal
action in terms of system action. By so doing, Parsons links the fundamentals of functionalist theory concerning social systems with a voluntaristic view of personal action.

By use of the pattern variables, the first system problem – adaptation
– may be described. Adaptation is the accommodation of the social
system to its environment, which might be problematic or even
threatening.[44] War is the supreme example of such a case, where two

---

42 This summary of the adaptation, goal attainment, integration and pattern main-
    tenance scheme is based on 'Phase Movement in Relation to Motivation,
    Symbol Formation, and Role Structure', in Parsons, Bales, and Shils, *Working
    Papers*. The scheme is found in almost all Parsons' theoretical works.
43 See *Toward a General Theory of Action*, p. 62, where Parsons discusses how
    he applies the general scheme to various 'levels' of analysis.
44 Sometimes Parsons uses the term 'mastery' of the environment, by which he
    means to emphasize the active nature of social systems.

societies threaten each other's survival. There can be no mistake about a war – an active enemy cannot be represented as anything but a hostile aspect of the environment, especially if he is dropping bombs on your cities.

Consider now warlike social behavior as characterized by the fundamental dilemmas of action in the pattern variables. First let us take universalism versus particularism. In warfare, the orientation of actors to objects is one of *universalism*, i.e. cognizance of the object (the enemy) as a member of a class of things (called enemies). Paying too much attention to one particular enemy soldier as an individual might result in your getting shot (failing to adapt).

However, adaptation in a war situation is not the same thing as wanton murder. The second pattern variable, specificity versus diffuseness, suggests that interest in the enemy is *specific*; only insofar as he is engaged in hostile action against you do you oppose him. Decisions about how to orient to him are not made according to his whole being, but rest on how his acts as an enemy are relevant to your goals.

The next pattern variable is quality versus performance. In adaptive crises such as war, social objects which have become troublesome are dealt with because of what they are doing, not because of what they are. This orientation to the object Parsons has named *performance*. Finally, note that it is inappropriate to attach affective or emotional sentiments to the object of adaptation. Everyone knows that soldiers do not usually think of their enemies as 'people' while they are killing them. The affective bond is withheld or never developed and the orientation is one of *affective neutrality*.

Let us review this quickly in somewhat less concrete fashion. When social systems face adaptive problems, the most effective solutions to these problems will be gained by social action toward troublesome objects, which is characterized by affective neutrality, specificity, universalism, and performance. It was said that we were being less concrete now, and here is what is meant by that: the four pattern variable choices appropriate for adaptation form a general pattern of orientation. Theory suggests that persons involved in action will behave according to this pattern for best results in adaptive dilemmas. There is nothing here, really, about the exact choice of concrete acts, or about concrete constraints on given activities or thoughts. However, the pattern is an abstract specification of modes of orientation and evaluation. Adopting these modes will place a social system in the best position to accomplish adaptation to its environment.

The other system problems are linked to the pattern variables in much the same way as adaptation. According to Parsons, for each problem of goal attainment, integration, and pattern maintenance, there is a unique combination of the pattern variables which satisfies the needs of the system in each of these phases. Including adaptation discussed above, the four system problems form what is probably the most famous of all Parsons' ideas – his four-fold conceptual scheme, found in Figure 5.1.

FIGURE 5.1

adaptation	goal attainment
pattern maintenance	integration

This four-fold idea can lead us further. The abstract definitions of the four system problems form the definition of a system. Any surviving system is consistently and continuously solving the four basic problems. Applied specifically to social systems, any existing social system may be regarded as consistently solving these four problems.[45] But recall the discussion of levels of analysis associated with functionalism. Since the four-fold scheme is completely abstract, Parsons can move it about. He can move it up in level of generality, or down, to account for the actions of whole societies, institutions, or even persons. Or he can define one of the four problems itself as being a system, and it will then display the four-fold scheme (see Figure 5.2).

In Figure 5.2, the goal attainment subsystem has been taken as the subject for analysis. It has been broken down into the same four constituent abstract elements as the larger system was, of which goal attainment was a part. The other three systems now become environmental to the goal attainment subsystem. Thus the idea of the general system can be used to analyze either a whole or parts of a social system, or abstract portions of the scheme.

D. *What kinds of systems are there?*

Parsons regards his basic idea as entirely abstract; by this he means that it is not intended primarily as a description of anything, but a mode of

---

[45] 'Solving' is not exactly the correct usage here. Parsons means that societies successfully cope with these problems. They do not solve them in a final sense. See Parsons and Smelser, *Economy and Society*, pp. 46-7.

FIGURE 5.2

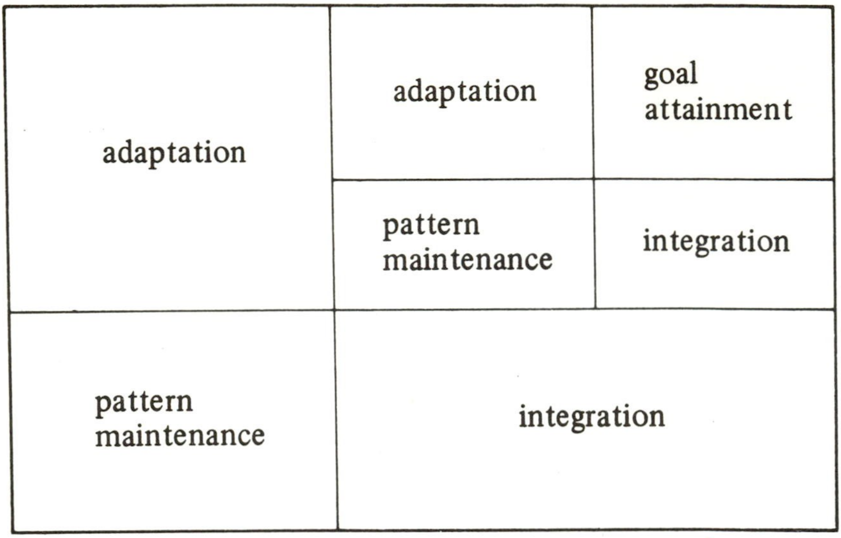

adaptation	adaptation	goal attainment
	pattern maintenance	integration
pattern maintenance	integration	

conceptualizing interdependencies and environments. In the examples and the discussion above, what was referred to by the term 'system' remained ambiguous. It turns out that Parsons has applied the idea to several levels of analysis, and these are now introduced.

The level easiest to grasp intuitively is that of the *social* system, a collection of interrelated social actions performed by persons in a society. Parsons' *The Social System* elaborates the application of his way of thinking to the action system of societies. But Parsons could have written other system books as well. For example, there is the realm of ideas and values, which played a part in the foundation of Parsons' ideas. In fact, says Parsons, social systems rely on *cultural* systems (systems of values, moral precepts, and ideas which are organized on exactly the same abstract principles as the social system). The four-fold paradigm, abstract and portable, can be applied to the cultural system, too.[46] Cultural systems have a unity, a coherence, and an internal logic quite like the action systems they accompany. Furthermore, the two systems are interdependent and influence each other. They are separate and environmental to each other, abstractly speaking.

Moving to another level of analysis, it is possible to think of the human *personality* as a system organized according to the four-fold

[46] Parsons, *Knowledge and Society* (Washington: Voice of America, 1968).

scheme. It, too, is separate from and environmental to the social system and the cultural system.[47] At yet a lower level of abstraction, it is possible to consider the *physical organism*, apart from personality, as being the system on which all the rest of social and cultural behavior is based.[48]

Taken together, the physical organism, the personality system, the social system, and the cultural system form a grand, mutually influencing array – they form a system.[49] Systems are the environments of systems, and as such they provide the potential for solving each other's problems, or they may be the sources of those problems. The whole picture (which might be called a 'vision' on Parsons' part) works as an integrated unit, yet each part is internally coherent and analytically separable.

Let us expand somewhat on the application of this abstract four-fold concept to the theory of society. Applying the abstract four-fold scheme to the array just described, Parsons identifies the *social* system with the abstract concept of *integration*. Integration means systematically relating the parts of the whole together. Interdependent social action does this, and society is interdependent social action. Thus, in the abstract four-fold scheme, the social system is identified with integration.[50]

Associated with *pattern maintenance* is the *cultural* system – an orderly part of the social system's environment composed fundamentally of the legitimizing principles on which normative acts are based. It is one thing to say, 'We act in a certain way'; and it is another thing to say, 'We act this way for a specific reason.' Ultimately, the only justifications for the ways we wish to act in a society are the deeply felt and strongly held values and principles which are more or less common to members. These things are systematically articulated in religious beliefs, myths about the nature of the world, art as emotional expression and embodiment of individuality, and the like. These aspects of culture are all in one way or another expressing a meaning for the enduring aspects of social life as lived, and the cultural system provides the highly abstract answers to the question 'Why is it like this?' Cultural patterns endure relatively long and lend coherence to diverse activity; hence they are pattern maintaining.

Associated with *goal attainment* in the general paradigm is the *personality* system. Personality is the learned mental organization of the individual. Persons do not entirely act on their own toward privately con-

---

[47] See Parsons and Bales, *Family, Socialization and Interaction Process.*
[48] See *Societies*, pp. 28-9.
[49] *Ibid.* p. 29.
[50] The integration subsystem of the grand scheme has taken on another name in Parsons' later writing, the 'societal community'. By this term Parsons indicates the sum total of integrative acts that take place among persons participant in the community. These normatively regulated acts spell out membership criteria as well. Those who act as though they belong, and are acted toward in a corresponding spirit, are by such action defining the societal community.

trived ends. Rather, their ends and the means which occur to them are ordered by the social relations in which people participate. Therefore, Parsons' concept of the personality system is one of a socialized, coherent personal organization dependent on both the social system and the cultural system. The social system requires cooperation from each individual. Hence, built into personality must be the desire to be rewarded by the things other people have to give, and the willingness to reward in acceptable ways. These desires, motives, and viewpoints (personality system) so necessary for integrated social action (social system) are, in turn, expressed and legitimized by the cultural system.

Associated with the remaining part of the general system, *adaptation*, is the purely physical aspect of the person and the organic and physical environment he lives in. Basically, Parsons' idea is that societies have to come to terms with their natural environments as a matter of survival, and the methods by which they come to terms are crucial. Collective social adaptation may be realized by the coordinated application of individual potential to collective problems, i.e. mobilization of *physical organism.*

So far Parsons has made a simple set of associations between the parts of the general system, stated in abstract terms, and the more concrete systems: culture, society, personality, physical organism. The accompanying table summarizes these associations.

Functions in general system terms	*Concrete systems*
Pattern maintenance	Cultural system
Integration	Social system
Goal attainment	Personality system
Adaptation	Physical organism

As a way of making the general system idea clearer and to show its classificatory powers, examine next a Parsonian classification of social *institutions*. Social systems must institutionalize solutions to the four problems of general systems. Why? Because if these solutions are not formulated, the system ceases to exist. Parsons shows that there are institutions of the social system associated with each of the four general system problems. Operating at the level of the social system (associated with integration in the general scheme), he demonstrates that its institutions perform the general functions of adaptation, goal attainment, integration, and pattern maintenance.

Classifying institutions by general system concepts, it is probably easiest to start with *adaptation*, the accommodating of a system to its environment. When Parsons considers adaptation, he asks about the methods of making social systems accommodate to their environments. It is natural, therefore, to find Parsons associating the *economy* as an institution with the adaptation function.[51] The economy produces the wherewithall societies need to accomplish anything. The health of the economic institution indicates the society's state of preparedness to cope with its environment. If orderly (institutionalized) economic activity ceased, adaptation would be impossible. It is no surprise then, Parsons would say, that we have an array of laws, agreements, trusts, basic understandings, and expectations which govern economies. It is precisely because of the centrality of the adaptation function that it must be regulated; institutionalized norms grow up to do just that.

Now let us pass on to *goal attainment*, but keep the adaptation function well in mind, because the two go together. Economies as productive engines do not, in the last analysis, determine what is done with the wherewithal they produce. There is a separate set of institutionalized and often quite formalized procedures for setting goals. This is the polity, or the *political* institution. In all countries, firms making up the industries which form the economy are regulated and controlled by laws which are not of their own making. Even though they may influence government, they are not the government. Social will is expressed through some regulating body of law and on-going governing system. This and custom determine what general directions will be taken by a society, what its priorities are, and who shall be the beneficiaries of economic activity, in what proportions.[52]

Integrative institutions are those which standardize other social relations of significance. In particular, legal norms which spell out clearly and precisely certain duties individuals have to each other are examples of institutions devoted to system integration. The institution we might call *the law* and its practice fulfills principally an integrative activity insofar as it standardizes expectations, passes decisions on justice, and defines particular duties and rights of citizens.

Pattern maintenance is associated with institutions which pertain especially to the articulation and analysis of what we might call 'basic truth'. *Religious* institutions are an example. Religious institutions make legiti-

---

[51] *Economy and Society* details especially the economic institution's role in this scheme of classified institutions. For a good secondary treatment of Parsons' scheme of institutional relations with particular emphasis on politics, see William Mitchell, *Sociological Analysis and Politics* (Englewood Cliffs, N.J.: Prentice-Hall, 1967).

[52] See Parsons' 'The Motivation of Economic Activities', in Parsons, Bales and Shils, *Essays in Sociological Theory* (New York: Free Press, 1949), pp. 50-68. Recall here that Davis and Moore see the rewards attached to various social positions as inducements to cause persons to take up various occupations. This is just what Parsons would have predicted. Collective decisions attach fruits of economic endeavor to stratified positions. This is necessary because of the relative importance of these positions and the scarcity of the means to fill them. The processes of collective decision-making and direction-finding are the special province of *political* institutions, not economies.

mate pronouncements on matters of high moral principle or ultimate reality as well as interpret these to men. This may be done in a round-about fashion, but ultimately behavior is culturally legitimized by reference to a cultural value. Parsons would say our pattern-maintaining institutions define for us an enduring 'rightness' of certain activities. This rightness forms the moral basis of socialization and education, and is the backdrop for the evaluation and control of social practices. The value of life, the Golden Rule, or the significance of social responsibility, cannot ultimately be upheld on grounds of rationality or efficiency. They are moral precepts that emerge from religious or sentimental feelings which are institutionalized as cultural values.

Now we may see how a social norm which regulates concrete behavior unites the elements of the general system. Norms are adhered to by socialized persons because they are satisfying and because proper conduct is rewarded by the role partner. Socialized persons accept norms and are happy to perform them because norms are actual behavioral expressions of cultural beliefs. In that sense, acting according to a legitimate norm helps to confirm the legitimacy of the cultural system. Also, when one receives the rewards for a performance adhering to a norm, one's role partner is seen to have right motives and desires and an adequate and properly organized personality system. Similarly, the personality which accepts the legitimately offered external rewards is confirmed and entrenched in the acceptance. Thus the social system, the 'scene' where the action takes place, unites the personality system and the cultural system into a total action system which contains them all.

E. *Cybernetic relations among the four parts of the general system*

Parsons needed a coherent way to summarize his thoughts about the relationships among the four parts of general systems. These parts do not stand alone; there is no cultural system in the absence of social system, personality system, physical organism; no social system in the absence of cultural system, personality system, physical organism; and so forth. What is required is a means to express their interdependent yet separate nature. Parsons has chosen to do this by borrowing ideas from cybernetics, a science originally developed by mathematicians and engineers to express relations of input and output between related entities, and to express the ways these mutual influences affect the total system in which they are found.

Consider two central ideas: information and energy. Information in a pure state is powerless. Pure ideas do not act, cannot act. Similarly, pure energy has no direction. If we think of energy in action, we always think of its doing some particular thing, and never of its doing everything at once. Usually, ordinary concepts of energy and information actually mix the two. Information and energy need each other, so to speak, for either to be conceivable in a concrete way.[53]

Cybernetic thinking spreads the concepts of information and energy out on two continua. The energy continuum goes between the pole of pure, undirected energy at one end to a lack of energy at the other; similarly, the information continuum goes from pure information on one extreme to no information on the other. When these two continua are combined, it turns out that the gradations go in opposite directions. If the two are put side by side, the end of the energy continuum representing pure energy is next to the 'no information' end of the information continuum. The 'no energy' end of the energy continuum is next to the 'pure information' end of the information continuum. Figure 5.3 summarizes this. Of course, the extremes of these continua are purely theoretical, but Figure 5.3 suggests an interesting schematic plan Parsons uses to display the components of the general system. It would be natural to think of social action, or any action in principle, as the utilization of energy. This follows from Parsons' concept of social action, too – it is a motivated expenditure of energy toward some goal. The energy available, the types, kinds, and the cost of it, are 'conditioning factors', which influence the decision about what actions may be taken. Similarly, as action is formulated, it is shaped, controlled, directed, and channeled. Information is combined with energy to do this. Information enters the act in the shape of 'controlling factors' which give direction. Note that no action is possible without both information and energy. Note also that, depend-

FIGURE 5.3

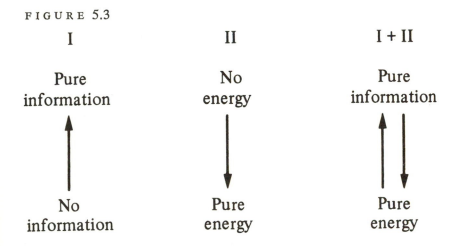

I	II	I + II
Pure information	No energy	Pure information
↑	↓	↑ ↓
No information	Pure energy	Pure energy

53   The following discussion is based on Parsons, *Societies,* Ch. 2.

ing on the point at which the action takes place on the continua, there is one specific mixture of information and energy implied. Parsons has conceptualized the 'inputs' and 'outputs' of each part of the general scheme as being information and energy. He locates the four parts in terms of what they take from and give to each other.

Refer to Figure 5.4. Note that on the left, in ascending order, are the names of the parts in the general system model. Opposite these, horizontally, are located the physical organism, the personality system, the social system, and the cultural system. To the right are repeated these systems, showing the cybernetic relationships in which they stand to each other in terms of inputs and outputs of information and energy. This arrangement is derived from the two hierarchies, energy and information, and Parsons calls these the hierarchies of *conditioning* and *control*.

Moving up from the physical organism, we note, as expected, that the physical organism contributes conditions and facilities for action to facilitate the working of the whole order, and that it receives normative controls as its input from the personality system. Notice that these controls are not directly from the cultural system. However, proceeding downward from the cultural system, in every case normative controls are the outputs from the systems above to the systems below. Hence, while controls applied to a physical organism and the personality system have a basis in culture, they are not directly related to culture. Rather, they achieve their relation through action's taking place in the intervening social system.

The social system is the system of mutually oriented interdependent social activities. Interdependent social action, in Parsons' language, is enacted in the *double contingency bond*.[54] In simple terms, the double contingency bond comes down to this: what I may do is dependent on two things. One is what I want to do; the other is what you want me to do. What you may do is regulated the same way. Now, for us to get together, I must want to do what you want me to do, and you must want to do what I want you to do. If this condition obtains, then each of us will be rewarded in our actions from two sources. We will have our self-respect and our internal satisfaction from doing what we wanted, and we will have external gratification as a reward from the other person. Social interaction has repercussions both inwardly and outwardly. In the inward direction, it finds its gratification in individual personality processes. These, in turn, appear in the personality through social learning and familiarity with cultural themes. Parsons often discusses these processes under the heading of 'need dispositions' when he means culturally influenced individual motivation. In the outward direction, social interaction is rewarded by other people who approve of the action.

The double contingency bond unites the systems below the social system with those above it (personality system and cultural system) in

---

[54] *The Social System*, pp. 36ff.

FIGURE 5.4

Parts of the general system model	Analytically separated systems	Cybernetic hierarchy
		Information (controlling factors)
Pattern maintenance	Cultural system	Cultural system
Integration	Social system	Social system
Goal attainment	Personality system	Personality system
Adaptation	Physical organism	Physical organism
		Energy (conditioning and facilitating factors)

I = controlling factors derived from pure information.

E = conditioning and facilitating factors derived from pure energy.

concrete behavior, and, by doing so, it contributes to the integration of these environmental systems with the social system itself. From the personality system the social system receives conditions and facilities, and from the cultural system it receives normative controls. To the personality system normative controls are sent and to the cultural system conditions and facilities are sent. Through union of information and energy in the social system, normative voluntaristic action can take place; and as it occurs, it affects the systems environmental to it. Parsons suggests that over time the four systems mutually adjust to be more consistent with each other, so that energy and information united in action embody legitimate cultural values and personal need dispositions. Thus Parsons argues it is natural to expect to find persons wanting to do what they are required to do. Orderly activity of the social system is no longer problematic. 'How does order come about?' is answered.

F. *Social evolution*

Parsons eventually became an evolutionary theorist. In the 1950s and 1960s, his theory was often criticized for giving too static a picture of social systems. It was said that his theoretical scheme, with its emphasis on well-ordered personalities, having clearly defined expectations and acting in an integrated social system, implied too much solidity and stability. Partly in response to such criticisms, Parsons sometimes applied his ideas more directly to the question of social change. Given functionalism's tradition and Parsons' systems thinking, it is not surprising that an evolutionary theory emerged.

Parsons' 1953 publication, *Working Papers in the Theory of Action* (co-authored by Bales and Shils) is of particular interest, especially Chapter 5, 'Phase Movement in Relation to Motivation, Symbol Formation and Role Structure'.[55] This outlines once again the four-fold paradigm and links it to the pattern variables. But here more clearly than elsewhere, Parsons *et al.* explain that the relationship between the four system problems involves a process of 'moving equilibrium'. It is true, he says, that abstractly speaking the four system problems can be seen as a unit which appears fixed in space and time, but in practice it is not so. He elaborates the idea of *phase movement* to express continuing changes in the relative importance of the four system problems in any total system, and the shifting nature of the relationships among them. Analytically, one instance of social change may be called a phase movement. A phase starts with an adaptation problem. The system as a whole has some need with respect to its environment. Appropriate to adaptive

[55] pp. 163-269.

crises is immediate and maximum instrumental adaptive activity (or, in plain terms, maximum effort toward solving the problem at hand). However, as the environmental problem is mastered, it becomes increasingly appropriate for the system to take a different orientation to its environment. A consummatory phase is reached in which the mastered environment is accommodated to the now altered system. This calls for a shift in collective attitude and orientation to the environment; there is a new relationship between the environment and the system, neither of which is exactly the same as it was before.

Following this is a further change, carrying the system out of the consummatory phase. After goals are attained, circumstances are somewhat altered. For one thing, energy has been used up. The system might be 'tired'. Similarly, it is not exactly the same system any more, and the environment-to-system relationship is changed. The system now has a different set of problems from the one it had before. Thus a new integration is required, a reordering of things. Finally, following reintegration of the system, a phase of solidification and entrenchment is required, one which will stabilize and maintain patterns of action and thought until the system encounters another adaptive problem. Then the cycle will begin again. Note that this analysis is simply the application of the adaptation, goal attainment, integration, pattern maintenance scheme in a dynamic rather than a static way.

Of course the environment might not wait for a full four-fold cycle to be completed before it presents further problems. The internal relationships among the four abstract system units might be continually in flux and several phase movements could be in progress at once. The point Parsons would want us to see is this: the system, as an abstract entity, remains the same. The four functions to be performed do not change. However, the actions implied by the phase movement, the particulars of each phase, and the solutions reached in each are unique. There is a continuing pattern and theoretical order, but the concrete system is changing. This approximates Parsons' view of what has come to be called *social evolution*. There is a moving equilibrium of the four defining characteristics of systems, and the emphasis on movement suggests that it is emphatically not a static conception.

Parsons later specifies that a continually more differentiated and specified set of social relations is evolved by the moving equilibrium. As problems are faced, techniques and forces to deal with them are contrived which then go into the repertoire of skills and roles a society has for doing its work. This amounts to greater specialization of function, which calls for different, perhaps more complicated, coordination of these differentiated activities – a more 'organically' interrelated set of mutual dependencies in the social system.

Parsons approaches close to organic analogies in this treatment of social evolution and in his specification of 'evolutionary universals'.[56] In principle, we might think social evolution would take so many forms that after some time in the life cycles of societies, it would be difficult to make comparisons among them. But Parsons sees things differently. His idea is that some forms of social organization are 'sufficiently important to future evolution that, rather than emerging only once, [they are] likely to be "hit upon" by various systems operating under different conditions'.[57] In other words, there are forms of social organization which Parsons predicts will eventually evolve in all societies. All that are required to set this process going are: a language, some kind of kinship organization, a religion, and rudimentary technology.

Parsons says the first structure likely to evolve is social stratification, a vertical dimension of social differentiation often loosely called 'social class'.[58] He notes that in primitive societies, ones without social class as he means the term, ascription of social status often depends upon biological relationships. Where status is distributed on this basis, there is no freedom for the system to select talent and to articulate social positions apart from persons. A person enjoys a status because of who he is rather than what position he holds. Where the tendency is for traditional lineages to be quite ancient, and for everyone to be related to everyone else, there is an inherent inability of the system as a whole to develop a hierarchy of positions, each with duties and rights. Parsons thinks that as time goes on, concern about personal advantage comes to outweigh kinship status, and there develops a tendency for families to be ranked. When this takes place, evolution toward an impersonal stratified system of ranks has begun. The end result will be an entirely impersonal emphasis upon rank as an indicator of preference and not family or lineage.

Closely associated with stratification as an evolutionary universal is the emergence of legitimate institutionalized definitions of the society as a whole, to which all can refer. As stratification develops, impersonal divisive tendencies are introduced which could threaten cohesive life in society. But parallel with stratification, Parsons believes, evolve more universalistic definitions and pride in 'we' feeling. Evolution of a new 'we-ness' gives a broader normative base. When a people is proud of its heritage, the evolutionary tendency is for this pride to be turned into increasingly explicit normative rules expressing the communal 'we-ness'. As these rules take form, normative grounds for universal social unification take the place of particular concrete obligations. With increased 'we-feeling', there are more adaptive freedom and more room for innova-

---

[56] See Ch. 3 above for a discussion of the organic analogy in sociological theory.
[57] Parsons, ed., *Sociological Theory and Modern Society* (New York: Free Press, 1967), p. 491.
[58] The following discussion is based on Parsons' chapter on evolution in *ibid*.

tion, hence more adaptive potential. There is more freedom to select talent and rationally fill needed positions without risk to the order uniting the whole.

Following these developments, Parsons sees an additional stage, that of evolving bureaucratic organization. Today, 'bureaucratic' is sometimes a term of abuse. But what Parsons means is not the alleged evils deriving from bureaucracy, but the adaptive advantage bureaucratic organization gives a society. For implicit in the bureaucrat's habit of acting impersonally is the idea that authority resides not in the person but in the office. In principle, two advantages flow from this. One is that the office (or, more broadly, status-position) is seen as acting in the name of the whole social unit. Given cultural legitimation, bureaucratic organization is an expression, a routinization, of the cultural themes uniting men. Hence, there is always a degree of acceptance of the bureaucrat's role as 'right'. The fact of its institutionalization gives this rightness a more solid foundation. In addition to offices' conferring established legitimate authority to act in the name of the group, the evolution of offices allows the system to apportion activities more consistently and rationally. A bureaucratic office implies duties and rights with respect to a closely circumscribed area of competence and power. Without bureaucratic specialization, authorities might carry altogether irrelevant status or importance. The freedom to allocate persons and act toward them according to their legitimate positions gives the system the competitive advantage of better utilization of talent, and more flexible responsiveness to environmental exigencies.

Evolving alongside bureaucratic organization are money economies and markets. The adaptive advantage of these is increased economic flexibility. A society must be readily able to transport its available resources to the industries and organizations most in need of support. This is best done when a common system of evaluation of goods and service is available, as in a money economy. Similarly, money markets liberate persons from entanglements which might otherwise hold them back. Ability and willingness to buy or sell goods and services are more inclusive criteria for economic action than are ascriptive or restrictive ones.

In addition to the sequentially developed practices of stratification, cultural legitimation, bureaucracy, and a money economy, Parsons sees generalized universalistic norms evolving, and democratic associations arising. Universalistic norms are those which apply to a position and are viewed as binding on persons taking that role.[59] Conversely, the role is left open for all who might occupy it, irrespective of extraneous distinctions, prejudices, or irrelevant selection criteria. Democratic association is the extension of this tendency into collective action. Universalistic

---

[59] Universalistic norms are perhaps best understood as an outgrowth of bureaucratic tendencies.

norms applied to a political system yield essentially democratic govern-
ments. Such norms, used to select the powerful and to monitor their performance, maximize political responsiveness and adaptive potential.

Parsons views these developments as universal in social evolution and
sees them as cumulative. The first ones are required for the emergence of
the others. But this is not to say that complete perfection of any is
required for onward movement in social evolution. Indeed, after a given
level of development has been reached, it appears to Parsons that several
social forms evolve together. Vestiges of previous practices may remain
within systems which operate in a predominantly different spirit.

If we revert to the general scheme again and ask about the origins of
present-day social change, one or two points may be added to this picture. So far, social change originating outside the social system has been
discussed. Social evolution is adaptive change in response to environmental conditions. That is why Parsons thought the first institutions to evolve
would be those making the greatest contribution to enhancing adaptive
potential. It is in this sense that social evolutionary change is originated
outside the system. In the absence of the need to adapt, social evolution
would not have begun. But once it starts, internal adjustments required
to accommodate a society to its own changing nature begin a parallel set
of internal changes. These do not originate directly in adaptive problems,
but come as a consequence of society's adaptation. It is internal changes
of this sort that we see about us in highly developed societies today. The
internal changes accompanying social evolution Parsons calls *strains*, to
differentiate them from the *stress* of externally generated social evolutionary change.

VII. *Research and functionalism*

There is so much research literature which could be called 'functionalist'
in inspiration that even to list the subjects of it would be beyond the
scope of this book. Nevertheless, some broad outlines about functionalist
research can be described.

A. *Levels of research*

The discussion has so far concentrated on functionalist theory applied to
total societies, or at least to large subgroups. Davis and Moore, for
example, work with the whole society; stratification is accounted for by
reference to society's natural requirements. Levy and Parsons theorize at
the same level. Hence, one would expect considerable research on total
societies, and it is extant. Especially in the areas of comparative social
systems, comparative institutions, and social change, functionalism has
provided a set of conceptual categories by means of which one can order

data about particular social systems. An example of this kind of work will be described presently.

But functionalism has been employed at lower levels of analysis. Factories, organizations of both formal and informal groups, schools, and hospitals are just some of the social arenas in which functionalism has become basic theory for research. Sometimes the objectives of functionalist social research change slightly when it is applied at different levels. Working from the basic functionalist theory of stratification, subtle variations on the theme have often been introduced. For example, in a paper by E. Burnstein, R. Moulton, and P. Liberty called 'Prestige versus Excellence as Determinants of Role Attractiveness',[60] functionalist theory is slightly altered in a revealing way. In general, the Davis–Moore argument says that positions of higher importance in a society have greater rewards attached to ensure recruitment of talented personnel. Burnstein *et al.* interviewed a variety of persons whom they could classify as having either 'high' or 'low' motivation to achieve. They questioned them on their feelings toward the jobs they held or aspired to, with special emphasis on jobs which demanded excellence and talent and jobs which conferred high prestige. The Davis–Moore argument would suggest that a given job would be rated high on both, or low on both, but that in all events the demand for excellence would accompany posts of high prestige.

Burnstein *et al.* found, however, that these were not necessarily the feelings of their respondents. When the gross distinctions of high and low prestige were refined, their subjects told them in effect that one could be more or less sensitive to the excellence demanded, independently of the prestige; and similarly, one could be sensitive to the prestige, independently of the excellence demanded. Furthermore, the determinant of whether one was sensitive to the prestige value or the excellence demand in a given job was one's 'achievement motivation'. Those high on motivation to achieve were characteristically more motivated by the excellence demanded, and rather less by the prestige value of the job. Conversely, those low on achievement motivation tried, in effect, to get the greatest prestige value for a given level of excellence demanded – they were sensitive to prestige before excellence.

This finding is theoretically significant; it shows that the Davis–Moore theory is overly simple because it apparently neglects psychological or personal factors. Burnstein *et al.* were effectively inserting a psychological factor into the hypothesized correlation between excellence demand and prestige. They wished to see if, when the psychological factor was varied, any significant variation occurred in the ability of society to motivate by offering prestige. Such was found to be true. Davis and Moore

[60] In *American Sociological Review*, xxviii, 2 (April 1963), pp. 212-19.

might argue that this variation was minor, on the scale of things, and that while variations of this kind might occur, the general rule would still apply if the stratification hierarchy were considered in its full range. And at least in part, the Burnstein *et al.* data support this. Burnstein *et al.* did find that prestige was a powerful motivator of persons having low or only ordinary achievement motivation. Burnstein *et al.* found confirmatory evidence for the Davis–Moore theory and contributed a theoretical refinement of functionalism.

B. *Research on functional alternatives*

Sometimes it is deduced from functional theory that the competitive advantage of a certain practice which has evolved over time renders that practice essential to society. In saying this, the theoretical emphasis is shifted from the function of the practice (its effect) to the concrete substance of the practice. Occasionally, the functional theory of stratification has been used this way – taken to mean that inequality of prestige and status is necessary to achieve basic recruitment. Indeed, in the discussion of Parsons' 'evolutionary universals' idea, we seemed to see this. However, it must be kept in mind that Parsons was saying that some system of stratification has to evolve, not one particular system.

However, there is no evidence in the world which could prove that a system of stratification would be necessary for social survival if there were alternative means of solving the recruitment problem. The ubiquity of stratification systems throughout the world is often cited as proof that a stratification system is the only way to accomplish recruitment. But this has not prevented sociologists from giving examples of functional alternatives – means by which to solve the functional problems of recruitment which do not involve ordinary stratification.

The idea of functional alternatives implies questions about functionalism's use as an empirically grounded theory. If functionalists can supply convincing explanations for social systems as they find them, or make comparative use of their data, well and good. But if functionalists say that whatever 'is' must be a functional solution to some basic requirement, then they are not really illuminating basic requirements at all; rather, they are turning functionalism into a tautology.

Schwartz has given an example of research into functional alternatives.[61] He compared two agricultural communities in Israel. One, organized on a collective basis, distributed goods and services according to need, and each person worked at assigned tasks. The other community was arranged so that land was divided among families. Each family was responsible for production, but it could proceed in any fash-

---

[61] R. Schwartz, 'Functional Alternatives to Inequality', *American Sociological Review,* xx, 4 (August 1955), pp. 424-30.

ion it liked. Using Davis and Moore's stratification theory as a guide, Schwartz expected the first community to have a high proportion of routinized jobs and little opportunity to practice social differentiation by means of unequal rewards. In the second he expected a highly developed reward system among members of the families. His findings did not exactly conform to predictions.

What he found were sociological adaptations in both communities which allowed them to work with neither too little nor too much individual initiative. In the first community, these adaptations involved mechanization, job rotation, and outside work which had the general effect of decreasing the subordination of the individual to the community, while maintaining the overall communistic social organization. In the second community, where Schwartz expected exaggerated social differentiation according to family rank and skill, he found instead cooperative enterprise among families and 'corrective' measures, such as training and education, to equalize the members. Additionally, there was migration in and out of both communities; personnel tended to change to fit the conditions.

Schwartz's data do not basically contradict the Davis–Moore theory of stratification. Schwartz shows that within the context of functionalist thinking, there are many alternative explanations for the observed stratification and differentiation practices of a given community. While functionalist theory is basically retained, predicted details are either reinterpreted or incorporated in some novel way. Work on functional alternatives has usually expanded the scope of functionalism rather than narrowed it, and as previously suggested, a possible danger is that functionalism may be made so broad as to 'explain' everything, and therefore explain nothing.

C. *Research on types of communities and societies*

Pattern theory is principally *typological* theory. This mode of thinking derives from German sociology in which ideal types are drawn up as conceptual models with which to compare actual situations. Of classical importance here is the *Gemeinschaft–Gesellschaft* typology employed in some form or other by Tönnies, Durkheim, Redfield, Becker, and others. Today, this sort of thinking survives in good health in Parsons' theories. One can view the pattern variables, for instance, as a modern refinement of the *Gemeinschaft–Gesellschaft* typology.

For these two classical types, the usual English translations are *community* and *society*. In the community (*Gemeinschaft*) type, relations based on kinship, location, loyalty, friendship, and tradition are indicated. In the society (*Gesellschaft*) type, relations based on law, contract, public opinion, and rationality are the key features. For Parsons and his pattern variables, the trouble with this typology was that many different ingredients were combined in only two concepts. Fine distinctions could not be expressed. Was it not possible to have some ingredients of each type? The pattern variables, as Table 5.1 shows, break down the old community–society typology into what Parsons regards as its main operative features. These four pattern variable pairs are independent of each other. He has refined the community–society distinction to make it more useful in the analysis of social systems and change.

T A B L E   5.1

Community (*Gemeinschaft*)		Society (*Gesellschaft*)
affectivity	versus	affective neutrality
particularism	versus	universalism
ascription (quality)	versus	achievement (performance)
diffuseness	versus	specificity

The pattern variables become a research tool for the analysis of types of social organization. McKinney and Loomis have done studies of this kind.[62] For example, they compared two agricultural villages in Costa Rica for size, type of routine, geographical layout, and accessibility. On some of these they found differences that indicated one village was less 'primitive' than the other. After this they identified persons in each community who had particularly important places in the power structures. In one village, these persons were the administrator and his subordinate; in the other these were persons of similar status.

McKinney and Loomis' idea was to examine the ways in which these persons in authority used their position, by characterizing their roles using the pattern variables. Did either pair behave according to the *Gemeinschaft* qualities of reliance on kinship and personal loyalty, tradition, and actions associated with emotions, or did they approximate the more rationalistic, legally based, and publicly oriented *Gesellschaft?* Their data supported the expected polarity. In the community which was harder of access, which had residents of longer tenure, where the farm practices were less determined by routine and schedule, and where the family units were of more central importance in social organization, the measurements taken with the pattern variables as guides gave *Gemeinschaft*-like indications. However, in the village which was less *Gemeinschaft*-like, the pattern variable array did not quite turn out *Gesellschaft*-

62 John McKinney and Charles Loomis, 'Systematic Differences between Latin American Communities of Family Farms and Large Estates', *American Journal of Sociology,* LXI (March 1956), pp. 404-12.

like. The responses from this village more approximated the center of the continuum between *Gemeinschaft* and *Gesellschaft*. In a way this is understandable, because both the villages were quite remote and rural, by North American standards; but the idea of a middle ground between these two social types raises theoretical problems which McKinney and Loomis do not address. We will return to this point when criticizing functionalist theory.

D. *Research on social evolution*

Buck and Jacobson have tested Parsons' theory of evolutionary universals in a creative and stimulating way.[63] Again we find that research with a given theoretical background results in refinements of the theory. Buck and Jacobson develop Parsons' theory of social evolution by showing variations in the evolutionary sequence foreseen by Parsons. Buck and Jacobson agree with Parsons that most existing societies have experienced at least some evolution of all forms. But when the idea of 'levels' of evolutionary progress is added to the theory, it is not unreasonable to expect existing societies to be at different levels and developing at different rates. A level is the same relative degree of development on each of the evolutionary universals postulated in Parsons' theory.[64] Buck and Jacobson's objective was to test Parsons' theory of evolutionary universals along with their extension of it – the concept of levels of development. Additionally, they developed methodological techniques for doing so.

A selection of fifty countries was made, probably according to the theoretically possible range of evolutionary development. Since the authors were interested partly in statistical techniques to measure evolutionary development, it was not thought necessary to select countries at random for analysis. Rather, the idea was to develop the measurement methods and apply them to a sample yielding information on both the level of development and on the usability of the scales.[65]

---

[63] Gary Buck and Alvin Jacobson, 'Social Evolution and Structural-Functional Analysis: An Empirical Test,' *American Sociological Review*, XXXIII, 3 (June 1968), pp. 343-55.

[64] The evolutionary universals were: stratification, cultural legitimation, a money economy, universalistic norms, and democratic associations.

[65] It is not necessary here to delve into the exact measurements used to check each of the characteristics of development mentioned by Parsons. Some of the information came from United Nations publications, part from other research. For example, anthropological evidence was employed in measurement of kinship systems, while technological development was measured as the *per capita* production of electric power, percentage of gross national product originating in agriculture, and percentage of labor force employed in industrial as opposed to agricultural or forest work. The 'democratic nature' of the societies was measured by the constitutional status of the government in power, presence or absence of a party system of elections, representative nature of the regime, and current status of legislatures.

With ten different measurements (derived from the ten indications of evolutionary development given by Parsons in his theory), it immediately became possible to test the idea of levels of development. Data were displayed on (1) communications, (2) kinship organization, (3) religion, (4) technology, (5) stratification, (6) cultural legitimation, (7) bureaucratic organizations, (8) money and markets, (9) generalized universalistic norms, and (10) democratic associations. If these data showed relatively consistent levels of development for a given country, the idea of levels of development on the ten indicators would be supported.

Basically, the ten indicators did show consistent levels of development for each country in the sample. Furthermore, it became possible to show that the sample of countries studied exhibited a pattern of 'upward progression' through the levels. For example, New Zealand, Britain, Australia, the U.S.A., and Sweden appeared at roughly the top of the list. Canada, Iceland, and West Germany grouped nicely in a position just beneath the top. Near the bottom were Nigeria, Uganda, and Tanzania. In itself, the fact that Parsons' theory could be scaled into ten indicators of social evolution expressed in levels confirms the usefulness of the theory. The empirical pattern encountered by the researchers was, in a rough and ready way, the pattern developed from ideas; this is what we expect from pattern type theory.

Of particular interest is the sequence of evolution found by Buck and Jacobson. In itself, the listing of countries at various levels of development only suggests the conclusion that these countries arrived at their levels by passing through evolutionary stages. It does not indicate whether they passed through them in the sequence Parsons postulated. Of course, it is impossible to gather data directly (except by extrapolations from history) on a developed society's sequence of passage through the different levels of development. But Buck and Jacobson were able to find variations in the data arranged in levels, which gives insight into this question. They note that in the lowest level (Level I), there are 'underdevelopment' and 'overdevelopment' on different universals. Some were less well developed than others; this is what they expected. But which ones? Theory alone would predict that the sequence, following basic starting points, would be stratification, then cultural legitimation, then bureaucratic forms, money and markets, and so on, ending with democratic associations.

However, within Level I, Buck and Jacobson found a different series. Most developed in Level I was bureaucratic organization; least was money and markets. Their explanation is that underdeveloped countries often import Western institutions more or less intact, and that colonial experience might overdevelop bureaucracy. But note here that the sequence is roughly in the order Parsons predicted: money and markets fall toward the end of the predicted series, and bureaucracy falls toward the beginning. In Level II, Buck and Jacobson discovered that the relative overdevelopment of bureaucracy had disappeared and some of the development which had led to Level II was actually impeding further social evolution. Established technology and kinship organization were not leading to social change in Level II; they were holding it back. In Level IV, there appeared a shift in relative development of the universals so that money and markets, technology and communications were leading the developments, while other previously developed institutional practices were impeding social change.

In general, this research shows that it is possible to establish facts empirically about the relative social development of various countries, and that this information generally suggests the sequence of evolution hypothesized by Parsons. The theory says that social evolution follows a given sequence. The data show that social evolution indeed is in progress, and that the sequence is in approximately the order Parsons predicted. Buck and Jacobson have improved things somewhat, however, by showing that, within levels of social evolution, Parsons' series is not always found. Hence, while the general theory has led to some good basic confirmatory evidence, it has also led to refinements which ought to be incorporated into the general theory to make it more accurate.

VIII. *Critical remarks about functionalist theory*

It is a credit to the field of sociology that functional theory, almost 'orthodox' throughout the 1950s and 1960s, was subjected to serious critical examination during that time. Functionalism has somewhat declined in popularity in recent years, partly because of damaging criticisms of it, and partly because of the fad-following that plagues most of the social sciences. But there are still large numbers of workers in the field who use some form of functional theory as their basic thinking. These may not all call themselves 'Parsonian' or 'Mertonian' as they once might have, but there is still evidence, as Davis has argued, that functionalism is the basic theory of sociology.[66]

As one would expect, the logic, substance, and method of functionalism have been criticized. These categories of criticism provide convenient organizing criteria for a review of critical remarks. But first we must consider criticism which alleges that functionalism is not really a theory.

A. *Is functionalism a theory or a model?*

It could be said that functionalism cannot properly be called a theory at all; rather, it is a set of methodological canons. Largely, this criticism

[66] Kingsley Davis, 'The Myth of Functional Analysis as a Special Method in Sociology and Anthropology', *American Sociological Review*, xxiv, 6 (December 1959), pp. 757-71.

addresses the highly abstract nature of functional theory, and the fact that its main principles are not really researchable. For example, the concept of 'system', especially in the work of Parsons, is a purposely abstract concept to be moved about, applied now to an institution, now to the personality, now to the relationship between the two. Since it is pliable in this way, there is virtually nothing which could be empirically proven about its applicability to a given situation.

Similarly, it is in the nature of functionalist theory to postulate things that cannot be proven wrong. Serious instances of this are the ideas of functional requisites, social evolution, and the four-fold scheme of Parsons. It is held that a social system, if it is to survive, must solve characteristic problems of social organization and institutionalized practice. This argument leads to the search for functional requisites. But we have no societies which are not, by definition, 'surviving'. Hence, it would seem that whatever these societies are doing are the necessary things. This line of argument, taken to its conclusion, suggests the charge that functional theory does not give an explanation of that society at all. Rather, it gives an abstract model suggesting that if a society were engaged in a survival struggle as outlined by functional theory, then the society would be solving certain functional problems. As a model, functional theory may suggest certain researchable areas of interest. But a model explains by analogy (see Chapter 3, pp. 43, 45-6); hence functional theory could be said to lack empirical grounding and only to suggest inquiry, not hypothesize relationships. The idea of functional alternatives leads to reinforcement of this criticism. For if there are an infinity of concrete ways to solve functional problems, then it will surely be difficult to discover the root reason for a given institutional practice in a given society.

If the actual mechanisms characteristic of functional theory are so hard to document and rigorously research, then we are left with the dictum that 'social structures have systematic effects on neighboring social structures, and possibly on individuals'. We ought then to search for these effects. This is not very enlightening; if such criticism is taken at face value, and functionalism's theoretical justification is left behind, then it emerges as only an arbitrary dictum to 'seek effects'.

B. *Criticisms of functionalism as a theory*

Obviously it is not unanimously agreed that functional theory exists. But among those who consider functionalism a theory, several types of critical material have been advanced. Some of the theoretical and logical criticisms of functionalism will be considered first, and then criticism of functionalism as a method.

1. *Logical and theoretical criticisms*

(a) *The problem of tautology*. Tautology means circularity.[67] Circular thinking is a matter of creating a closed system by defining one thing in terms of another so that both seem to be separate entities, yet are actually the same thing or are analytically inseparable. Abstractly, if we define *A* as *X* and define *X* as *A*, then *X* and *A* share all attributes in common. If they have any distinguishing attributes, the definition of neither is sensitive to the distinguishing marks.

Functionalism is charged with making this kind of mistake in logic. The most notable and central point at which this happens is in the definition of a society. For example, Levy's definition of a society includes:

1 a plurality of actors oriented to the system, who
2 are self-sufficient for the action of the collectivity, and
3 the whole system is capable of existing longer than the individual members who make it up.

But there is no means to decide when the system is the same as the previous one involving these or other actors. There is no way to determine whether the third characteristic is being met. The definition of a society becomes an assertion about the empirical nature of the system one is studying. It is asserted that since we are calling some system a society, then it must be outlasting individual members. Giving characteristics to one's data by definition and then 'finding' these empirically means only that the characteristics were true by definition. Such an exercise suffers from logical circularity.

(b) *The question of teleology*. A teleological explanation is one that gives an explanation of the parts of some system (be it social science, biology, or mechanics) by making reference to the purpose of the parts with regard to their future relatedness within the whole. (See Chapter 2, pp. 30-4. It seems that functionalism does this despite conscious attempts to avoid it. An example is found in the functionalist theory of stratification, where the general argument is that stratification has beneficial effects on the system and is retained by the system because of these effects. To make such an argument, logic requires that all the effects of the given structure be known and that the precise nature of the system in which these effects occur be known as well. In the human body, for example, if the heart stops, we have enough knowledge about the interrelations of body parts to say that the body dies because the contribution of the heart is lacking. In social sciences, there is greater difficulty in demarcating the precise extent and effects of structures. It is, therefore, hard to tell what the teleological explanation of a social structure should

[67] See Ernest Nagel, 'A Formalization of Functionalism', in *Logic without Metaphysics*; Carl Hemphill, 'The Logic of Functional Analysis', in Llewellyn Gross, ed., *Symposium on Sociological Theory* (Evanston, Ill.: Row, Peterson, 1959), pp. 271-307.

be. Furthermore, the exact nature of the contribution must be known and it must be known that the structure does not have deleterious effects. For example, it is by no means agreed that stratification has the effects claimed by Davis and Moore, and that it does not have destructive effects instead. Yet this theory of stratification continues its teleological explanation as though logical criteria for a teleological explanation had been met.

But perhaps teleological explanations are not desirable in sociology. In the introductory remarks about functionalism, it was noted that function-alists consciously avoid imputing motive or purpose to abstractions like 'social structure'. Still, it may be argued that it is in the nature of man to have purpose, and therefore an explanation of social institutions in terms of intentions is proper. This argument might have some power when applied to explanation of the manifest functions which are intended. But functionalism seems to show its greatest strength in explaining manifest functions which are not intended, or in explaining latent functions. When the concept of social evolution is added, the inherent teleology in func-tionalism becomes more apparent than ever. Durkheim suggested in *The Division of Labor* that the eventual consequence of a certain threat to social solidarity was the evolution of an alternative solidarity. This sug-gests that, unknown to the participants, society was 'protecting' its soli-darity. It had its own purpose in mind, as it were. This makes society into an entity having powers of choice. Surely this is absurd. Persons have minds, but do societies? Making the assumption that society is some kind of entity allows the teleological explanation to proceed, but invites criticisms about the justification for doing so.

Related to this criticism, it has been noted that functionalism seems to reverse the chronology of cause and effect.[68] Since we do not observe cause, but only impute it, we do not know for certain that the cause of a thing lies in its history and not in its future. Yet from 'common-sense' observation it would seem silly to say that the cause of an institution's particular form lies in the future effects that institution will have. Partic-ularly for sociologists concerned with methodological positivism and the establishment of cause and effect, the reverse chronology seemingly implied by functionalism frustrates rather than facilitates inquiry.

(c) *Reductionism and functionalism*. Toward the end of the 1950s, theorists who were especially impressed with exchange models of society made a damaging criticism against functionalism and started a debate which lasts to the present. They claimed that functionalism is not a theory because everything functionalists try to establish can in turn be reduced to propositions about individual motivation. Hence, the only real theory in sociology is psychological theory, since it is in psychology that

[68]   William Catton, Jr., 'Flaws in the Structure and Functioning of Functional Analysis', *Pacific Sociological Review*, x, 1 (Spring 1961), pp. 3-12.

the motives of men are established and codified. Because they were reducing functionalism down so thoroughly these critics were called *reductionists.*[69]

One of the objectives of functionalists has been to separate the theory of society from the theory of man. This entails explaining societal forms and institutions by reference to ideas about the societies themselves, and not by reference to the motivations of the people who populate them. The justification for doing this is that people may have various and unique motives, but they act collectively. Hence, there must be something about their actions that is not reducible to their individual motives.

Immediately, motivation became a problem for functionalism. If it was to be the institutional structure, at its own level of abstraction, which explained, functionalists had to account for why persons act normatively with respect to these institutions. Wrong has complained that this led to an 'oversocialized' concept of man as essentially an empty bucket into which society could pour all of its requirements for social action.[70] Not only was man theoretically oversocialized, but society was theoretically overinstitutionalized, since obviously, by this model, there had to be an institutionalized norm for every action. We got a brighter picture of man from functional theory when we saw him competing for prestige and material benefit in Davis and Moore's theory of stratification. But did this very theory of stratification not imply a psychologically self-interested man? If so, it was only a short step to the conclusion that the stratification system could be explained in individual competitive terms without need of functional requirements, social evolution, institutional systems, and so forth. So went the argument.

But as pointed out in Chapter 4 on exchange theory, these reductionist critics of functionalism had an equally devastating problem on their hands. Where did the individual desires and motives come from which were supposed to be the reducing agents that dissolved functionalism? Either they came from instincts, 'deep' inside the person, or they were fashioned in experience. Homans largely took the second alternative. But this is just what functionalism was trying to say - that the commonality and unity of collective experience fashioned motives in men, that motives were to be explained by institutional structures.

So, is it that functionalism is to be reduced to psychology, or is psychology to be 'expanded' to functionalism? It appears that sociology cannot easily do without the concept of motivation, unless it simply becomes a study of comparative institutions. Similarly, psychologistic

---

[69] For example, see George Homans' 'Contemporary Theory in Sociology', in R. E. L. Faris, ed., *Handbook of Modern Sociology* (Chicago: Rand McNally, 1964), pp. 951-77.

[70] Dennis Wrong, 'The Oversocialized Concept of Man', *American Sociological Review*, XXVI, 2 (April 1961), pp. 183-93.

theories in sociology cannot easily put aside structural thinking. Here the matter should probably rest.

(d) *Problems related to the concept of system.* System is usually found in functionalism as a 'closed' concept, that is, a system is thought of as a bounded, sealed entity. There is good reason that this should be true. The logical necessity of a boldly demarcated system has already been explained.[71] The question is not settled, however, because it is this very requirement which has come under fire from critics who would have functionalism an 'open' system. An open system is one which admits easier penetration from outside it and one which is less static. Openness of the system, the argument runs, would be beneficial because greater flexibility could be achieved in empirical application. There would be less fuss in taking in new ideas; the pattern of the theoretical model would be more sensitive to 'reality'. All this sounds good. But making the system open in this way invites indeterminacy and vagueness of boundaries. What emerges from this argument is a paradoxical quality about systems thinking in social science. The paradox is that the logical and the empirical requirements of functionalism run at cross-purposes. To be made more empirically sensitive, the system should be open, it is suggested. To be made logically defensible, the system should be made more securely and definitely closed.[72]

An example of this problem can be found in the way equilibrium is construed in functional theory. By way of equilibrium, functionalists justify the concept of functional interdependency. Furthermore, the idea of a moving equilibrium suggests that social change and historical flow could be analyzed with functionalism. These are seen as an orderly matter of the interplay of equilibrating tendencies. In principle, the equilibrating tendencies a society possesses might be fast or slow to work. But in fact, this theoretical point appears to suggest that functionalism is logically ill equipped to handle questions of rapid and substantial social change – situations in which equilibrium is extremely hard to see.

Another logical problem related to the concept of system was raised by Black and others in questioning Parsons' concept of the pattern variables.[73] The ingredients of a pattern theory should make sense *vis-à-vis* each other. That is the way a pattern theory explains; it 'marks the occasion' on which the pattern may be invoked. Black says that the pattern variables do not form a coherent or stable set of concepts within Parsons' array of related ideas and theorems. He calls the pattern variables 'chameleon concepts' performing first as normative patterns, later as

---

[71] See p. 131 above.
[72] See Walter Buckley's critique of functionalist use of 'system' in his *Sociology and Modern Systems Theory* (Englewood Cliffs, N.J.: Prentice-Hall, 1967).
[73] Max Black, 'Some Questions about Parsons' Theories', in *The Social Theories of Talcott Parsons.*

need dispositions, and even later as role expectations. What Black wants is a specification of what the pattern variables pattern. To precisely what do they apply? To the extent that there is ambiguity about this in Parsons' writing, Black's point is well taken. However, in defense of Parsons, it ought to be said that in his mind the pattern variables probably apply to attributes of purely abstract systems. We have seen that this system concept is alternatively, yet simultaneously, applied to the physical–organic, the personality, the social, and the cultural systems. Hence one would expect the 'chameleon concepts' to do duty in each of these systems.

However, there is real ambiguity about where these concepts come from in the first place. Moreover, it is far from agreed that they form a complete and exhaustive list of the dilemmas of orientation and valuation faced by actors. Mitchell noticed that even Parsons concedes that the pattern variables may not be an exhaustive list.[74] He cites Parsons' statement to the effect that there might be six pattern variables. But in the same article Parsons argues, mainly on terminological grounds, that there are really only four, and that a fifth, the self versus collective orientation, is really a special case of the other four.[75]

(e) *Research using pattern variables criticized.* There is evidence of the ambiguity of the pattern variables as methodological guides in the work of McKinney and Loomis in comparing peasant villages. They attempted to scale informants' responses to questions based on the pattern variables. But Parsons means the pattern variables to be polarities. He does not think that there is a middle ground between affectivity and affective neutrality, for example. One is either being gratified by an object and releasing motivational energy toward it, or one is not. Yet McKinney and Loomis used the concepts as continua, along which they found responses distributed.

Of course the question arising from this is to what extent, if at all, could it be said that McKinney and Loomis 'tested' the value of the pattern variables as a theoretical idea? Holding to Parsons' conception of the pattern variables, the answer is that McKinney and Loomis mistook Parsons' intent, and hence no test of derived hypotheses was made. But there is an additional point which shows something about Parsonian pattern theory. McKinney and Loomis' findings show that even if the pattern variables are fundamentally misconstrued from a logical point of view, they give illuminating knowledge of the ways in which the two vil-

---

[74] Mitchell, *Sociological Analysis and Politics*, p. 32.
[75] Parsons points to the four described earlier: affectivity–affective neutrality; universalism–particularism; specificity–diffuseness; quality–performance. The four rather than five or six have been chosen because this is consistent with Parsons' usage in his *Working Papers* article on phase movement and the definitions of the four-fold typology in terms of the pattern variables. See *Sociological Theory and Modern Society*, p. 334.

lages differ. The theoretical scheme does receive some support from their findings.

C. *Criticisms of the substance of functional theory*

In addition to the critical fire leveled at functionalism by logical and methodological opponents, critics have pointed to errors of either omission or commission. Some critics are concerned less with the logic of the theory than with its apparent descriptive accuracy. Appreciate that these are different questions. A 'true' picture, empirically justifiable, need not be logically construed; a logical construct, of course, is not necessarily accurate.

1. *The oversocialized concept of man*

Wrong suggests that the functionalist view of motivation neglects individuality and implies the overinstitutionalized society. But this criticism is somewhat polemical, since nowhere does functionalism seriously argue that it accounts for all behavior. Nevertheless, there is really very little behavior that most sociologists would not claim as at least partly their 'territory'.

The polemic exposes theoretical failure. For instance, the sociology of risk, decision under uncertainty, decision-making among unstructured alternatives, uniqueness, and, generally, the nonregulated aspects of everyday life are not well accounted for by functionalism. Socialization and social control are commonly explained in functionalism as the effect of institutionalized sanctions. In empirical applications where these sanctions are confused or nonexistent, there is a real theoretical problem. Recall Merton's theoretical work on types of individual adaptation to overstressed success goals. Merton's accomplishment is that he logically outlined the pathways an individual might follow if he did not choose conformity. But Merton was conspicuously silent about using sociological theory to predict which pathways would be followed, and by whom. Just when Merton's theory was getting productive, it failed him.

2. *Power, force, and voluntarism*

Partly deriving from the 'oversocialized' criticism, and partly as a complaint about functionalism's emphasis on the interdependence of institutions, is the criticism that *power* and *force* in human affairs are not well portrayed.[76] Power is the capability of one person or group to cause

---

[76] See Ralf Dahrendorf, *Class and Class Conflict in Industrial Society* (New York: Free Press, 1956); C. Wright Mills, *The Sociological Imagination* (New York: Grove Press, 1959); John Rex, *Key Problems of Sociological Theory* (London: Routledge and Kegan Paul, 1961).

another to do its bidding. But functionalists view the role relationship as a situation in which expectations and rights going with a social position are legitimate in the eyes of those involved. One makes demands and the demands are met, not out of force, but from both parties' sense of the appropriateness of the demand. These legitimate demands are said to have *authority*. Authority derives ultimately from the cultural system to which the social system is connected, and it is the sharing of belief in similar cultural values that assures legitimate authority. This is the foundation of Parsons' concept of the double contingency bond, institutionalized norms, and pattern-maintaining social systems.

The double contingency bond concept and the idea of legitimate authority are directly traceable, especially in Parsons' work, to a desire to create a theory which emphasizes *voluntarism*.[77] This refers to the cognitive, evaluative, and emotional basis of personal decisions to act in a given fashion. Personal decisions are confined by training and selective rewarding, as well as by value-attitudes. Hence, every act is seen not as a predetermined step, unrelated to the individual's will, but as a step into which a predictable and controlled will enters. In this sense, for all the talk of collective action, systematic patterning, and the like, the Parsonian system is individualistic.

When the individual is construed in this way, it is difficult to account for action outside the legitimate authority of role systems, or action which forces others against their will. How can such situations be theoretically explained by functionalism? To treat such problems may require a new set of starting points, a new definition of action, and perhaps a new sociological theory. Functionalism simply does away with the question of power by subsuming it under the idea of authority. By arguing that even in the most constrained of situations there is always some alternative (one could always take the poison rather than submit), functionalism evades the question of force and power theoretically, but not convincingly.

3. *Change and conflict*

Here are areas in which functionalism stands up somewhat better to its critics. It is sometimes said that functionalism is unable to theoretically explain *change*, but this criticism is possibly confused with the assertion that certain functionalists are not concerned with change as a theoretical problem. Functionalism embraces the concept of social evolution very closely. Even if functionalist works do not emphasize change, functional theory may be applied to questions of social change and historical dynamics.[78]

[77] See p. 155 above.
[78] Lewis A. Coser has considered conflict as in some ways 'functional'. See his *The Functions of Social Conflict* (New York: Free Press, 1956).

But functionalism's concept of social evolution implies slowness and a lack of control over social change by participants in it. Yet there is no reason, in principle, why social evolution could not take place rapidly and as a result of planning. Also, planned events often do not turn out as the planners intended. Even if the changes are rapid and planned, social systems might actually react to such changes in ways resembling more the evolutionary picture than the planner's vision.

More serious is the charge that functionalism is incapable of explaining changes which are consequences of the use of power or open *conflict*. The theoretical idea of power is not well suited to the functionalist theory. It might be possible to argue that a system responds to power-originated change by bringing its evolutionary adaptive machinery into play. But this does not account for the change agent, and leaves functionalist theory essentially lacking.

4. *Criticisms of the theory of stratification*

The Davis–Moore paper on stratification reaped a bumper crop of criticism.[79] In general, critics have noted that the functionalist picture of stratification is insensitive to inheritance of status and to nepotism and special advantage.[80] Because they emphasized incentives and abilities required to fill positions and the individual's route through the social system, the authors were accused of neglecting important structural facts about society. Similarly, it was said that the theory neglected the possibility that an existing stratification order would actually limit the opportunities to discover talent by not encouraging it. Davis and Moore have said that the stratification system did encourage the talented. This criticism rests more on observed differences of motivation among persons of different classes than on theoretical ideas. But from the basic charge that stratification decreases talent available, rather than increases it, several other criticisms followed. One was that societies are handicapped by stratification systems because full use of talent is not being made. Another was that unfavorable self-images are systematically created among less successful persons which impede their progress more than external disadvantages do. Related to criticism about self-image was the charge that stratification systems decrease loyalty to the social system as a whole,

---

[79] The paper was answered by Tumin, whose paper was criticized by Moore and Davis. Tumin reappeared with further criticism. Others entered the debate, including Buckley, who in turn was answered by Davis. Several papers generally related to the functionalist theory of stratification appeared which did not criticize the Davis–Moore paper directly, but certainly examined some of it in a critical light.

[80] Dennis Wrong, 'The Functional Theory of Stratification: Some Neglected Considerations', *American Sociological Review*, XXIV, 6 (December 1959), pp. 772-8.

encourage hostility, and so forth. It was also suggested that stratification systems give a manipulative opportunity for the higher classes to retain their positions in spite of free competition hypothesized by the model. All in all, these arguments were intended to suggest that, theoretically, stratification should be considered a hindrance rather than a benefit to society.

In somewhat different fashion, it was argued that if stratification were as Davis and Moore had said it was, disruptive consequences would follow.[81] There would be constant and fierce competition for places at the top, and the rotation of persons in and out of positions would be deleterious in the extreme. From this it was concluded that the Davis–Moore theory is not accurate because what it predicted is not happening. There is not rapid and continuous rotation of personnel as talent emerges, people do not all consistently compete for high positions, and so forth.

Developments later on in the theory of stratification suggested that the Davis–Moore theory has some use, but that it tells only some of the story. For instance, Lenski thought the functionalist theory of stratification gives the true picture only among 'non-elite' groups in the service of controlling elites; the latter have their positions for reasons unexplained by functional theory.[82]

5. *Is functionalism conservative?*

Related to the debate over stratification is the charge that functional theory in some fashion 'justifies' the *status quo*. Davis and Moore resist this charge, and have pointed out that they are trying to understand societies 'as they find them', not give justifications for the institutions they discover. In the sense in which they seem to mean their defense, there can be no doubt that they are right. Sociologists of every political persuasion have noted that the institutions of advanced Western countries depend heavily upon competitive forces which catch up individuals and sometimes treat them with brutality. Sociological indictments of the business and commercial ethic in the United States usually castigate the extreme emphasis on 'getting ahead', professional success, and the like. In a way, those who criticize such institutional systems on humanitarian or political grounds are in fact offering evidence for the Davis–Moore theory and functionalism. They are complaining that stratification does, indeed, induce striving. They also are complaining that various institutions are geared together, forming a comparatively integrated whole.

But the more crucial theoretical point in this debate is raised by those who wish to talk about power and force. Some argue that stratification

---

81 *Ibid.*
82 Gerhard Lenski, *Power and Privilege* (New York: McGraw-Hill, 1966).

systems exist essentially because they are caused to exist by powerful interests. Tumin says the stratification system does have functions, but that Davis and Moore have not pointed to them all.[83] In fact, Tumin and other critics imply that stratification has essentially nothing to do with the functional interdependence of institutions, talent recruitment, and the like. Rather, it is an order imposed by those already in possession of wealth, position, and prestige.

Those who call functionalism conservative are usually those who are impressed by the theory of power in human affairs. Their main criticism is that by drawing attention away from power and focusing instead on authority, functionalism sweeps a significant question under the rug. It ignores abuses of power. Functionalism characteristically addresses social reform in ways that do not imply rapid upheaval, complete social redirection, or radical shifts. But it is clearly wrong to conclude that functionalism cannot illuminate problems of social change, social dislocation, and the like, especially if such problems result from institutional flux, technical change, and so forth.

Theories are neither conservative nor radical, but men are. The spirit in which a theory is approached can give it the appearance of justifying some political viewpoint. As long as theories are kept properly in their place as conceptual technologies by which persons reconstruct and order their experience, emotional debate about their political nature can be minimized, and useful criticism enhanced.

IX. *Conclusion*

Just as with exchange theory in Chapter 4, we have found that functionalism comes off rather badly when criticized. Theories in sociology are normally not very rigorous. But just as with exchange theory, the conclusion is not that we should abandon functionalism, but that we use it cautiously. Knowing the weak spots, we can give them the most attention in theoretical research, and we can benefit from such knowledge in interpreting findings. Similarly, when evaluating research, it is often handy to be aware of the theoretical strengths and weaknesses from which these findings are drawn.

And there is much in functionalism that is not weak. As long as it is the aim of sociologists to explain social structure apart from individual motives, functionalist conclusions are bound to crop up, one way or another. When we ask a question about the relationships among institutions, again functionalist answers will be tempting. Especially as it is applied by Parsons, the systems concept can be a valuable tool to sociologists, and not only to functionalists. The concept of 'system needs' seems very fruitful, even though hard to justify logically.

[83]   Melvin J. Tumin, 'Some Principles of Stratification: A Critical Analysis', *American Sociological Review*, XVIII, 4 (August 1953), pp. 387-93.

Functionalism is a theory that generates reasonably coherent patterns. These 'explain' by appealing to the sense of insight one gets when a reconstructed picture fits the facts. This fitting is a matter of reconceptualizing observations into abstractions which have an inherent coherence of their own. It is a kind of translation from the language of what is seen in the raw into the language of how such things actually coexist and influence each other. Of course, in principle functionalism could be stated in propositional and deductive form, but its great strength is that it is not in that form. Propositional form is eminently useful for the generation of logically true hypotheses, but it tends to break up the coherence of patterns. Pattern theories, on the other hand, have less rigorous clarity, but maximize the ability to portray broad vistas. Hence, functionalism as a pattern theory has a strong intuitive appeal as an organizer of ideas, an orderer of data.

KEY CONCEPTS

function	structure	boundary
equilibrium	functional requisite	functional alternative
system	pattern maintenance	goal attainment
system problem	pattern variables	structural levels
social evolution	environment	values
voluntarism	teleology	adaptation
affectivity	affective neutrality	specificity
diffuseness	quality	performance
universalism	particularism	integration
system needs	social system	power
theoretical pattern		
socialization of motivation		
war of all against all		
cybernetic relations of systems		

TOPICS FOR DISCUSSION

1 In what sense is functionalism in sociology a scientific theory?
2 What are some of the theoretically important facts about Parsons' pattern variable scheme?
3 Describe a 'system' by reference to its boundary and its environment.
4 A system can have environments both 'inside' and 'outside' itself. Explain how.
5 Social evolution is said to be a continuous development of social systems toward more adaptive forms of organization. Suggest concrete examples.
6 The functionalist theory of stratification is based on the economic

ideas of supply and demand. Discuss. Does this suggest that social stratification approximates a 'free market'?

7 Discuss the success of functionalism in explaining social organization by describing it as an abstract theoretical pattern.

8 Discuss functionalism's evolutionary perspective on social change. Is evolution a bad concept to use if change is rapid? Why or why not?

9 In what sense might functionalism engage in teleological explanation?

10 To what extent do you think Parsons succeeded in retaining voluntarism in his theoretical scheme?

ESSAY QUESTIONS

Compare Parsons' ideas of the double contingency bond with exchange theory. How does the double contingency bond differ from or approximate the meaning of exchange?

Discuss the research projects reviewed in this chapter, and come to a conclusion about whether or not they actually confirm functionalist ideas.

Do Parsons' idea of social evolution and Davis and Moore's idea of stratification complement each other? Write an essay in which you explore the extent to which these two ideas are similar in theoretical inspiration.

Using the pattern variables, characterize the orientation a professor should take toward a student when marking an exam paper.

How does Parsons' idea of cybernetic relations between cultural and social systems help prevent his theory from becoming culturally deterministic?

Apply some of Levy's ideas to modern role differentiation by age. Do recent changes in political or social behavior of youth confirm or deny Levy's theory?

Examine the relationships between the educational institution and the economic, using functionalist ideas to describe the 'inputs' and 'outputs' from each to each.

Functionalism cannot explain social change. Discuss arguments for and against this assertion.

Is there any *theoretical* reason why functionalism must be considered conservative or radical?

FOR FURTHER READING AND STUDY

Bendix, Rinehard and Seymour M. Lipset (eds.). *Class, Status and Power: A Reader in Social Stratification*. Rev. ed. New York: Free Press, 1966.

Black, Max (ed.). *The Social Theories of Talcott Parsons.* Englewood Cliffs, N.J.: Prentice-Hall, 1961.

Davis, Kingsley, 'The Myth of Functional Analysis as a Special Method in Sociology and Anthropology', *American Sociological Review*, XXIV, 6 (December 1959), pp. 757-71.

Demerath, Neil S. and Richard A. Peterson (eds.). *System, Change and Conflict.* New York: Free Press, 1967.

Fallding, Harold. 'Functional Analysis in Sociology', *American Sociological Review*, XXVIII, 1 (February 1963), pp. 5-13.

Levy, Marion J. *The Structure of Society.* Princeton, N.J.: Princeton University Press, 1952.

McKinney, John C. *Constructive Typology and Social Theory.* New York: Appleton-Century-Crofts, 1966.

Merton, Robert K. *Social Theory and Social Structure.* New York: Free Press, 1949.

Mitchell, William. *Sociological Analysis and Politics: The Theories of Talcott Parsons.* Englewood Cliffs, N.J.: Prentice-Hall, 1967.

Moore, Barrington. *Political Power and Social Theory.* New York: Harper, 1958.

Ogles, Richard. 'Programmatic Theory and the Critics of Talcott Parsons', *Pacific Sociological Review*, IX, 2 (Fall 1961), pp. 53-6.

Parsons, Talcott. *The Social System.* New York: Free Press, 1951.
   Societies: Evolutionary and Comparative Perspectives. Englewood Cliffs, N.J.: Prentice-Hall, 1966.

Parsons, Talcott (ed.). *Theories of Society.* New York: Free Press, 1961.

Parsons, Talcott, R. F. Bales and E. A. Shils. *Working Papers in the Theory of Action.* New York: Free Press, 1953.

6   Symbolic interactionism

I. *Introduction*

The subject of this chapter is the sociological perspective called *symbolic interactionism*. First the distinguishing marks of a 'perspective', as opposed to a deductive or a pattern theory, will be described; then a systematic introduction to the basic ideas of symbolic interactionism will be developed. We have seen that the theory of sociology is usually built upon a philosophical base of some kind and that the particular elements of the philosophy color the resultant theory. This is as true for a perspective as for other viewpoints, and it is crucial to recognize this fact in the case of symbolic interaction.

In fact, it was a philosopher, George Herbert Mead, who brought the study of society together with a philosophical program more completely than any other person. To obtain an understanding of Mead's intent, it will be necessary to introduce some discussion of his philosophical ideas and some of the background which influenced his work.

A perspective is not quite the same as a theory. A theory often has more ambitious aims, considers logical and conceptual rigor more crucial to success, and has explanation or prediction as its goal. These are the objectives of most sociological theorists; and even among symbolic interactionists these words are used. But often for the latter group, the idea of explanation does not mean rigorous deduction from logically prior first premises. Similarly, a symbolic interactionist may indeed be able to predict, but this is usually more a matter of his native wit and insight into human affairs than the manipulation of variables and constants in deductive series arriving eventually at logically true hypotheses.

A perspective, however, may be just as coherent as any other theoretical stance. To say that symbolic interactionists pay less attention on the average to the standard aims of science is not to bring a pejorative case against them. Rather, it is to point out that essentially different processes are at work in interactionism. The interactionist's aims are different. These aims are, in general, the application of a set of basic principles to specific cases of human action with the intent to 'understand' the action somewhat as the participant himself understands it. While the participant in the action would probably use different language in describing his activities and feelings from that used by the symbolic interactionist, the general intent is to discover the actor's predicament and situation as he sees it. This is the prime purpose of sociology from the symbolic interactionist's point of view.

But symbolic interactionism does not stop at this. In addition to the sympathetic insight which is sought, the interactionist has at his disposal what the man in the street does not usually have: an additional overview of the situation, knowledge of institutional forces or constraints, a broader vision with which to make comparisons, and so forth. Putting together his view of the world with that of the actor he is studying, the interactionist's program can result in a description of life-as-lived, as a developing process influenced by individuality and institutions, morality and mores. This description is often nearly equal parts art and science, or sometimes mostly art. It is really the use of creative imagination that makes for good symbolic interactionist work, and the language of the arts is often used to describe action and situations. Especially drama, with its stagefront and backstage action, its roles enacted by creative players who both say the lines and enliven them, its scenes, often to be 'managed' by the actors as they carry the play, and its presentations, fanciful yet real in the emotions and predicaments of the actors – drama has lent its language to symbolic interactionism. There is much in common between the kinds of knowledge one receives from the drama and from symbolic interactionist work. To experience a play is to observe the action progressing, becoming intertwined within itself and attached to other action in a flowing procession of detail. This is very different from the quality of knowledge one gets from close reading of functionalist or exchange literature, where the action is made to derive from abstract first principles.

The basic components of the symbolic interactionist perspective are not testable ideas, as is supposed to be the case with scientific theory. Rather, the perspective is taken as a given, somewhat as an understanding of the intent of drama is taken as a given by the playgoer. With symbolic interactionism, the activity as observed is fitted to the perspective. Nearly everything has an interpretation within symbolic interactionism's framework; but this is not taken as a sign of logical weakness, as it would be, for example, in deductive theory. Rather, interactionists assume that their main organizing concepts are correct as basic descriptions of reality, and that the practice of their craft requires that the inherent truth expressed in them be made clear. Thus, 'testing' symbolic interactionism is not really the intent of research, and while interactionism has spawned empirical work, it is usually not the investigator's purpose to test specific hypotheses.

It is possible to have a fair variety of sociology going under the name of symbolic interactionism. One of the strengths of this school is that it does not restrict sociologists too much. It gives them a kind of commandment to 'go forth and do sociology' but it also throws them on their own devices much more than do other theoretical stances. There is an amazing array of subject matter treated under this heading, as a look into almost any symbolic interactionist 'reader' will show. But it is given some coherence by the fact that most interactionists are followers of Mead, C. H. Cooley, William Thomas, or, to a lesser extent, John Dewey and William James. Additionally, symbolic interactionism is not terribly far removed in time from these 'founding fathers'. Mead died in his working prime in 1931. One of his most famous students, Herbert Blumer, has seen to it that Mead's work was carried on and is still actively doing just this. Today, we are only a few generations from the founders of the field, and this fact, plus the proselytizing of Blumer and others, has kept the interactionist perspective from becoming excessively diverse.

Nevertheless, additional influences since Mead's death have entered the picture. Often it is hard to tell if a man's work is really symbolic interactionist or not, and it is almost impossible to solve questions of this kind. For instance, Erving Goffman, whose formal academic training is in the arts and anthropology, has contributed significantly to the field.[1] His subject matter has an everyday quality about it which is typical of interactionist work, and he has adopted the language of symbolic interactionism and added to it, attending particularly to aspects of self and identity, typical interactionist themes. But it would be hard to make the case that Goffman bases his work on Meadian theory in any philosophical sense.

Some sociologists who take Mead as their mentor have attempted to make their work scientific and rigorous methodologically. Kuhn's name is linked with this move, and he and his students have developed tests of self concept, self presentation and the like, as a variation on the basic themes of interactionism.[2] However, Kuhn has found it convenient to leave out some of what other interactionists would call basic material from Mead. Thus, it is not altogether clear whether or not Kuhn's 'self theory' is indeed symbolic interactionism.

In itself, the problem of precisely who is an interactionist does not need to worry us. The problem is to make a judicious choice from among the many recognized contributors to the wide and diverse field so that the resultant description retains coherence, yet includes sufficient unifying detail. To achieve this, first an examination of the problems addressed by the founders of the field will be conducted. This is the phil-

---

[1] See *The Presentation of Self in Everyday Life* (New York: Doubleday, 1959).
[2] See Manford Kuhn, 'Major Trends in Symbolic Interactionism in the Past Twenty-five Years', *Sociological Quarterly*, v, 1 (Winter 1964), pp. 61-84.

osophical base mentioned earlier. Secondly, Mead's ideas, especially as expressed in *Mind, Self and Society*,[3] *The Philosophy of the Act*,[4] and numerous papers will be described. In addition to this, the follow-up work of Blumer as well as that of Kuhn will be outlined, since these two are leaders of their respective schools. Some critical remarks have from time to time been made which have resulted in defenses by interactionists. Some of these defenses have added materially to the perspective, and will be described. Additionally, some research literature taking symbolic interactionism as a foundation will be reviewed.

II. *Pragmatic philosophy and symbolic interactionism*

Pragmatic philosophy arose in the United States in the last third of the nineteenth century. Some say it was a peculiarly American philosophy because it took a disapproving view of pure abstraction for its own sake and because it put considerable emphasis on action, as opposed to thinking, logic, and in general, the mind. This is supposed to be an American philosophy because America was a place where there was considerable action, movement, building, and change, and where traditional philosophical concerns received little attention. But pragmatism, to its philosophical adherents, did not mean simply 'If it works, it's good', as is sometimes said. This may have been the crude rendition of the pragmatic rule by the farmer or the businessman, but, philosophically at least, pragmatism was a movement which used the traditional concerns of philosophy as a point of departure from which to defend a somewhat novel way of looking at these problems.

A. *The mind–body problem*

The mind–body problem goes back eons into philosophical history. The problem is this: each of us has consciousness of his own 'mind'; hence, it seems reasonable to suppose that 'mindedness' is a natural condition of people. However, there is no known physical entity or process in the body which corresponds to mind. Surely there is the brain, from current evidence a kind of computer. But mind is the quality which seems responsible for things like fantasy, imagination, sympathy, emotion, and feeling, as well as mental creativity such as novel-writing, music composition, and so on. Furthermore, moral and ethical understanding appears to be a property of mind which has the power to control the physical body. In fact, if one takes the 'rational facility' as a starting point, reasoning toward an account of conduct results in a strange anomaly: the quality called mind, which is unaccounted for, seems to be in control.

---

[3] Ed. Charles Morris (Chicago: University of Chicago Press, 1934).
[4] Ed. Charles Morris (Chicago: University of Chicago Press, 1938).

In general, there were two types of thought on the mind–body question, excluding the viewpoint that became pragmatic philosophy. One was that there was no sense in questioning the existence of mind, since it seemed certainly to be there somewhere. It was mind that controlled persons in their action, and some thought a kind of aggregate mind could exist, uniting the activities of groups or nations. Group will, national spirit, and a variety of other expressions of this sort formed one way of handling the mind–body problem. From this viewpoint, action is preceded by thought, or 'mental activity'. Insight, or mental penetration into action, is required before the action can be carried out. Logically, some controlling power lays a plan for the action prior to the action, and directs it in its course. The more behavior comes under the power of mind, philosophically speaking, the more the body becomes subservient to an entity, mind, which can itself be accounted for only in terms of spirit, divine essence (or which cannot be accounted for at all). Scientifically, to strict behaviorists this is an outrage, since such a 'spook' in the machine of the body could not exist. In fact, charges can be made to the effect that the word 'mind' is a symbol with no referent, since the entity to which it refers is undescribable. This being so, no philosophical discourse can be carried on about the mind, since the definition of the subject cannot precede its discussion.

It is worth emphasizing that action, social action as well as every other kind, which takes mind as its determining factor puts the action itself in a derivative, secondary position. The act comes after the thought. Thus the activities of people are in a way determined by, depend on qualities of mind, and have no actual life of their own. Used in this deterministic and logically prior sense, mind demotes action. Additionally, it seems to demote the idea of the individual, since action appears really to be under the control of an entity into which the actor has little insight and over which he has little control.

The alternative way of disposing of the mind–body problem is to simply say that mind does not exist, or that it is an illusion of the nervous system. All that exists is the material body. In this view, experience enters the nervous system through sensation and becomes coupled with actions being performed at the time. There being no mind, action is, in principle, completely explicable from this mechanistic viewpoint. It can be argued that if we only knew enough detail about the physical brain and the pleasure and pain experiences of Beethoven, we could explain his writing of symphonies, sonatas, and his opera.

The 'no-mind' group certainly had a case to start with, since the superficial fact that mind could not be empirically accounted for was well known. But to assume the extreme position that the physical body is in complete control over human creativity seems to result in an absurdity. Similarly, the 'mind over matter' position yields the empirical absurdity of there being mind in the first place. The 'no-mind' argument also advances a similar temporal order about human action to that character-izing the 'minded' position – it places action in a derivative and deter-mined position relative to sensation, physical processes, and the like.

B. *Rejection of metaphysics*

The pragmatists came upon the scene with this philosophical battle raging, and they simply swept it aside. Much of what underlies symbolic interactionist theory today is contained in their critique of the way the mind–body problem was framed as a philosophical question. Fundamen-tally, the pragmatists said that it is unwise to make the distinction between mind and body. The mind–body problem is more a matter of the human tendency to artificially separate things for analysis than it is a matter of there actually being two separate locations, facilities, entities, or determining factors. Instead, the thing we call mind arises in the action of the body and its senses. There can be no separation of the two, since to divide them is to cut off the sustenance of both. In fact, even to talk about a philosophical distinction between mind and body is non-sense, since to make that distinction is to give names to two things that are really one thing. To make philosophical distinctions between things that do not have separate existence is to build conceptual castles in the air. 'A difference that makes no difference is no difference.' Thus, the pragmatists took a swipe at both traditional philosophical speculation and the way the social sciences tended to frame their questions. By argu-ing that both the mind and the no-mind positions led to absurdly placing action in a secondary, derived position, giving it an 'explanation' by rely-ing on a fictional abstract distinction, the pragmatists were on a new tack. This was to take human action as the basis. Do not attempt to derive it, or to explain it away; instead, start from it.

Similarly, there had been the traditional question of the primacy of either the individual or the society. Should we see persons as the primary element, societies being built up out of them as a building is made up of bricks; or should we first take society, and deduce individual action out of it? Pragmatic philosophy handled this question in much the same way as it dealt with the mind–body problem: there could be no meaningful distinction between society and the individual. Individuals are obviously created and formed in and by society, but just the same, it is creative, human, individual action that makes society what it is. To say anything else is either to reify society into something it is not, or to give individu-als a primary controlling position over society, which individuals clearly do not have. When these abstractions, the individual and the society, are taken together as one, the question of human social action becomes how to work motivated acts into a unity exhibiting facets of each person, partly constraining him and yet being influenced by him. This position does not make persons 'role players' exactly, unconsciously saying the lines society has written on their scripts. Neither does it overemphasize the primacy of individual desires, values, or motives.

C. *Symbols and communication*

1. *Centrality of the communication concept*

The line of argument being followed here leads away from traditional ways of conceptualizing the individual and the group. So far, we have seen that the pragmatists have asserted that the person and his group are cumbersome when unnaturally divided for analysis. Now the question obviously is, what facets of life do we examine to follow up this assertion? Certain answers to this question are untenable. Rejected are answers which would follow one or other of the discarded abstract analyses of the individual–society and mind–body problems. Hence, seeking instincts, deep-seated unconscious drives, stimulus–response conjunctions, and so forth, will not do. Neither will answers following from realist philosophy, such as group mind, collective coherence, will to power, or the like. In fact, what we have left to go on is what people experience themselves, and the only way to know this is to hear what they say about their experience. *Communication*, more than just a method of reporting, is thrust into the foreground of the whole theory. The argument is that individual lines of action are worked out among persons when they communicate their desires and intentions among themselves. Persons act on the basis of these abstractly communicated aspects of social life. It is not that people react to the acts of others, but that they act on the basis of communicated intentions of others, and they construct their action partly by communicating their own intentions to themselves, and partly by observing the adjustments made by others to the intentions they have communicated.

The observer of all this is in a place directly analogous to that of the participants. In order to conceptualize the action, the observer must gain from it the meanings being communicated among the participants themselves. This is taken as a confirmation of the principle that symbolic communication is the basis of all social action, as well as the foundation of any methodological system for finding out about action. All persons are in analogous positions, in that their actions are adjustive processes in situations in which they interpret action symbolically. Communications are at the very center of action, and must form the basis of a proper perspective on social events for the observer.

Communications assist persons to define their situations. Of course any actual situation has a certain existential reality – it exists, apart from what anyone knows or does not know about it. But things unknown or

forgotten about situations by the participants are not part of their definition of the situation. The salient features of situations are those seized
upon by the persons involved in giving that situation meaning. The
definition of a situation, as distinct from the existential situation (the two
may or may not be similar), is the operative factor in how persons construct their actual behavior. It is in a situated context that meanings
come to be agreed upon and stabilized. Thus a situation, as it comes to
be defined among group members, surrounds each member with a meaningful context of action. Meanings for acts are derived from action, and
action is invested with meaning.

2. *Art as an example of this view of symbolic communication*

Much of what has been taken over by symbolic interactionists about
communication has grown out of the pragmatists' philosophy of art.[5] We
have seen that the essence of social life, from this perspective, is precisely
its symbolic representative quality. Art is accounted for according to
similar principles. Artistry is the construction of works that have exactly
the same symbolic character as ordinary communications, but it is able
to articulate this symbolic meaning in ways that are not common. By
dramatizing, emphasizing, or clarifying the vagaries of situations or
ideas, artists bring out meanings that may be obscure or less appreciated.
Hence, there is really no new creation in art, but only new and more
insightful ways of expressing collectively derived meanings, grasping the
significance of situations. It is clear from the study of art, too, that the
term 'meaning' is not to be construed too narrowly. Emotions are
engaged by the artist. Collective emotional responses to symbols are as
much a part of this as are cognitive responses. Art is not only making
things cognitively clear. It is also the making plain of emotional consequences; it is the knitting together of a complete human response to a
portrayed act or development. For example, the artistry of the novel
unfolds human predicaments and shows the consequences of making certain decisions. It shows how different responses affect the whole course
of events, and it commonly heightens the reader's sense of involvement
and participation by cleverly engaging his interest. In short, a good novel
draws the reader into the on-going action, gives him an account of it, and
simultaneously presents him with a description of the consequences of
the actions, the circumstances leading to these actions, and the personal
and social relatedness of the actions to each other. A novel can do this
with completely imaginary characters; fiction becomes art through the
symbolic, representational nature of the human conduct displayed in
characterization, situational analysis, and moral dilemmas.

[5] For a secondary treatment, see Hugh H. Duncan, *Communication and Social
Order* (New York: Bedminster Press, 1962), pp. 55ff.

3. *Language*

To the pragmatic philosopher, ordinary language does for its users things similar to what artistic representation does for the artist. Language is the manipulation of 'significant symbols' which portray the action at hand and the completed expected consequences of it. The meanings of symbols arise in the context of the action, and it is said that symbols have meaning for several parties when all involved derive the same understandings of the acts and intentions from a given symbolic gesture. While mistakes are perfectly possible, they are made less likely by the fact that meanings are closely associated with collective experience among those who use the symbols. Those sharing experience can find the means to symbolically communicate about it to each other on the basis of their common insight derived from it.

It is clear from this that meaning is not based on personal preference; it is not a private matter. Meanings are not invented by persons to describe mental events or to communicate these to others; there are no logically prior mental events. The meaning is in the action; the action becomes symbolized as a matter of communication in the personal adjustment process by which people interact, and the content of communication is the meanings derived from action.

D. *The act; social conduct*

Up to now action and behavior have been mentioned but not discussed directly, but from the description of language and symbols it should be clear that action, to the symbolic interactionist, is something quite special. Yet there is a problem to solve which is of the pragmatists' own making. If human action is not to be accounted for by forces of either outside determinism (as with forms of sociologism and cultural determination), or from inside (via the infinite build-up of reflex arcs), and if it is to be regarded as coming about in a symbolic context of meaning, and if it is directed as it proceeds by the person doing the acting, the question of what causes action must be faced, and there is a need to describe how communication and language play a part.

The pragmatists settled on the concept of *impulse* to help solve this problem. Impulses are not instincts. 'Instinct' denotes an innate force which has a one-to-one correspondence with some activity, as with nest-building of birds. Birds do not learn to build nests; they just know how, innately. The driving force causing the bird to build is apparently not changeable, plastic, or portable. Neither is it symbolic. Impulses, on the other hand, are subject to modification and they are rather more diffuse. But they still arise as a matter of 'human nature'. The question of why man does anything at all is not up for discussion. It is assumed that some active principle gives rise to some action or other, and the problem of importance is the direction and control of that action in humans. The question about the act which is of significant importance is, what processes control action? rather than, why is there action?

Mead uses the term *conduct* to indicate social behavior in the ordinary sense, and it will be wise to adopt this usage now, since the more general terms 'behavior' and 'action' can mean non-social activity. Conduct is the series of acts which is being controlled by the actor toward certain ends, or with reference to emotions, and so on. Remember that we are to avoid determinism. Pragmatists do not think that conduct first arises in the mind and then is brought into manifestation. Rather, conduct starts as impulse which the person is not aware of, or notices only dimly.

While a given piece of conduct may actually be of exceedingly short duration, say, the pronunciation of a word or a significant gesture with the hand, it is analytically separable into a succession of parts. The first part arises in impulse, and brings out some action directly. This action, once it becomes manifest, enters one's consciousness as a recognition of oneself in action. But note that this entering of consciousness is a kind of memory, since, analytically speaking, what is now in consciousness has already happened as a result of impulse, even if it happened only an instant before. When these two stages have been completed the formation of conduct becomes possible, since the symbolic representation of what has occurred opens the way for modification of the action. The possibility is now open for redirection of the already started action because the person can now see the probable result if the action were to continue on its present course. If he does not like that result, modifications of the course can be made. This is something like the situation in which a person starts talking and notices that what he hears himself say is not just what he 'means', so he starts again, lengthens the sentence to include modifying clauses, alters the sentence so that it indicates something different from what it appeared to mean at the beginning, and so on. The sentence is a piece of conduct constructed in stages by stringing together pieces of action, by monitoring those actions as they come out, and by constantly making adjustments toward the end product of a completed bit of conduct.

Note the central importance of symbolic representation in social conduct. It is because a person is able to grasp the meaning of his own gestures (his impulse-related acts) and direct their course that conduct is possible. In just the way the person grasps his own meanings, those sharing his symbol system grasp them. Thus the on-going conduct, continually regulated in a mutually adjustive process, constructs itself as it becomes manifest – or, more accurately, is constructed and controlled by the persons involved through the medium of symbolic representation.

Imagery has the additional property of being able to call out action, which can end up as conduct. A symbol or constellation of symbols can bring out the action which is the beginning of conduct. Such imagery can be habituated, say the pragmatists, so that more or less predictable action will be called out by a given symbol. But note that this is just the beginning. This is not to say that the conduct resulting from a presentation of imagery will be predictable from the image alone. Presentation of the stimuli and the production of the first reaction to it are purely stimulus–response behavior. In this, man does not differ from the rat. But in the symbolic representation of that action as memory, in the eventual modification of the action by the shaping of it into directed conduct capable of calling up conduct in others, and in the mutually adjustive processes that symbolic representations of consequences make possible, man and rat differ very much. At the heart of the difference is the symbol and the reflexive use of language as a symbol-organizing technique for transmitting meanings.

E. *The self*

A concept is required which is capable of organizing the pragmatists' ideas about human conduct, symbol manipulation, and communication, and which locates the focus for these activities in the person. The concept *self* performs these duties. A self is not something a person possesses as a matter of inheritance or biology. Rather, self arises in the context of symbolic associations among other people. People are endowed with the capability, via their symbol-manipulation powers, of having a self, but the self is not something that is carried about until used. It is an integrating reflective quality which becomes actualized in performing conduct. When action becomes manifest from impulse, the controlling and shaping force which directs this action into conduct by way of cognitive reflexive power is the self.

In addition, the word 'self' has come to mean the physical possession of the impulses and the sensory machinery which initially give rise to conduct. Self must contain these features as well, since one of the outcomes of pragmatic thinking on social life is that self-directed conduct is really the marriage of impulse with controlling factors. Also, the emotional feeling of possessing an entity called a self enters this picture, often as a unifying bond between the impulse and controlling forces. Cooley begins his discussion of the self in this context.[6] But he soon makes clear that what is actually understood by the self is really only partly private. The other part is the representation inwardly to the self of the wishes and valuations of others in whose company the self is acting or has a history. It is in a symbolic context that the self is active, a natural

---

[6] Charles H. Cooley, *Human Nature and the Social Order* (New York: Schocken Books, 1962), pp. 186ff.

consequence of the interactionist's position on language, meaning, significant gestures. Hence the thing impressing us as being our private self is really in some measure a property of the group, made by it and partially under its control. The term 'self' indicates a kind of group reality which arises in interaction and becomes attached to a particular person.

This kind of thinking about the self accounts for the pragmatists' early interest in psychology, face-to-face groups, and small-scale situations in which the contours of social conduct are very personal and perhaps intimate. Symbolic interactionism is still largely a perspective appropriate to social psychology, rather than to larger-scale studies. Part of this concern for small-scale social analysis is derived from fascination with the self for its own sake. Thus Cooley explores the self by describing it in various characteristic phases, such as vanity, honor, pride, and so on. All these he understands to be aspects of the congruity between a person and his surrounding situations in which these feelings arise.

This fascination with the self deserves further attention. In Dewey's *Psychology*[7] several chapters are devoted to 'feelings', by which he means the varieties of modes of experiencing the self in mood, attitude, and temperament. These explorations are indeed unified by the pragmatic philosophical tradition. However, it appears to have been an early characteristic of interactionists, just as it is a characteristic today, to become interested in the experience of selfhood and internal feelings quite apart from whatever philosophy might underlie the derivation of the concept. The self assumes a central position in symbolic interactionists' perspective largely because of the richness of the idea itself. And as we will see, the additional sociological concepts of perspectives, such as society, interaction, minded behavior, and so on, really come back to the self as the touchstone which unifies the whole effort of depicting social life.

F. *Self as object*

Putting aside all the fascination with the self as an intriguing element of subjective human experience, we must turn now to the objective part the self plays, for it is as an object that the self is viewed as a unifier of persons in mutual conduct.[8] 'Object' as used here means that no matter how much it is in reality an abstraction of both social and personal elements, the self tends over time to be experienced as a unified, coherent, and firm entity, and it comes to impress others in this way as well. In this solidified form, the self can enter the experience of another as an object. It becomes a target toward which communications are directed and the per-

[7] New York: Harper, 1890.
[8] Mead, *Mind, Self and Society*, pp. 135ff.

ceived part of the acting person. This self-as-object enters relationships between people, or between the self as knower and the self as known. Here, the English language sometimes obscures the analysis. What is meant is that the self can take its own 'self' as an object, so that meaningful gestures can be directed at it, just as they can be directed toward other persons. It is this ability to get outside the self and experience it as an object which makes possible other than an entirely egoistic view of life. Getting outside the self and looking back at it, so to speak, allows for the possibility of viewing the self as others do. Taking this objective, exterior view of one's self allows for a kind of verification procedure. While having such a view of the self, it is possible to compare one's own inner feelings about identity, conduct, and so on with the apparent evaluations of others, and thus the adjustment process can proceed from the viewpoint of another. The same verification procedures are opportunities for change, since finding discrepancies between the other's evaluations and one's own offers the chance to accept or reject the other's views. When the self arises in a person, it is this objective-yet-subjective monitoring of one's own conduct which is the mechanism for fitting together one's intentions, feelings, and actions with those of other persons in a workable, organized way.

To summarize, the symbolic interactionists interpret all conduct as arising in a context of meaningful objects, which are in many cases persons-as-objects, but are also other things. In fact, an object is anything that can be indicated symbolically by a person. Thus the world of objects in which all interaction proceeds is a symbolically defined world of denotations including the self-as-object. Objects take their meaning from a given person's viewpoint, according to the relationship that person has with the object.

From this line of argument, we see a conjuncture of the pragmatic philosophy of symbols and art, language, the mind–body problem, the self, and the act. Conduct is built up toward objects which have significance for the person. The way to know this significance is to have meaningful ways of denoting the essential features; that is, we have to define the objects. Hence what matters is not the inherent characteristics of the objects, but the abstracted relatedness of the objects to the person. This is also true with respect to the self, when it becomes an object to itself. The person has not so much a given 'nature' from which all his activities spring and by which they can be explained, but a capability for adjusting and defining his world, taking on features of it as needed for action and gaining his 'content' from the surrounding constellation of group definitions of objects, including himself.

Mutuality in interaction is derived from these principles. A true sociology based on them must argue that interaction cannot be explained as deductions from first principles about the fundamental nature of social systems or of persons, but rather, it must describe the working out of suitable interrelations of individuals, all engaged in precisely the same process of definition and conduct toward the self and others. In fact, the key word here is 'process', rather than 'structure' or 'nature'. The interactionists mistrust concepts of social structure, institutions, and the like, when these are given as explanations for conduct. Most interactionists would agree that something like these structures exists. But they would say that reference to them as a means of explaining conduct misses the point. Structures and institutions, for the interactionist, become just more objects to be adjusted to. They do not assume prominence among all objects; they are not more significant.

III. *George Herbert Mead*

Mead was not a professional sociologist, but a philosopher with an interest in understanding social processes. As a philosopher, he was occupied by questions like the mind–body problem, the nature of consciousness, the bases of human rational powers, and the interpretation of what man is. His viewpoint was fundamentally that of the pragmatic philosopher and he was impressed with the philosophical works of James and Dewey, but he was not exactly a follower of anyone. It is simplistic to say that all philosophers of a given school think alike. Mead was concerned with making use of pragmatic philosophy in rather a different way from the others. Fundamentally, he used pragmatism to interpret the mind. How did people differ from other animals? If we all started out as creatures capable of clever responses to stimuli and impulses, how was it that people ended up with mental facilities which seemed to go beyond those of clever apes? Mead did not forget the fundamental difficulty of the mind–body problem. It was insufficient to merely name the rational facility, call it 'mind', and then say that people had it and that was that. To do so would be to 'solve' the problem by giving it a name. This trick pragmatists in particular could see through at a glance. Mead intended to tackle the mind problem along lines set out by the pragmatists in their studies of symbolization, their philosophy of communication and of art; and he wanted to stay within the critical spirit of pragmatic philosophy. He was not trying to compose the simplest possible theory in order to get on with studying social behavior, as Homans did years later. Mead found that his philosophical concerns carried him into the world of social psychology and sociology, and for this reason he has come down to us as a social theorist.

For an influential thinker, Mead did not actually write a great amount. It is hard to grasp a sense of the development of his work in the sociological field because what we must use is mainly the published lecture notes of some of his students.[9] For all we know, editing may have re-

---

[9] *Mind, Self and Society* is itself such a set of notes compiled from the lecture notes of several students.

arranged certain parts, emphasized points, and neglected others, so that we are not sure we are studying Mead as Mead would have had us do. But in those lecture notes we do have Mead's conclusions. His main ideas are clear enough.

Mead knew that to answer his main question about the nature of mind, he would have to criticize the existing theories of mind.[10] Additionally, he would have to develop his own to replace the old ones. Following pragmatic philosophy concerning the meaningfulness of symbols arising in collective responses would involve him in the discussion of the social group, and in a theory of communication. Finally, there would need to be an account of the possessor of 'mind' – an account of the process of mind attaching to persons and the communicative processes involved. There would have to be a discussion of the nature of the self. While it is not clear in what order these basic ideas came to Mead, or exactly what his mode of solving preliminary problems was, the three main facets of his work centered on mind, self, and society.

A. *Psychological parallelism and behaviorism*

Mead was most familiar with the psychology of Wundt with its very physiological orientation.[11] This psychology consisted very largely of the study of perception and of experiments which investigated stimulus–response associations with muscle movements. In fact, emotions, feeling, mood, and the like were regarded as being analogous to muscular movements; they could all be triggered by appropriate stimuli.

When the question of consciousness was raised among psychologists of this persuasion, answers usually came in the form of what Mead called 'parallelism'.[12] Consciousness could be accounted for by physical, behavioral responses to stimuli. Running parallel to the bodily course of events was consciousness, which, to this viewpoint, was coming to awareness of what the body was doing. Consciousness was parallel to action in the sense that it followed, side by side, wherever the physical organism took it. But it was always consciousness 'of' bodily action; action stood in a prior and superior position. This line of argument demoted consciousness and swept it away entirely as a psychological problem. It was a way of saying that, eventually, behavioral psychology would explain even consciousness by physiology; but until it did, consciousness would be allowed to run subservient and parallel to to the really important thing – bodily response and external stimuli.

This parallelism, to Mead's way of thinking, contained errors as well as certain appeals. In the first place, it emphasized in empirical form the

---

10   *Mind, Self and Society*, pp. 1-7; 42-50.
11   *Ibid.* pp. 42ff.
12   *Ibid.* pp. 18ff.

mind–body distinctions the philosophers had debated. Clearly the parallel account of consciousness is based on a philosophy which analytically separates mind from body (falling into all the philosophical traps by doing so). It then treats these abstractions as separate entities. Mead was suspicious of this from the start. Yet it was clear that 'body' was certainly responding to stimuli, and that there was no empirical way to cause 'mind' to do the same. Were these psychologists right? It seems that Mead took from this question a profound insight that the mind–body distinction was indeed wrong and that he needed to find a way of deriving mind out of body while giving mind a more prominent place. In a way, fighting physiological psychology on its own ground, he would have to show that mind was indeed a behaviorally responsive entity which could influence action just as material stimuli could do, and which could be accounted for by more than the lame assertion of a spiritual force, an inborn rational facility, or the like.

Mead begins here with the critique of physiological psychology. In his behaviorism we see the answers starting to form up – answers which were central in the subsequent construction of *Mind, Self and Society*. In the first place, behaviorism is to Mead a kind of correlational enterprise. It seeks to show the correlations between the experiences of an individual and the conditions under which these arise. Mead criticized making an arbitrary division between the activities of the central nervous system and what we call 'consciousness'. In any case, if consciousness runs parallel to bodily processes, any physical or emotional conditions correlated with bodily responses are also correlated with conscious process. Hence, the program of behavioral psychology discovers correlations among all states of body, including consciousness. Secondly, it finds that common features of the world result in responses common to all. Mead says that behaviorism needs to find a language to express such common responses so each can recognize that his private experiences are explicable by reference to the conditions giving rise to them.

In Mead's critique of physiological psychology, we see the main features of his alternative.[13] His willingness to accept this main paradigm of psychology and seek stimulus–response patterns shows his uneasiness with blatant abstractions that might go unresearched. However, Mead would not go along with this psychology in denying a real role to conscious processes, for he knew that to treat consciousness as a residual parallel category is to ignore it. Consciousness is just as much a fact as is a muscle twitch. Mead brought together the undeniable fact of consciousness as an active element with empirically based psychology as a correlational technique by which to discover the conditions under which experience arises. Bringing these two things together led him to the basic point

[13] *Ibid.* pp. 61-7.

that active conscious mind could be accommodated to behavioral psychology by concentrating on the ways mental powers arise in people through their behavior in groups. Hence Mead concentrated on consciousness arising in certain conditions, the self as object of stimuli, and the centrality of communications.

B. *Mind, gestures, signification, and meaning*

Mead's discussion of mind is actually devoted primarily to an account of symbols and communication. He did not intend to elaborate states of feeling, the meaning of intelligence, insight, or other standard topics often discussed as 'mind'. Rather, he was interested in giving an account of how the concept of mind can be understood. Mead begins by discussing the meaning of symbols and communication among animals, and then shows how the human process differs from this.

Looking back, Mead notes that imitation has been a key feature of thought about linguistic behavior, suggesting that one animal simply does what it sees and hears another do. The imitation argument holds that one person observes others who make certain sounds in given situations. The observer connects these sounds made by others to features of the situation, and then comes to hold the association with respect to himself. This explanation of language is not sufficient. Perhaps something like this occurs, but in fact human communication (as distinct from rudimentary symbolization) could not be built up in this way. Communication could not be merely imitative, since one person would simply imitate another and the conversation would never get off the ground. What is the kernel of truth in the imitation argument? It is simply that a symbol, a vocal gesture or some other kind of signification, comes to stand for a complex relationship between the person using the symbol and some feature of his situation. What is this complex relation? To begin with, the amount and diversity of stimuli around us at any one time are very great indeed. Surely this large amount of environmental stimuli is not all represented by a gesture. That is, a situation holds many things that are not actually very important as far as the given person is concerned, and a situation could have more than one kind of significance, depending on other circumstances. Thus Mead concluded that symbolization of environmental quality in gestures must necessarily be selective. We pick out aspects of the situation which are of particular importance. It is the selected part that is symbolized.

Selection raises a problem that is quickly solved in pragmatic philosophy. Which aspects of an environment will be associated with a given gesture? It is the relationship between the symbolizer and the environment that is the key. It is because of an overt act with respect to a particular object that the term 'chair' has to do with sitting down on something, and this explains why extremely diverse objects may all be indicated by the word 'chair' when the intended action is basically the same. Similarly, the word 'chair' may mean something entirely different when the relationship is different between it and the symbolizer, as in the case where 'chair' indicates discussion leader or committee head. We tend to say that, in the second example, the word 'chair' is used symbolically, while in everyday speech we do not think of the first usage as symbolic. To Mead, they are both symbolic in exactly the same way. Both usages denote a relationship between a symbolizer and an object.

Recall also that objects are not all tangible things to pragmatists. In the example above, 'chair' could refer to a social position as well as to a thing. In referring to a social position, the term is used to denote certain features of a situation particularly important to the action at hand. It is not important whether the person in the chair (the group leader) is tall or short, dark or light, Polish or Australian. The point is that the term denotes an intangible and abstract quality of the situation to which it is important to refer with a symbol. Abstract as this is, it is still concrete in that the relationships being denoted are experienced by the symbol user. It is his relationship with the objects that lend meaning to symbols. The *mind* enters this discussion not as an entity, but as a process. It is 'minded behavior', as Mead sometimes calls it, that is denoted by the term 'mind'.[14] Minded behavior is the concrete action associated with symbol use. Mind is not an entirely abstract thing unconnected with action or physiology. It is an associational quality which depends on the processes of selective attention and perception to organize a set of action elements with respect to an external object.

Raw gestures are the sounds or movements or other productions that can carry meaning, as in language, but this does not suggest that all gestures do carry it. A gesture is not significant if it communicates no intelligible intent either to a hearer or to the gesturer himself. But *significant gestures* are another matter.[15] These are the symbols that, as Mead says, call out a similar response in both the hearer and the gesturer. Significant gestures are the basic stuff of linguistic communication. A sound associated with fear or hope to one person which also indicates fear or hope to another is a significant gesture because the same thing is indicated to both. This calling-out for Mead is a matter of similar experience, imitation, and stimulus–response learning. For, at this point, he is still discussing something that he considers appropriate to both animals and humans, although he believes that animals make far less use of this than men do. Calling out a response is a matter of dragging up old associations to a symbol and, in a way, of having a memory of one's predicament at the time when this symbol was committed to memory. One's predicament refers to one's relationship with certain selectively perceived

14 *Ibid.* pp. 124-34.
15 *Ibid.* p. 68.

aspects of the environment at the time. Significant gestures call up associations primarily as aspects of relationships.

To understand *meaning* as Mead did,[16] it is necessary to recall something of the pragmatists' philosophy of art. Meaningful communication is symbolization which collapses into the present both the past and the expected future of a given situation. Viewing paintings is a matter of looking at the present, but 'seeing' the consequences and the associated feelings and motives as expressed by the artist. This quality of bringing into the present both the genesis of a thing and its consequences is what Mead had in mind when he said that significant gestures bring together the symbol that stands for the act with the intended consequences of that act. Another way of saying this is that signification through symbols indicates a whole, a completed thing which has not yet occurred, or which is just in the process of emerging. Thus, the use of symbols indicates what one understands by the whole relationship, or at least some substantial part of it.

We must now complicate this somewhat by making a qualification. Recall that 'conduct' was in fact the process of directing action as it emerged from impulse by the use of adjustive mechanisms. So *signification* is the process of symbolizing and then adjusting the meanings of additional symbols as they emerge, to indicate an intent. A flow of symbols starts in impulse, just as an animal cry starts in impulse. This cry brings forth associations in the person who then, perhaps while the cry is still in process, performs adjustive actions on it to redirect its meaning to better indicate intent. A series of these symbols, all rooted in associated experience of relationships between speaker and situation, ends up as an indication of the expected consequences of the situation for the actor.

Recall further that persons have the capacity to indicate to themselves, as well as to others. They hear themselves speak as others do, and are capable of making the adjustments necessary to express themselves. This is Mead's idea of mind as minded behavior; it is behavioristic in the sense that it is always rooted in stimulus–response associations and perception, and it is minded in the sense that as soon as a symbol emerges, it does not go to completion without having been interpreted and directed. The interpretation comes as a consequence of the nature of symbols. Symbols indicate in the present the expected consequences of the act symbolized. It is possible for me to direct symbols, rather than simply emit them, because it is possible to tell in my experience whether or not the symbols I find myself emitting are actually indicating the intended consequences. When the hearer understands by a set of significant symbols the same consequences and situated actions the speaker intends to indicate, then the symbols are called meaningful by Mead, and the communication is established.

[16] *Ibid.* pp. 75ff.

Implied in the foregoing is an additional element of mind – reflective intelligence. Thought is the recognition of the significance and consequences of on-going, already progressing acts and situations. This viewpoint does not set mind over against the acting organism, nor does it exactly demote mind to a mere accompanying feature. Reflectiveness of mind suggests that mind is always in the process of arising as the need for mental activity is at hand and that it is always later in time, analytically speaking, than the action it cognizes. Reflective thinking is coming to a consciousness of what has been and measuring the consequences of this action for the future.

C. *Self*

Mead's view of the self follows directly from his ideas about mind and communication. One could say that the self is another way of applying exactly the same points about language and communication and then drawing another set of conclusions.

1. *The 'I'*

Symbols arise, as we saw, in impulse, and are later directed. Mead found it useful to divide the concept of self into the 'I' and the 'me', especially to indicate the two phases of conduct, the arising in impulse, and the consummation in directed action.[17] Use of the 'I' concept has not been consistent among the pragmatists, although Mead, James, Dewey, and Cooley all found need for some kind of 'I' and 'me' to distinguish between phases of the self. For Mead, the 'I' indicates the aspect of self which is intimately attached to us as our individuality. We identify with it, as he says. But it is true that, in learning how to act, the person acquires attitudes and behavior patterns from others. These attitudes or activities are first present in imitation or as stimulus–response activities that are not yet under the control of the person, or, as Mead might have said, are not yet in his consciousness. Then the I enters the picture. It is the I that becomes aware of these appropriate actions and attitudes. The process of the self's arising is the process of the I's coming to be acquainted with the behaviors that the person is emitting. Having arisen in consciousness, the awareness of the activity is the I. It is the recognition that the person is behaving in a given way on this occasion. Hence Mead says that it is the I with which we identify, since we see that it was ourselves who acted. But I comes in as 'an historical figure', which has already acted.[18] This is the reflective nature of consciousness, of mind. Having arisen in self, the I reacts to the already performed behavior. It affects it, again not in forethought but in a kind of corrective or adjustive

---

[17] *Ibid.* pp. 173ff.
[18] *Ibid.* p. 174.

action to the behavior just ended. Sometimes the I is also identified with impulse alone and not with reaction to other impulse. If the genesis of a given action is needed, it can be found in the I.

2. *The 'me'*

The 'me' is the other half of the analytically divided self, in Mead's thinking.[19] It is here that Mead locates the forces of the outside world as they affect the person. A me is a set of 'organized attitudes of others which one himself assumes'.[20] From others it is learned that given attitudes or tendencies to evaluate or act are appropriate for given occasions. It is the me to which the I reacts, since it is the me which commonly guides the behavior of a socialized person. It is also the me of which a person is aware when thinking about himself, since, following Mead's terminology, the I only enters consciousness as a me.

Surely this is confusing, but the point remains that we do not experience the I, but only what the I has become in action in the past, which is to say that at the present moment of experiencing the self, the I is already doing something else we are not yet aware of. Hence, we observe that we have just acted similarly to or differently from a given behavioral standard which we ultimately gain from others, and so the I has entered consciousness as a me of recent vintage.

It is no accident that there has been confusion over the place of the I and the me in Meadian social psychology. The words themselves tend to come so fast upon each other that the meanings become confused. However, if the basic philosophy behind them and the main points about the origins of significant symbols are kept in mind, the sense of the I and the me concepts can be easily worked out. Also, it is well to keep in mind that Mead intended the terms 'I' and 'me' simply to be ways of denoting the phases of the self as it is generated in action. They are not real as parts of the anatomy, brain, or person. Mead's problem was to develop a way of talking about the phases of the self that distinctly separated the operation of self-action which was not yet conscious (he called this the I) from the influence of others in actual consciousness (this he called the me). Finally, Mead needed to show the relationship between these two in any conduct.

3. *Acquisition of self: role-playing and role-taking and the theory of stages*

In discussing how individuals come to have powers of communication, self-recognition, reflective thinking, and the like, the focus shifted away

[19] *Ibid.* pp. 192ff.
[20] *Ibid.* p. 178.

from the analytical discussion of how to conceptualize the person fully formed and toward a developmental account of how persons become formed. Often it is noted in this connection that Mead was influenced by Darwinian thinking, since there is in Mead's account a kind of developmental thesis.[21] But actually there is little Darwin here, except the historical viewpoint. Mead does not have in mind a species analogy within which there is struggle or natural competition; instead, he sees a cumulative developmental model in which persons follow a pattern by which they become capable of interacting symbolically as adults.

(a) *The stages of self development.* Some commentators find three stages in Mead, some four. Mead himself mentioned only two: the *play stage* and the *game stage*.[22] By the detailing of the requisite conditions for reaching the play stage, three stages in all have been identified; and by the separating of the game stage into two parts, four stages are possible. In all of the accounts, however, the main idea is the same. To come to experience one's self as an object, one is required to take the viewpoint of another toward the self. From that imaginary exterior standpoint, one views the self as it is and becomes aware of its reality as it appears to others.[23]

By 'play', Mead means acting as though one were someone else. In play of young children, however, instabilities and mistakes are the rule. It is not possible for the child to know the actual role of its own father in any depth, for example. In early play, certain parts of this father role might be grasped. The child may refer to himself in the third person, as his father would refer to him. When a sentence such as 'Johnnie is a bad boy' is spoken by Johnnie himself, it is taken to mean that he has grasped the fact that he is an object which can have certain qualities (goodness or badness) when viewed from another's point of view. Of course, Johnnie's father behaves in a very complex way toward Johnnie. The fact that Johnnie can grasp some of the significance of viewing himself from another's point of view as an object while playing father does not mean that he is fully capable of performing such a role adequately. It is perhaps true that we never get to the stage where this can actually be done completely. Nevertheless, there is progress for Johnnie to the extent that he eventually comes more fully to take in the complexities of his father's role and to grasp the states of feeling and motives that lie behind his father's conduct.

To the symbolic interactionists, role-playing is this incomplete or perhaps superficial placing of one's self in the role of another. The idea of playing a role suggests that the role is not truly 'me'. To play the role is to have sufficient insight into it to act overtly as though one were some-

---

21 Charles Morris, Introduction, *Mind, Self and Society*, p. x.
22 *Mind, Self and Society*, pp. 152ff.
23 *Ibid.*

one else, but this is not to say that the characteristic attitudes of this role have become incorporated into one's natural repertoire. As Johnnie plays father, he might also play fireman or some other superficially adopted position. As he does so, he learns fundamentally two things. The first is how the other person is expected to act in the role that Johnnie is now playing. This can include insight into how the person is to feel and emote, as well. If a little girl is sad because her doll is sick, this suggests understanding that sadness and sickness are related in the grown-up roles concerned with such things. The more interesting thing that is learned by this kind of play is the distinction between me and not-me. For in the process of playing, taking a make-believe position, what is expected of the actor is dramatized. To the extent that one must mentally strip off what he is in order to enter the role he knows he is not, the person is required to know the salient facts of how his reality differs from the role he is playing. Make-believe in play has the function of showing up this difference between me and not-me so that the residual becomes clearer; the residual is what is me. There are superficial and profound ways of doing this, and with practice, the child comes to have greater insight into others' roles and, concomitantly, greater insight into his own being.

Note here that self-insight comes from an exterior person's view of the self, and not from introspection or contemplation alone. This emphasis is consistent with the pragmatists' assertion that selves grow up in contexts of symbolic denotation which form the new selves, and it is not the other way around. While persons do, of course, have influence on group action, the genesis of persons is explained by the group. But also, such social formation involves learning self-insight, which sets the individual free to make his own judgments of himself. This idea skirts a middle course between social determinism and the errors of extreme individualistic determinism.

One feature of the play stage is that the player normally has only one alternative role in mind at a time, or perhaps a composite mixture of various roles. These enter consciousness during play as only one point of view. It is rather like looking in a single mirror and seeing one's own face. But there may be other mirrors. A multiple mirror can show the face from several angles at once. In the *game stage,* Mead has something like this multi-mirror analogy in mind.[24] In a game, several players are in action in concert, and it is the problem of game-players to grasp the organized and united requirements of all the players so as to understand their own action. Playing shortstop in baseball has to do with fielding, throwing, tagging runners, and so on; but it also has to do with some organized and more general duties related to the relationships between the infield and the outfield. 'Infield' is an abstraction, for there are not infield players, but only basemen and shortstop, pitcher, and catcher.

24 *Ibid.* pp. 158ff.

The job of the infield is an abstracted derivative of all the jobs of all the concrete players who occupy positions in the infield. Thus, to occupy adequately an infield position, it is required that the game be understood as an abstract thing which calls for a generalized knowledge of what team partners will probably do in a given situation. To know individually the expectations between shortstop and second baseman, shortstop and first baseman, and so on does not add up to a knowledge of what infield play is, since infield play is in fact the interrelations of all of these acting as a unit.

In the game stage, Mead thought, this abstracted way of viewing the self from a generalized exterior point of view is developed. The self as a reflection of others' attitudes and points of view takes on a more complete, rounded form, and it takes on a three-dimensional quality on an abstract level. The game differs from mere play in taking on the exterior perspective of an aggregate number of other persons and viewing the self from this abstracted collective viewpoint. Play leads to game, and game leads to depth of understanding.

Role-playing is the key concept in this picture of the developing self obtained through reflecting on the self from the standpoint of others. The more profoundly one accepts the definition of self derived from the viewpoint of others, the more the role is taken as one's own and not just played. This more complete, enduring acceptance of a coherent set of viewpoints on the self is called *role-taking*.[25] In play and games, there is a continuing make-believe quality which is useful in learning and self identification. But role-taking suggests more than play and suggests something which is the opposite of make-believe. Whereas role-playing has an instructive function, role-taking has an identificational one. The person, say the interactionists, comes to develop so well-rounded and consistent a set of self definitions through symbolic interactions with those in his environment that he finally comes to see himself as consisting of the person portrayed by the reflections. His own conduct then tends to confirm these impressions in his mind. In a stable system of others' definitions and self's definitions, the person's self emerges as a patterned repertoire of conduct that is 'me'.

However, according to Mead, the self is not passive and receptive, as the foregoing description might have suggested. It is not a simple matter of accepting others' definitions of one's self that makes one have that self.[26] The additional ingredient Mead calls for is the 'realization' of the self in action.[27] Taking the role, as opposed to only playing it, means doing it. This follows, of course, from the basic pragmatic philosophy of knowing the self only in reflection. Taking a role means doing it and

[25] *Ibid.* pp. 150-2.
[26] Recall the *active* nature of the 'I'.
[27] *Mind, Self and Society*, pp. 200ff.

observing the self in action, and grasping the interpretations about the self that others make. Taking a role is an active process, with not imagination but reality as the arbiter.

Finally, role-taking and self-realization are bound up in Mead's scheme with the concept of the *generalized other*.[28] This idea develops out of the concept of the other as the viewpoint from which the self is seen objectively. The other, in a way, became the general viewpoint of a stabilized and organized collective in the game, and it becomes in abstracted form the basis from which to reconstruct evaluations of the self's performance. While the generalized other is composed of concrete evaluations and attitudes of real people, it is portable from situation to situation in the 'mind' of the person, and hence it is actually more stable and consistent than any actual set of others. Sometimes the generalized other is equated to the superego or to society. To some these terms indicate something powerful and unyielding in control of the individual; but Mead means a generalized set of attitudes and value positions that are actively worked through in the invention and completion of conduct.

D. *Society*

Symbolic interactionism has concentrated its greatest weight of argument on the ideas of self, communication, individuality in action, self-attitudes, and self-change. But in addition to this, Mead stood ready to give an account of *society* in terms of his theory of the self and the mind. It is, of course, based precisely on the same key ideas as are the mind and self, and the same processes are central. Just as the self was implicit in Mead's treatment of the nature of mind, so society is implicit in Mead's understanding of mind and self. It is sometimes argued that symbolic interactionism does not handle the idea of society in a convincing way. Indeed, in the critical section of this chapter such an argument will be advanced. But it is worth remembering that the interactionists have let this challenge go unheeded and mostly unanswered because of their essential interest in other things, rather than for lack of resource to argue the case. It is because of interactionism's inherent ability to argue at least some case about the nature of society that it qualifies as a sociological perspective. With the discussion of society, Mead comes to the conclusion of his sociological work, having drawn up his theoretical picture of man, society, and the man–society relation.

Mead's main principle in his theory of society is that communication involves the participation of one person in the life of another.[29] This point goes back to the theory of mind and the assertion that mind arises in communication. Hence, there is a dualism contained in the interac-

28 *Ibid.* pp. 160ff.
29 *Ibid.* pp. 200-9.

tionists' conception of society and minded self. It is that whereas society was a prerequisite to the development of selves having mental powers, so the same individuals with these selves and powers are the explanation for society. This argument is frankly tautological, and will be regarded by logicians with a jaundiced eye, but to the interactionists the truth of the whole idea shines through. The point has not been to build a picture of the genesis of society or discover its origins in some state of non-society, but to describe a process which is seen as given, as on-going at the present moment. Interactionism does not speculate about where the first society arose which was capable of producing the first selves, as it were, but tries to understand social organization by applying the communications theme.

The principle of symbolic communication involves the appearance of one self in another, through the mechanisms of role-taking and reflective thinking. Hence the concept of intention, or the symbolic representation of an act together with its consequences, when mutually applied to two or more people, suggests that their communication will entail mutual adjustment. The mutual adjustment process in this context is often called 'self criticism' by Mead.[30] By this he means that the conduct of the self is fitted to the conduct of others. An integrated action unit results. Furthermore, Mead says that this is not merely a method or conventional means of regulating individualities which might otherwise be on collision course. Two arguments apply here. One is that individuality is really the appearance of generalized community attitudes and a person's reaction to them; the second is that there can be no conduct at all without a set of generalized community attitudes and a community perspective from which to sustain each person. Hence being involved in a mutual adjustment process is to be self-criticizing. To be regulated in one's conduct by the forces of collective society is to be living the only life possible. This general conclusion comes close to those of other theorists, although the others have often worked from different premises. But the important thing is not that different theorists reach similar conclusions, in this case at least. The important thing now is to notice that Mead's idea of society is rooted in the pragmatists' solution to the philosophical problem of mind and body, that a stimulating new series of ideas has been constructed to reach a conclusion that everybody already knew – men live in societies.

More specifically, we can note some of Mead's ideas about society. For example, let us explore his idea of *institutions*. Flowing from the main point about communications, persons' conduct is mutually keyed together. If these multiple conducts are geared to a common purpose, and remain stable for some time, Mead calls this an institution. Institutions are not things, but a certain lasting and specific quality of interac-

[30] *Ibid.* p. 255.

tion. Note that the institution is not really a 'common' response by all, even though *Mind, Self and Society* uses this term.[31] Mead has in mind mutually supportive and additive social relations organized around interests which all share. For example, the educational institution does not involve everybody in classroom teaching, but in a variety of lines of action with a root purpose. Mead would say that the general grasp of the root purpose comes as a result of each person's ability to take the roles of others in the system, so that each can see his own conduct fitting into a grander organization, the general aims of which all share. Mead sees institutions as flexible and 'progressive', changing with changing definitions of situations or the changing nature of the problems under attack and the like, although he recognizes that institutions do appear to have an ability to become rigid and inflexible. He does not carry out an analysis of how institutions could do this if their nature were as he says, but nevertheless he believes that, inflexible or not, institutions do change in the end, and individual creative acts of common purpose win out over ossification.

Mead is not pitting the individual against society here. It should be obvious by now that this is so, but Mead clinches the argument by pointing out the fusion of the I and the me in society.[32] He says that when persons are engaged in collective action toward common goals, their impressions of the sharply defined distinction between self and other becomes blurred; the effort in common brings out an extremely close identification of the person with the group. In this kind of action the me is so completely in concert with other people's me's that there is a weakening of an individualistic I. Actually, it is not a matter of reduction of the I; rather, the similarity of conducts makes it appear so. Because it lacks individuality because of intense common effort, the impression of a separate I recedes in favor of a common me. Hence the most complete identity of individual and society is in extreme cases of commonality, in which the most profound examples of the other appearing in the self occur.

IV. *Mead's influence*

George Herbert Mead's work eventually had an immense influence on sociology. It was novel and insightful in its own right, and it complemented work already in progress. Yet Mead's thought did not immediately become a major force in sociology. Rather, it remained a minor theme in the field, finding particular use among persons interested in special areas such as collective behavior, fad and fashion, or social psychology as it applies to face-to-face groups.

[31]   *Ibid.* p. 261.
[32]   *Ibid.* pp. 273ff.

Mead's influence grew and developed steadily over time, largely because of the efforts of his students. While the fundamental points of what is today symbolic interactionism have not changed a great deal since Mead's seminal work, the job of rounding out the perspective, applying it more universally, and filling in certain gaps fell to Mead's followers. Of particular importance in this work of turning a Meadian perspective into a more fully developed sociology were three areas of concern. (1) A better account of 'society' was necessary if symbolic interaction was to become a general perspective for sociologists and not remain an adjunct of a wider discipline. (2) A full-fledged methodology appropriate to Mead's thought needed to be worked out and defended. (3) A richer conception of motivation was needed. We will see that the issue of methodology is yet unsettled among followers of Mead, and that it divides into a striking duality. Some take a particularly operationalistic line, seeking empirical tests for explicitly defined concepts, while others who claim Mead as their mentor insist that this method cannot be derived from the main Meadian theory. An account of society on a more equal plane with the detail and richness of the concept of self has failed to appear. The problem of motivation still remains, although it has been addressed specifically and some dark spots have been brightened.

A. *Herbert Blumer*

Blumer was a student of Mead's at the University of Chicago. Because of this close association, Blumer is often thought the natural heir to the leadership of the field. Of course, Mead had other students, but Blumer has taken a leading role and made his career as a sociologist by elaborating and extending what Mead said. Blumer made his most significant empirical contributions to the field of collective behavior. But specifically in the theory of symbolic interactionism and its methodology, his contributions will probably be more lasting. These are, in principle: (1) a description of how symbolic interactionism regards society and (2) a criticism of sociological methodology with a view to showing the particular appeal of symbolic interactionism as a theoretical stance.

In his methodological work, Blumer has sharply criticized the scientific approach to research and substituted a somewhat different angle on the relationship of theory to data. The discussion of society as symbolic interaction is more conventional Mead. Let us take a look at each of these contributions in turn.

1. *Blumer on society*

As academics go, Blumer appears to be a man of few words, at least in print, although these words are not wasted. His explicit consideration of society as a topic does not cover many pages.[33] And to a great extent, it repeats the main arguments of symbolic interactionism – interpreting action in progress by capturing the meanings persons attach to their conduct, taking the role of the other in gaining an objective view of the self, constructing action as an intelligent response. Out of this argument come three basic points which deserve attention. First, society is best conceived of as a vast series of individual selves fitting together their individual lines of action. This means that the symbolic interactionist does not imagine persons as being caught up in social structures at all. They are not participating in something they do not make for themselves, even though the resultant actions may become habitual and what other sociologists could call structured. Secondly, Blumer makes the point that situations (concrete times and places for practical conduct) are the features of social life which people must define and the contexts in which they must align their activities. Hence the concepts of institutionalized values or norms of action at an abstract level or as a matter of cultural determination do not play a central part for Blumer. It may be true that institutionalized norms are features of action manifest in situations, but the components of the immediate situation, and not principles of behavior, guide persons in their choices concerning how to conduct themselves. Of course, this point is a broadside aimed at theories of social action which emphasize culturally legitimized norms as a basis of social life. But what must be kept absolutely clear is that Blumer does not deny social institutions exist. Rather, he relegates them to a rather minor place in explaining social conduct. Thirdly, Blumer insists that a cognitive grasp of the situation is a necessary condition for social conduct in it. Before a situation becomes meaningful, and hence before it is possible to act toward it, a person must come to an understanding of it insofar as he grasps his place in it and the likely consequences of any action he might be contemplating.

Cognition, situation, and mutual adjustment, then, form the basis of Blumer's model of society. It resembles very much his idea of a social movement, or his framework for understanding public opinion and its fluctuations. While institutionalized action does occur, he sees it as a matter of expedience. Persons would be in far more of a muddle if they had to construct all their activities from scratch than if they could take over great chunks of defined situations. These labor-saving chunks of definitions are Blumer's picture of institutions or of social structure.

But more should be said about structured social relations. Indeed, institutions could be an all-important feature of situational definition. Obviously, legally defined behavior proscriptions, for instance, set

---

[33] 'Society as Symbolic Interaction', in Herbert Blumer, *Symbolic Interactionism: Perspective and Method* (Englewood Cliffs, N.J.: Prentice-Hall, 1969), pp. 78-89.

boundaries within which situations must be defined, unless action is taken surreptitiously. (This in itself is one way of taking cognizance of legalities bearing on a situation.) Blumer is not downgrading institutions, but he is trying to take away from them the priority and necessity he feels other social theories allocate to them. While institutions can and do profoundly affect action, they do so not because of their existence as another order of being, apart from human action, but simply because they condition the situations in which individuals have to construct their personal conduct.

2. *Blumer's critique of scientific method in sociology*

In a series of papers Blumer has shown an abiding interest in the methodology, even in the philosophy, of science, and in the methods specifically appropriate for the social sciences. Blumer feels that what he calls *variable analysis* is particularly unsuited to sociology because it is incompatible with the processual build-up of conduct and the mutual adjustment process.[34]

By 'variable analysis' Blumer means the designation of some factor or factors in a situation for particular interest, either as a cause or as an effect, so that these factors receive special attention. Blumer argues that in doing this several mistakes are made. First, the situation in which the variables are important is unnaturally construed. By designating what he is interested in, the scientist makes a legitimate claim to examine the situation for certain features, but he makes an assumption in doing this. The assumption is that the action studied proceeds according to previously defined activities of variables, and that the resultant conduct can be accounted for in terms of the variables examined. Blumer says that this kind of reasoning might approximate a scientific posture, but that 'science' is not the result. A preconception is placed between the observer and the action which does not allow the observer to contact the reality; he notices only the variations on certain preselected scales, measures, or indicators.

Associated with Blumer's rejection of variable analysis is the more important theoretical point that action is mediated symbolically and that variables and constants designated beforehand cannot pick up the subtleties involved. It is the interpretation of action that is all-important to the symbolic interactionist, and a particular variable might in fact have many interpretations for those actually experiencing it. Hence, indications from test scores and the like are quite beside the point. In the absence of knowledge of how the participants interpret the action picked up by the indicators, no explanation of the action is possible.

[34] 'Sociological Analysis and the Variable', *American Sociological Review,* XI (December 1956), pp. 683-90.

For example, it may be that a birth-control program and the birth rate in a given city are related, in that the introduction of the program correlates with some shift in the birth rate. But what Blumer would consider key features of the situation are not yet known. These would be the symbolic meaning of the program, the type and style of presentation of the program, whether or not it was seen as an insult or a threat to a given subgroup or social class, whether or not some persons used the program's information to have children more often instead of less, and so forth. For Blumer, no indication as derived from rigidly controlled variables can capture the meanings of the actions people take, and hence, in spite of all the research findings piling up in sociological journals, little progress toward cumulative understanding of conduct is being achieved.

Finally, Blumer is struck by the vagueness of even the most rigidly and precisely defined variable in sociological analysis. He makes a forceful case for the point that sociology has gone on for years talking about key ideas like community, solidarity, and norm, when in research these things are subjected to unstable and imprecise measurement. The result is that research is not cumulative; findings allegedly concerned with the same idea are not comparable across research projects and insight into conduct remains at a low level.

It must be emphasized here that Blumer has hit upon one of the continuing paradoxes in sociological methodology, and he is trying to turn it to account for symbolic interactionism. The paradox is that while we might wish to know action in its fullest sense, in order to know any of it we must define our concepts about it precisely and rigidly. This means drawing up clear boundaries between what each concept refers to, and keeping concepts separate. Doing this in research practice forces the use of methodologically stable indicators for concepts – things like tests, controlled observations, measurements, and the like. In short, all the things that would move sociology toward an ability to use scientific research tools actually move it away from what Mead and Blumer consider centrally important: the shifting, adjusting, interpreting, symbolically mediating nature of social conduct. To become more scientifically precise is, to Blumer, to become less capable of capturing reality as it is.

Blumer's solution to this problem is to refashion the idea of the *concept*.[35] In scientific methodology, as noted, concepts must be clear, precise, and stable. In sociology, Blumer claims they are not. The reason they must be so in science is that standard use in research requires it. Blumer believes that if the traditional objectives of science were abandoned in sociology, the rigid strictures could be put aside as well. If variable analysis were not required, then the necessity for concepts to have empirically reliable indicators would also disappear. The result would be

---

[35] 'What Is Wrong with Social Theory?' in Blumer, *Symbolic Interactionism*, pp. 140-52.

that concepts would become 'sensitizing' agents for the researcher. A sensitizing concept is not something that can be built up by rigid definition. Rather, it is an idea that enters the researcher's mind as an abstract principle. He knows, for example, that a person's interpretation of events is to be considered important, so he will look for what he considers 'interpretations' without any preconceived idea of what he will find. Through practice, anticipations and predictions might indeed be possible, but these will not be scientific in the ordinary sense. Rather, the researcher's common-sense experience will come out via his familiarity with the situation. The concepts of sociology, then, amount to a universe of discourse which takes on fairly stable meaning among those who know the language, because 'knowing the language' means experiencing the conduct indicated by the concepts themselves. It does not mean knowing the abstract derivation of the concepts logically or by definition.

Perhaps it is obvious that Blumer's viewpoint on the proper nature of concepts for sociology is uniquely a product of his own theoretical stance, derived from Mead and the pragmatists. Conduct is a matter of stringing together acts while monitoring the developing meanings, and shifting actions so as to impart or derive meanings from situations according to definitions which themselves derive from the action on hand. Hence the concepts in use by the person doing the acting are pictured by the interactionists as 'sensitizing' these people to their surroundings and enabling them to pick up the meanings developed in the situations.

It then follows that a committed symbolic interactionist ought to practice what he preaches in research by developing the concepts of social science in a similar fashion. These concepts will be uniquely social science concepts. The natural sciences do not deal with entities that have the capability of interpreting their own actions; hence the concepts of natural science need to differ fundamentally from those of social science. Blumer would argue that social science is a profoundly different kind of science from natural science, because the key feature of his theoretical perspective is precisely the interpretive nature of social action. From this it follows that the objectives of social science are different, the methods are different, and the results are different. And finally, the nature of scientific knowledge about the social world will be different from any other kinds of scientific knowledge.

B. *Symbolic interactionists as positivists*

Blumer's view of the proper approach to sociological data, as we have seen, was based on the emphasis Mead gave to meaning and interpretation. There could be no predicting activity and no scientific explanation of it without doing violence to this main point. Therefore Blumer wished to reconstruct the idea of a concept, making it into a sensitizing principle but allowing it to remain devoid of specific behavioristic content. His contention was that no other kinds of concepts were even possible in social science.

But Blumer's argument to this effect rests at least in part on showing that, until now, no scientific positivist of the social world has done a satisfactory job of setting out stable behavioristic categories, nor has anyone done an unassailable job of theoretically linking these. So far, many sociologists might agree with Blumer. But if the objective of sociology remains to seek these categories and order them theoretically, Blumer's criticism can be answered by saying, 'Because it has not yet been done does not mean that it cannot be done.'

1. *Operationalism applied to symbolic interactionism*

If the objective of sociological theory is to remain explanation and not just sensitization, then the same problems associated with the application of theory to data will arise for symbolic interactionism which have arisen in other attempts with other theories. Of prime importance in this regard is how to establish empirically verifiable indications that what symbolic interaction theory says is true. This question really breaks down into two distinct but related questions: (1) what, precisely, does symbolic interaction theory say that is of empirical importance? and (2) how can experimental operations or observations be made applicable to these assertions?

Manford Kuhn has tried to show that symbolic interactionist theory drawn from Mead as well as others can be construed to mean actually nine separate, subtly different theoretical ideas.[36] Mainly, these differences arise from ambiguities about the actual point in conduct when interpretation occurs, the time relationship between an event and its effect on the self (which might be instant or occur over a protracted period, for instance), and the question of indeterminacy of the result of action. 'Indeterminacy' refers to the question of whether a given event always has the same kind of effect on the social action it influences.

Blumer had much to say about the idea of the variable in social science. But Kuhn argues in return, hoping to justify a more rigorous methodology, that there is really no alternative to variable analysis. The divergence between Blumer and Kuhn on this point would be less serious if symbolic interactionism were another kind of theory, one which did not involve the subjective experience of the acting person. But the fact is that this is a key feature of interactionism. Kuhn puts it succinctly: 'It is most difficult to establish generalizations valid for human behavior

[36] 'Major Trends in Symbolic Interactionism in the Past Twenty-five Years'.

without methods wherewith to make precise checks on intersubjective perceptions of events'.[37] It is indeed most difficult, but it is just this problem that anyone attempting more traditional positivistic methodology faces with symbolic interactionism. It is precisely the internal subjective experiences and interpretations of events that make symbolic interactionism what it is, and these are least accessible to positivistic methods. Blumer said it was impossible. Kuhn says it is possible, but difficult.

2. *The problem of non-empirical concepts*

It is ironic that a sociological perspective based on pragmatists' mistrust of metaphysical notions should contain so vast an array of central points having no possibility of empirical verification. For instance, the dichotomy of the I and the me is such a point. No matter how much one is sensitive to the proposal that action develops through an internal conversation of gestures, initiated through impulses released by stimuli, the I cannot be contacted empirically because it is not there. While the nervous system may be investigated positivistically, the I, in and of itself, cannot. It is not an entity, only a concept. Of course Kuhn finds concepts which are empty of empirical content frustrating. Hence there is a tendency in the positivistic use of symbolic interactionism to simply forget about the I and concentrate instead on the me. The me is troublesome enough, but in principle it may be empirically investigated because it refers to the internalized expectations one holds for himself. These expectations are, in turn, derived from the behaviors of others displayed toward the self, and these can be observed. In principle, correlations between the way others conduct themselves toward a person and the way that person behaves in their presence can be found. Hence, the concept of the *reference group* has assumed importance for Kuhn's version of symbolic interactionism.[38] While the concept of reference group is implied by the 'generalized other', the concreteness of an actual group whose activities can be observed tends to take the question out of the theoretical world and into the empirical.

In addition, the scientific use of symbolic interactionist principles implies a tough decision on the question of determinacy. If one accepts the argument that situations are indeterminate in their consequences, for whatever reason this is accepted, the result is the same: there can be no scientific characterization of such situations. That is, similar causes are not expected to lead to similar results. On the other hand, determinacy as a principle has been found in symbolic interactionism, at least by implication and ambiguity, and positivistically minded interactionists find

[37] *Ibid.* p. 74.
[38] 'The Reference Group Reconsidered', *Sociological Quarterly,* v, 1 (Winter 1964), pp. 5-21.

that they must accept some version of this principle as a basis for going ahead with positivistic research. They have no alternative, except to abandon their efforts in this direction. Returning to the example of reference groups, and applying the principle of determinacy while neglecting the I, the self emerges as the personal manifestation of a series of me's, displayed in a predictable way as a result of internalizing others' expectations.

Following through on this version of interactionism, a schematic version of any social action emerges in which the self plays a central part as the acting manifestation of externally determined self-attitudes. Conduct is explainable because it is self-constructed action, meaningfully interpreted as the behavior appropriate to the situation in which the action occurs. And this meaningful interpretation made by the self is in turn explained by the self's having been formed as the internalization of external expectations. Essentially, a given bundle of me's makes a self, and selves of a given kind act in given ways in given situations. Hence, working backwards, action is explicable as a manifestation of self, which is in its own right a product of community attitudes. Clearly, the same general approach to action is found here as in Mead's dictum that action is both personal and social, in a complex mix of community-determined attitudes and self-constructed conduct. The differences lie in the fact that the non-empirical I is gone, and with it the elaborate vision of the process of action construction. Additionally, action construction as unique interpreted responses to situations has been narrowed to become the action which is predictable, knowing the determinant me's for a situation. Thus we see that the problem of non-empirical concepts is solved by scrapping them. Those for which a positivistic case can be made are retained, along with the general form of the argument with a slightly altered concept of the self at the center.

C. *The question of motivation*

It has been noted by many that symbolic interactionism is a theory of social psychological importance but lacks a convincing account of *motivation*. Of course this is a serious problem. Motivation is important, perforce, in a theory heavily weighted with concern for the individual, because the reasons why action is taken, or why there is some particular action and not another, are questions which go straight to the heart of the whole social action topic. If we are to make a theoretical perspective which emphasizes the creative conduct of individual persons, and if we are to account for the institutional structures persons create and call society by reference to individual lines of action, then the theoretical explanation of why persons take certain lines of action is paramount.

It is not strictly true to say that symbolic interactionism had no theory of motivation from the very beginning. In Mead's concept of the impulse, for instance, there is the assertion that action originates simply because people are active beings. Mead's point in raising the question of impulse is to show how action which is just 'there' is shaped into guided conduct. In other words, he was interested in discovering the mechanism by which conduct becomes formed and in describing the process by which this occurs. He was assuming that there would be a basic activity of some kind. But there is more to the problem of motivation than this. In addition to the question of why there is action at all, which Mead ignored for the obvious reason that there simply is action, there is the question of what gives action its direction; what forms its goals?[39]

It is important to note that a description of the ways in which conduct might be formed and controlled does not amount to an explanation of why some particular line of conduct is selected. For example, Mead's central point about social life's being the fitting together of persons' conduct according to a generalized concept of expectations raises a blunt but important question. Why should anybody care about the 'generalized other', or indeed, any other? It is something to account for group life by showing the mutual adjustment process which leads to a given form of collective action; but this is not the same thing as an explanation of why it is this form of collective action and not some other.

In Miyamoto's paper on motivation in symbolic interaction theory, the self plays a central part, as it ought to do.[40] Since it is the self which can experience itself as an object and act toward itself, it is this which is the central figure in conduct. The self constructs action. Hence it is the self which is motivated. Miyamoto's key question is this: by what criteria could the self be expected to evaluate its own actions? If an account of the criteria could be given, then an account of motivation would be at hand, since we would then know the dimensions of any action important in determining whether the self would choose or reject that action. Miyamoto borrows initially from Parsons' modes of orientation, noting that, in principle, three modes appear to answer the question of how selves are judged. These are the *evaluative, cognitive,* and *affective* modes. The evaluative mode concerns questions of 'good' and 'bad'; the cognitive concerns questions of 'definable or nondefinable'; and the affective concerns questions of 'gratifying or not gratifying'. Miyamoto thus narrows the field from essentially an infinity of possible criteria for self-evaluation to three.

In addition to this, Miyamoto draws on more traditional symbolic

---

[39] This is a completely analogous question to that confronted by Parsons in his rejection of the randomness of ends assumed in hedonistic utilitarian theory.

[40] 'Self, Motivation and Symbolic Interactionist Theory', in Tomatsu Shibutani, ed., *Human Nature and Collective Behavior: Papers in Honor of Herbert Blumer* (Englewood Cliffs, N.J.: Prentice-Hall, 1970), pp. 271-85.

interactionist concepts to describe three *perceptual settings,* or fields of activity in which the three criteria of self-evaluation may be applied. These are: the self as an attitude object; the self as a task-performing object; and the self as a role-performing object. The self as an attitude object may receive evaluations which refer to its general qualities – it is kind or harsh, quick-witted or dull, and so on. Task-performing objects are objects which do specific things. Miyamoto suggests that the self is evaluated in part relative to specific tasks that a person performs. In the third perceptual setting, the self is evaluated with reference to its occupation of a specific social position, a broader concern than that of task performance.

Returning to Mead for inspiration, Miyamoto notes that it is only in the communal context that a person can survive. Hence it must be as a matter of survival that the self comes to view itself as desirable (evaluative mode), definable (cognitive mode), and gratifying (affective mode). It is required that the self come to see itself to be an object in these ways, because these are the ways others, who hold the key to survival, will see the self. Hence, motive is understood as tendencies to evaluate possible actions by the self according to the effect they might have on the self's desirability, definability, and the ability to gratify.

Of course, desirability, definability, and the ability to gratify are not always of equal importance to the survival of the self. It is for this reason that Miyamoto introduced the different settings of action (attitude, task, and role). These settings tend to place one or another of the self modes at a premium from time to time. The point is that whatever is at a premium in the situation, in the setting of the action, must be maximized by successful selves. Of special interest here is that by trying to systematize the criteria of self evaluation and motivation, Miyamoto has taken a long stride toward the conclusion that organizational necessity plays a large part in determining what action will be taken. This stride is away from the intense individualism of previous symbolic interactionist theory.

V. *Research and symbolic interactionism*

The symbolic interactionist perspective has generated considerable research of one kind or another. Partly this can be attributed to its inherent admonition to sociologists, never far from the surface, to get close to their data, their informants, and their subject-matter problems. Since interactionism lacks a highly developed theory of social structure of its own such as functionalism has, there is relatively little in it to occupy the mind of a 'pure' theoretician in the discipline of sociology. An informal differentiation has emerged in the field between theorists and researchers which usually locates symbolic interactionists on the side of research. This does not mean that symbolic interactionism is anti-theoretical. Nevertheless, the interactionist program has basically rested on research articles devoted to results with 'sensitizing' concepts or with measurements devoted to testing the self, the situation, the definition of others, and the like.

Being in principle a social psychological perspective, interactionism has led its adherents to select research topics that avoid expositions of social structure, institutions, social evolution, or things of that kind. Instead, the emphasis is on topics in which personal performances are particularly crucial. For example, the standard alternative to the functionalist portrait of the deviant is drawn from interactionists' interpretation of the process by which a person takes on deviant attitudes toward himself and how these spawn deviant acts. The wider problem of behavior change has been addressed from the interactionist perspective, as in the cases of studies in professionalization of medical students,[41] rehabilitation of convicts, analysis of status passage and ceremony, and the like.

Interactionism makes contact with certain branches of psychiatry as well. The interest Mead had in explaining the process of acquisition of self is similar to medical interest in exploring how socialization goes wrong, or how the processes can lead to painful results. Thomas Scheff's *Being Mentally Ill: A Sociological Theory* is an attempt to explain the influence of social interactionist factors in convincing persons, or confirming them in their fears, that they are indeed physically sick with mental disease.[42] Numerous research studies with normal children have focused on role-learning topics, sex-role identification, and the like.

Behavior as it occurs in particularly interesting situations has also formed a part of interactionist research. Schools have come in for study, sometimes to find how different participants in the situation define it. Policeman–suspect interaction, the doctor–patient relationship, courtship and love, family organization, old age, and generation-gap studies have all been done. These tend to point out salient features of the situations which make the action itself of professional interest, and then describe the conduct in terms of interactionist factors. Related to this is some of Goffman's work which reports on everyday life instead of particularly novel or crucial situations.[43]

Obviously there can be no criticism that symbolic interactionist theory does not inspire empirical work. However, some questions can be raised about the exact relationship between the perspective and the research. The basic question of the applicability of interactionism goes back to Blumer's criticism of the scientific method, and his refashioning of con-

---

[41] Howard S. Becker *et al., Boys in White: Student Culture in Medical School,* ed. Ann Green (Chicago: University of Chicago Press, 1961).

[42] Chicago: Aldine Publishing Co., 1966.

[43] Goffman, *The Presentation of Self,* and Goffman, *Behavior in Public Places: Notes on the Social Organization of Gatherings* (New York: Free Press, 1963).

cepts into 'sensitizing agents'. The basic problem is this: how do we know that my sensitivity to the situation is the right one? And if mine differs from yours, how do we decide who is right? In liberating interactionism from a firm, stable hold on specific definitions, admittedly for a good cause, the perspective runs the risk of enfeebling itself as a research base. Related to this point, research with this perspective tends to be the elaboration of ever-different situations and activities, with a consequent lack of emphasis on relating these works into a coherent view of whole societies.

Aside from the fact that interactionism could come apart at any time through different practitioners' making divergent conclusions with the interactionist approach, there are associated problems of a more technical nature. For example, in planning a research project, the researcher never knows exactly what he is looking for, and hence he can never fully equip himself to follow up action in all the directions it might lead.[44] Researchers are faced with a constant series of snap decisions in the field – whether or not to count some incident as central or peripheral, important or trivial. There is also the question of when enough data have been collected. Obviously, people do not finish their performances and ring down the curtain. The analogy to drama obscures the fact that situations do not come in discrete, defined packages, and in fact there may be more than one situation relevant at a given time in the lives of the participants. The actors' conduct is never finished, and neither is the imperfect record of it kept by the observer. This problem usually calls forth a solution in terms of time, effort, and expense, rather than on the basis of clearly defined research goals.

Of course, it is the awareness of problems like these that causes some interactionists to take a more rigorously positivistic approach to research. But here, many of the same problems crop up. It does not matter what approach to research one takes; situations remain, in one sense, everlasting. It will be even harder to prepare for research, if this means questionnaires or controlled observation, when there is insufficient clarity of research expectations. On the other hand, however, the results will be less open to criticisms of non-repeatability or idiosyncratic selective perception.

There is a sense in which these general criticisms apply to all sociological research, from all theoretical angles. But it is still true that these are particularly serious problems for the interactionists because the nature of the concepts and the general looseness of the perspective emphasize questions of standardization and unique observation. Imprecise definition

---

[44] See J. Kitsuse's discussion of behavior imputation as a case in point in 'Societal Reaction to Deviant Behavior: Problems of Theory and Method', in Howard S. Becker, ed., *The Other Side: Perspectives on Deviance* (New York: Free Press, 1964), pp. 87-102.

of concepts is a count on which Blumer criticized alternative theoretical viewpoints, but making a concept into a 'sensitizing instrument' does not solve the problem of precision, even if it does change the research aims.

A. *Using sensitizing sociological concepts*

Fred Davis has given a classic example of insightful sociological treatment of a particular kind of interaction.[45] His aim is to elucidate the process by which people experience and project impressions of themselves – the self-identity issue which is so central to symbolic interactionism. His particular research interest is visibly handicapped persons. The problem of identity projection and management for such persons is exaggerated because often there is a suggestion made by normals that handicapped persons are 'deviant'. This may take the form of an imputation that handicapped people are significantly different from normals, and hence are a special case of interaction management. Even if the 'deviance' is imposed, as with wheelchair cases, the stickiness of interaction flow and the uneasiness which may beset both the normal and the handicapped can become an impediment to even the most superficial social interaction. Davis' intention is to show some of the problems involved in management of self among handicapped persons and the process by which visibly handicapped persons disavow the 'deviant' definition of themselves. The Davis paper fits snugly into the mainstream of interactionist literature; it is organized around the concept of self and how selves are thrust into situations in which they must cope.

Additional features make this classic interactionism. The settings in which Davis is interested are typical. He wishes to elucidate everyday face-to-face interaction which is prolonged enough to actually establish a relationship, but not so long as to be governed by norms of extreme familiarity or deeper sentiments. The interaction cannot be too stylized; if it were, the interactional dynamic would be restricted by formality. However, the interaction cannot be completely unpredictable. That is, the normal rules of behavior and etiquette ought to apply, since these give a general boundary and set a tone for a developing situation.

Obviously, these strictures are not rigid. What Davis is trying to say by delineating the kind of interactions he wants to describe is that these are the normal bounds within which most social interaction occurs among people who are neither intimate nor total strangers. A rather loose and undefined set of behavior rules governs activity, but considerable room for novelty and impression-management exists. Individuality has its fullest room to develop as it constructs mutual interaction via controlled self-projections and interpretations of self.

[45] 'Deviance Disavowal: The Management of Strained Interaction by the Visibly Handicapped', in Becker, ed., *The Other Side*, pp. 119-37.

What is Davis' specific research problem? He wishes to understand how visibly handicapped people subtly erase the impression of their being 'deviants' from the minds of those they contact socially, and replace this with a delicately balanced definition of themselves which acknowledges their essential normality, yet clearly denotes their limitations. Davis says it is almost always obvious to the handicapped that they are being defined as deviants. Davis' discussion of this points up the interactionists' emphasis on symbolization of attitudes as key features in interaction. He notes that the way handicapped people know how they are being defined is by reading the signs left by *faux pas*, revealing gestures, slips of the tongue, and inadvertent remarks, as well as by the pace and flow of the interaction itself. These are all symbolic of a set of attitudes, a surrounding array of ideas, which define the situation and the relationships of the people in it. A lot has been said about language in this chapter, but this should make it clear that the interactionist means far more than words and sentences when he uses the idea of symbolic communication.

Davis notes that the handicapped person is always potentially threatened in his social interaction, because the handicap itself may become the exclusive focal point, cutting off further avenues and restricting the relationship. Additionally, the sympathy most people feel for the handicapped might actually overflow its normal bounds and overcome the normal restrictions on everyday feelings. Smothered in sympathy, the handicapped person may actually be prevented from engaging in more normal activity. Finally, the handicap can pose a threat to the person's being defined as normal in every other way, and this, coupled with the ambiguity which accompanies it, is at best a nuisance to handicapped people, and at worst a barrier to their forming normal social relationships and definitions of themselves.

Davis notes from his interviews with the handicapped that the process of deviance disavowal has three stages. The first of these makes use of everyday manners by causing them to work in the handicapped person's favor. In early stages of interaction, it is common to accept people as they would like to appear, and to make no reference to obvious differences from ourselves. This 'fictional acceptance' is a possibility open to the handicapped as a starting mechanism for interaction. However, the second stage is more delicate. If the interaction is not to end in waves of sympathy, or stumble over the handicap itself, the handicapped person must manage the interaction so that it facilitates role-taking around the normal aspects of the self being projected, yet clearly denotes the limitations posed by the handicap. If this is successful, says Davis, the psychological effect in the normal person is a receding importance of the handicap, to the point where it disappears from his consciousness for normal interactional purposes. One of Davis' informants called this 'breaking through'. The breakthrough is acceptance of the preferred definition of self. This definition forms the basis from which role-taking is performed in the ensuing relationship. 'Crippled' or 'blind' cease to be the salient features of the person, and more normal dimensions of definition, such as 'knowledgeable', 'attractive', 'witty', may take over to provide a potentially expansive relationship. The final stage of this process, Davis notes, is an institutionalization of the favored definition of self for most purposes, and an accompanying normalized recognition of the limitations on the relationship which the handicap causes. When this process is complete and successful, a disavowal of the 'deviant' self-definition has been made and it has been replaced by a more normal one.

We have already noted how this research report is typically symbolic interactionist in its emphasis on self definition, the centrality of the self in the process of role-taking, and the subtle employment of the idea of communication. Additionally, we should note Davis' research style, which was to interview a small number of handicapped persons and ask them general questions about themselves and how they managed social interaction, following these questions further as the opportunity presented itself. No controlled questionnaires or battery of tests here. Similarly, Davis' natural tendency is to conceptualize a solution to his question as a process. He says that deviance disavowal by handicapped persons is a process which passes through stages on its way to completion. It simply is not in the interactionist's repertoire to view Davis' research question as one having a solution in a specific set of normative prescriptions, morally legitimate role expectations, or the like. The interactionist is more likely to see all questions of self-identity, situation definition, and interaction stabilization as processes, developing in time through the alignment of individual conduct in a mutually acceptable pattern. This parallels Mead's insistence on the progress of stages as an explanation of the self-formation sequence, and it echoes Blumer's emphasis on society as the fitting together of individual actions in a never-ending adjustment process. Finally, it is worth noting again that all this is viewed by the interactionists as a symbolic communications process, and Davis has given examples of how he understands the projection of attitudes and denial of deviance as actually proceeding via inadvertent noises and inappropriate sympathy, and via management of self projection using norms in a way that will work to the best advantage of the person involved.

B. *Empirical investigations of the self*

A continuing problem for most sociological research, as was pointed out in Chapter 2, is the subjective versus the objective point of view. Whereas sociological theory often implies the subjective point of view, as symbolic interactionism does, the methodology employed to discover these subjective entities is sometimes external and objective. All divining of other people's subjective states is in some sense objective, since understanding comes to the observer via external cues, descriptions, situational behavior, and the like.

Fred Davis, in the sociological work just described, followed Blumer's dictum about research rather closely. Davis applied none of what modern sociologists would call 'empirical' tests, and he had no particular hypotheses. He had no structured research techniques or specific procedure for working on his data after they were gathered. But, as we have noted, there is an alternative approach to research on symbolic interactionist theory, one which takes the major points raised by the pragmatists about self, communication, and society, and applies more structured procedures to them.

Manford Kuhn's name is linked with this attempt to research more systematically symbolic interactionist theory in sociology.[46] His thinking runs something like this. The self is at the center of sociological theory. Taking Mead's work as a basis, the self is formed in social interaction by the internalizing of various self-attitudes from the others with whom one comes in contact or of whom one is somehow aware. In fact, for research purposes the self may be conceptualized as a more or less stable set of attitudes about one's own identity. Since attitudes, in Kuhn's view, are tendencies to act, the self-as-attitudes argument leads to the conclusion that if we knew in sufficient depth the actual identity of a person as he knows himself, then we might have at hand adequate information to both explain his activities and predict some future action. If we could not actually predict in the individual case, then at least some tendencies or proclivities could be made clear, some alternatives eliminated. Furthermore, Kuhn has discovered that Mead's statements concerning the self are not wholly consistent and are in some ways ambiguous. The I–me problem is of interest here. While the I plays a theoretical part in the analysis of conduct, it seems that the me is actually the internalized attitudes of others which give action its shape and direction, its social coherence. Therefore, if the question simply is, 'How do we conceptualize the self for research purposes?' then the self as a set of attitudes is the answer – the me. Kuhn has argued both that the self ought to be conceptualized as a set of attitudes, for reasons of clarity, and that the others from whom the self-attitudes are derived have had less research than their importance calls for. His own work has followed up these points.

Kuhn faces the question of the subjectivity of the self by asking people for their attitudes toward themselves. This is an objective attempt to discover subjective identity. Kuhn's Twenty Statements Test (TST) was developed for this purpose. Fundamentally, the TST is simplicity itself.

[46] See M. Kuhn and T. McPortland, 'An Empirical Investigation of Self-Attitudes', *American Sociological Review*, xix, 1 (February 1954), pp. 68-76.

Kuhn gives people a paper with twenty numbered blanks on it and asks them to quickly write down their responses to the question, 'Who am I?' as if the responses were to one's self and not to an impersonal research worker. It is the analysis of the results of this exercise that makes the TST of interest to symbolic interactionists.

In a series of papers based on the TST, Kuhn reports that he first found the results of his test readily divided into answers which were either 'consensual' or 'sub-consensual'. The consensual category includes all those items of identification which are obvious to others, or which could be obvious. Things like religious membership, sex, class member-ship, and so forth, are in this category. In the sub-consensual category are those items of identification which we might think are more 'private', such as happiness or sadness, optimism or pessimism, and the like. Later, Kuhn reported that further studies with the TST put salient self-attitudes into five categories: social group and classifications, ideology and belief, interests, ambitions, self-evaluations. Note that the basic dichotomy of consensual and sub-consensual still remains.

As a confirmation of Mead's basic idea, Kuhn found some interesting things. One was that, in making the twenty statements, most people thought of the consensual identifications of themselves first, and only later went into their more private (perhaps less communally validated) world to identify themselves with sub-consensual statements. This is readily interpreted. Since supposedly people gain their self-identification through contact with others, and since the theory of the me says that self-attitudes are a product of what other people think of us, the self-atti-tudes of most importance to us will be consensual ones. These are the attitudes other people most influence by their evaluations of individuals and which are gained in associations, groups, and the like. Kuhn calls this tendency to think of some self-attitudes first and rapidly the *salience factor*. Salience refers to readiness to identify one's self. The more quickly an identifying attitude comes to mind, the more salient.

So far, so good. Most sociologists following Mead would have pre-dicted this. Interactionist theory tends to suggest that all persons in all situations gain their self-attitudes in this way. However, Kuhn has dem-onstrated (and this is the importance of this research) that not all people think of the consensual category of self-identification first, and that people vary a great deal in this depending on their age, sex, amount of schooling or training, degree of involvement with groups, and so forth. Furthermore, with a standard tool like the TST, the degree to which people vary from each other can be gauged and correlated with their other characteristics. Kuhn interprets these variations more or less in line with the interactionists' general theoretical perspective.

For example, simply by measuring religious salience by noting how high on the list people make religious references about themselves, and how often they make them, Kuhn has shown that persons having 'stand-ard' religious affiliations (Roman Catholics and members of established Protestant churches) have a lower religious salience in their self-identifi-cation than those of more sectarian faiths, and all these have higher reli-gious salience in their self-identification than do nonbelievers. Another interesting finding is that sex identity apparently increases with age, up at least to middle age. At any age, females identify more by sex and by kin-ship relations than do males of the same age, and females identify less by race than do males. As one would expect, occupational identification varies directly with years of involvement with the work.

These findings with the TST are important in understanding symbolic interactionism because they clarify an area left relatively untouched by the theory in its original state. Taken alone, the findings might be trivial. We do not really care, theoretically speaking, if Protestants or Catholics identify more by religion than do Jews. The theoretical importance of this lies in the qualification it places on the theory of the self. The Meadian hypothesis about self-acquisition is that one takes his cues from others by taking the role of 'other' to the extent of finally coming to an understanding of the 'generalized other'. Kuhn's work has forced a quali-fication of this. Where there is great heterogeneity, selective factors enter into self-identification which are predictable by other sociological factors such as age, sex, religion, nationality. This is something that symbolic interactionism, in its enthusiasm for the individual and his uniqueness in situations, has tended to undervalue. Similarly, it has tended to ignore institutions, social class, and religion. Kuhn's simple demonstration that factors like these might have considerable influence on the development of self has re-emphasized the value of more standard sociological think-ing. It has elevated the concept of structured social relations, but within the context of symbolic interactionism. Yet, as Blumer would say, the subtleties are missed in Kuhn's work. Surely it is not possible for Kuhn with twenty statements to conclude that he 'knows' a person to the extent some other interactionist, using other techniques, would say that he knew him. But here is where the arguments between the objectivists and the subjectivists in symbolic interactionist research miss each other. Kuhn is trying to give a theoretical description of the self as self-attitudes and describe the relatedness of these to sociological factors. Most other inter-actionists are researching relationships and the formation of them. The focus of Kuhn's work is on the self directly, while for most other interac-tionists the focus is on the uniqueness of the relationship and less directly on the self as a determinate entity.

VI. *Conclusion and criticism*

In appraising symbolic interactionism in sociology it is necessary to recall again that this is a perspective and not, strictly speaking, a theory. While individuals might make stronger claims for symbolic interactionism than it can actually sustain, being fair to the interactionists entails at the outset the recognition that their theoretical efforts are not usually toward the standard aims of scientific explanation and prediction. Parsons claimed in mid-career as a theorist that his work was actually preliminary to the building of real theory; Homans has claimed rigorous deductive theorizing for the exchange theory principle. But the interactionists still basically eschew scientism in sociology, opting instead for more interpretive forms.

Nevertheless some criticisms of the interactionist tradition may be offered which do not ignore the interactionists' real intentions. To begin, we should go back to Mead, particularly to his concept of language, since it is language more than anything else which unifies interactionists' work. An adequate account of language should stand behind any derivations from Mead. But it is curious to note that most modern interactionist literature does not really pay close attention to what Mead said about language. Normally, the point simply is made that language is important, and that people use it to adjust their activities. There is usually no more inquiry into basic principles than that.

Mead's concept of language is indeed behavioristic in tone and intent. Linguistic expression is the causing of a symbol to represent action and the consequences of action. Today, we might call this the 'sign' function of gestures – that a verbal gesture is the sign of a certain kind of event in certain circumstances. But what is intended by most modern interactionists is not this at all. They usually mean far more interesting things than Mead's theory of language could account for. How does one know, for example, that a situation is like another? If this is requisite knowledge for the use of a given gesture to represent given actions and consequences, then some principle of transference or generality of gestures should be found in the account of language. Mead attempted to answer this problem by pointing out that perception is selective, and that signifying is a selective process; but of course the unanswered question is, 'On what principles or from what basis does this selection occur?' Mead's work leaves this question unanswered.

A more serious problem with the Meadian view of language centers on the question of novelty in language, and the related question of language structure. Mead's treatment of language is so behavioristic as to closely associate given actions with given gestures. But it is surely true that most people have never heard the sentences they utter every day. The sentences are new and will probably never be said in exactly the same form again. Similarly, situations are new, even if similar to older situations. The deeper point here is that Mead gives no suggestion of how hearers of language could divine the significance of gestures when the hearers' understandings have been built up in dissimilar situations, with other people. Add to this the fact that the language being spoken is not likely to have been heard in the same way ever before, and the Meadian view of language starts to look quite inadequate.

Criticisms like these lead up to a basic point that modern linguists would make at the outset: language is a structured way of communicating. Mead's rendition of how language comes to exist and how it works provides an explanation of how actual words might become attached to actual conduct, but he suggests nothing of how strings of these utterances can convey thoughts across situations, across time, and between people who manipulate words in infinitely various ways. It is indeed the structure of language that allows this to happen. Everyone knows that a child who is completely innocent of the rules of grammar can speak sentences in his native language which are formed more or less correctly. He will say, 'Ginger is a horse standing in the field.' He would never say, 'Horse standing is field Ginger a in the'. The same words are used in both 'sentences'. What that child knows is both the words to express his observation and the grammatical rules for the formation of an adequate English sentence. The real significance of communication by way of language is in the determinant structured usage of utterance. Mead's concept of language does not account for this.

Also missing from Mead's concept of language is an account of purely abstract terms and usages. Mead's overriding concern to link gestures to action caused him to neglect important classes of terms that do not refer to action at all. Purely abstract concepts such as 'beauty' or 'justice' have no concrete referents. One can say, 'That canary is beautiful', and the term 'beautiful' is not used in the same sense that a concrete term might be, such as in, 'That canary is yellow.' The difference is that 'beautiful' refers to an abstract quality not residing in a category of concrete things. As anyone knows who follows theatre, film, or music, concepts like 'beauty' are far from being concretely applicable with precision, accuracy, and decisiveness. Language conveys more pure abstraction than most people realize, and a firmly behavioristic account of it can hardly serve as a characterization of everyday speech.

Another question related to Mead's rendition of language is the paradoxical relationship between the individual and the ongoing group. It is true that Mead did not wish to spend time on such questions, but it may not be idle to ask how the individual comes to play so small a part in developing the meanings of gestures, and how the group, made up of individuals, has the power to generate language and implant it into the group's new members. Locating this power of linguistic formation with the abstract group, while not conceiving individual members as more significant in this regard, remains a problem. Lest it be argued that Mead did not mean this, recall his insistence that the self's reflection coming from other people in the community, making up internalized me's, was the necessary requirement for group participation and presumably the existence of the group in the first place. Particularly if the I is neglected, as it tends to be in some interactionist work, this makes the person a bundle of me's constructed by his group, and very little more. The group becomes exterior and logically prior. A kind of crude sociologistic fallacy is the result, in which the individual is smothered in group determination. In fact, it was probably Mead's intention to enhance the place of individualism in theoretical thinking, but here emphasizing group importance as a means of explaining individualism leads to paradox.

More generally, we can note again that interactionism consistently fails to give an account of social structure. Rather, it usually takes structured normative relations as given parameters from which to begin, as Davis does in his discussion of deviance disavowal. What Davis says is that persons use the norms to their advantage as best they can. But should the sociologists not also wish to know why there are these norms? Saying that they are simply agreements among people who have worked out livable relationships flies in the face of the fact that, among many, normative rules are a direct constraint, and that, among many others, an extreme feeling of powerlessness and alienation toward normative order exists. It may be true that, given prior normative order, people work out modes of coping; but this does not amount to a full-fledged account of social structure – rather, it assumes social structure as a prior condition of coping.

This leads directly to the question of motivation, especially since Miyamoto has given a symbolic interactionist account of motivation, suggesting that group requirements are at work which have heretofore been neglected by the interactionists. We would wish to know why people consistently choose to act in given ways in certain situations, instead of in all the other ways they might possibly have acted. The reasoning drawn from Mead is that the community standpoint is taken into account, and the person acts to fit in. But why wish to do that? Miyamoto's answer is that successful activity in a given role, given task, or given self-identification depends upon the individual's making decisions about how to act which maximize his effectiveness in these activities. Miyamoto wishes to cast this in terms of group approval, but how far is this from saying more abstractly that expectations are laid down by others because they wish to have the task performed? This is close to saying that acceptance is contingent on proper performance. And this is very close to saying people require certain activities because they are crucial, either to existence or to well-ordered social affairs in the community. If this is what Miyamoto implies, then he is saying that the question of fitting in with the wishes of the group is in reality a matter of defining the individual's place according to some criterion set abstractly by the group itself. Indeed, this takes the question of how to account for motivation out of the hands of individuals and places it at the group level where activity, efficiency, survival, orderliness, or some other structured criterion is the basis for decisions on motivation. This takes symbolic interactionism a long way toward recognizing its relatedness to structural theory, rather than enhancing its view of itself as an alternative to such thinking.

There is also the possibility that symbolic interactionism, as advocated by Blumer, runs the risk of removing all specific subject matter from sociology. This is an old question which has gone out of fashion. When sociology was establishing itself, debates were sometimes held on what unique subject matter sociology could rightfully claim which was not history, political theory, philosophy, and the like. Blumer's position on the nature of sociological research, and on sociology as a collection of sensitizing concepts, makes this question relevant again. If sociology is simply another language in which to talk about social intercourse, and 'doing sociology' is simply the mastering of that language as a way of describing observations, then in fact there is no particular subject matter – such as social structures – for sociology to claim. Sociology would then face the question of whether or not its insights compare in quality and resolving power with those of other disciplines.

On the positive side, it is clearly true that some of the most fascinating sociology is in the symbolic interactionist tradition. People are probably naturally interested in themselves, and an elucidation of how one's self is of crucial significance in society is bound to be interesting when the story is told with flair and a modicum of human insight. This quality is almost completely the province of the interactionists. Sometimes it is said sociology's studies and findings are trivial. Indeed some may be, and when they are dull as well, the effect can be devastating. But the interactionists have a knack for seeking out and elucidating relationships of theoretical importance which can be of practical interest, too. An example of this is the work on professionalization of medical students done by Becker. Here is a study which to some extent unmasks the high professionalism of the medical profession, and which is informative about how doctors come to regard their patients, how they judge the importance of cases, how they come to differ from other people in attitudes toward disease, suffering, intimate exposure, and so forth.

Is there no sense, then, in which symbolic interactionism can be said to 'explain' social life? It does not do it very successfully by rigorous deductive methods, or by establishing covering laws and yielding hypotheses. Yet as a method of making one understand by telling a tale in terms of a perspective on human affairs, and all the while asserting that its perspective is really 'the way it is', interactionism achieves a 'soft' explanatory style which is valuable to sociology in its own way.

KEY CONCEPTS

perspective
self
other
pragmatism
mind
society
role-playing
role-talking
language
significant gesture
TST

play stage
game stage
social conduct
me
I
parallelism
variable analysis
perceptual settings
sensitizing concept
salience factor
reference group

TOPICS FOR DISCUSSION

1   Debate the various merits of the positions on symbolic interactionist research taken by Blumer and Kuhn.
2   In what ways did the pragmatists reject metaphysics in their attempts to understand the mind? What had this line of thought to do with behavioral psychology?
3   Answer the question, 'Who am I?' in twenty statements and then compare answers to see if consensual or sub-consensual statements appeared first in most cases. What is the significance of your findings?
4   Think through the process of self-acquisition and then discuss the necessary sequence of events leading to significant self-change.
5   Describe the theoretical reasons why motivation is said to be weakly explained in symbolic interactionist theory.
6   What are the main features of a perspective in sociology, and why is this term applied to symbolic interactionism?

ESSAY QUESTIONS

What is the controversy about determinacy of self-attitudes? Discuss the debate and come to conclusions about which side of the dilemma seems correct.

How does the research work by Kuhn and others with the TST help show the relationship between symbolic interactionist explanation and more traditional structuralist sociology?

How is the idea of minded behavior different from the idea of mind?

What questions would you have asked if you were doing Davis' research on visibly handicapped people? How would these have improved the result?

Discuss role-taking and role-playing by showing the differences in theoretical meaning between the two ideas.

Why does the I only enter consciousness as a memory? Discuss the
theory of the I and suggest, if possible, ways of doing research on
the concept.

FOR FURTHER READING AND STUDY

Becker, Howard (ed.). *The Other Side: Perspectives on Deviance*. New
York: Free Press, 1964.

Blumer, Herbert. *Symbolic Interactionism: Perspective and Method*. Englewood Cliffs, N.J.: Prentice-Hall, 1969.

Cooley, Charles H. *Human Nature and the Social Order*. New York:
Schocken Books, 1962.

Goffman, Erving. *The Presentation of Self in Everyday Life*. New York:
Doubleday, 1959.

Huber, Joan. 'Symbolic Interaction as a Pragmatic Perspective: The Bias of
Emergent Theory', *American Sociological Review*, XXXVIII (April 1973)
pp. 274-84.

Kuhn, Manfred. 'Major Trends in Symbolic Interactionism in the Past Twenty-Five Years', *Sociological Quarterly*, v, 1 (Winter 1964), pp. 61-84.

Lindesmith, Alfred R. and Anselm L. Straus, *Social Psychology*. 3rd ed. New
York: Holt, Rinehart and Winston, 1968.

Manis, James and Bernard Meltzer (eds.) *Symbolic Interaction: A Reader
in Social Psychology*. 2nd ed. Boston: Allyn and Bacon, 1972.

McCall, George and J. L. Simmons. *Identities and Interactions*. New York:
Free Press, 1966.

Mead, George H. *Mind, Self and Society*. Ed. Charles Morris. Chicago: University of Chicago Press, 1934.
    The Philosophy of the Act. Ed. Charles Morris. Chicago: University of
Chicago Press, 1938.

Miyamoto, S. Frank. 'Self, Motivation and Symbolic Interaction Theory', in
Tomatsu Shibutani (ed.), *Human Nature and Collective Behavior:
Papers in Honor of Herbert Blumer*. Englewood Cliffs, N.J.: Prentice-
Hall, 1970.

Shibutani, Tomatsu (ed.). *Human Nature and Collective Behavior: Papers in
Honor of Herbert Blumer*. Englewood Cliffs, N.J.: Prentice-Hall, 1970.

Stone, Gregory and Harold Faberman (eds.). *Social Psychology through
Symbolic Interaction*. Lexington, Mass.: Xerox College Publishing,
1970.

7 Formalization; theory construction; ethnomethodology

I. *Introduction*

Sociological theories are rather complicated bodies of ideas, held together by a mixture of logic, rhetoric, journalism, and a few data. It is no use to suggest otherwise; sociological theory at present does not exhibit the clarity, precision, or exactitude many would hope for. Even in the forms presented in preceding chapters, where some effort was made to systematize main features, it can be seen that there are many murky areas yet to be clarified in each of the three main theories in modern sociology. Criticism is the primary engine of forward movement in the field of sociological theory. Essentially, in this context, criticism means making things clear and exposing weaknesses.

But there are several ways to 'make things clear'. Basically, a rather ancient tradition has been followed in this book which holds that sound knowledge is had by scholarly consideration of an idea, and that the procedure for this work must be left for the scholar to decide. Native wit, basic intelligence, and a general knowledge of the issues have been sufficient to produce good critical work in most fields of the arts and humanities for some time past. However, sociology is only part art. It is also a science, at least in mental atmosphere and inspiration. This is the weakest possible claim for it as a science. It is said by some to be much more of a science. And sciences do not work very well on the critical principles appropriate to the arts and the humanities. Science is more precise, its goals are more clearly defined, it is not held back by philosophical debate or by questions having no empirical importance. It requires clarity of thinking in the extreme, and it is radically intolerant of ideas with an ideological or an emotional basis. Hoping to bring sociological theory into line with this kind of definition of science, some modern sociologists have opened up new approaches and new methods of theoretical work. Partly resulting from interest in the philosophy of science applied to sociology, two separate but related movements in modern sociological theory and criticism have emerged. The penetrating, sometimes arid expositions of logicians and the cutting analysis of philosophical criticism have made sociologists and others wonder how sociological theories would stand up to the bright lights that logic and philosophy could shine.

II. *Formalization of theories*

One of the annoying facts about the way large theories are usually written is that their authors follow no particular plan. They have a vision of things, a notion of how the world is, and they sit down and write it out. This may take years, of course, but often the approach to presentation is no more systematic than this, and of course it is influenced by completely irrelevant facts of the author's career, his changing insights, and the like. Similarly, when 'schools of theory' develop, which may have several major contributors, each having slightly different emphasis, each making unique contributions, what the theory actually does say can become distressingly vague. At this point, terms such as 'functionalism according to Parsons' and 'exchange according to Blau' emerge which amount to a way of admitting that there is obviously some general relationship between the particular author and the school of theory, but that the precise nature of the relationship is complicated and somewhat obscure.

A. *Objectives of formalization*

Efforts to formalize theories have been directed at warrens like this to untangle the mess.[1] Formalizations are not themselves theories. Formalizations are operations performed on an existing theory in order to see what the theory actually does say. The formalizer usually wishes to make certain standard things clear. Of particular interest is the distinction between (1) statements in the theory which define the concepts and the field of study; and (2) statements which are empirical propositions. Consider the following example: 'Man was born free and is everywhere in chains.' Obviously Rousseau was not speaking literally when he wrote this in *The Social Contract*, but how was he speaking? Does he mean to define social order as being bondage, or does he mean this as a kind of empirical generalization, in which he asserts that bondage has become a concrete fact, like the weather? Commentators on Rousseau might give several answers; the point remains that if Rousseau means his statement to be a definition of the nature of social order, then it would be impossible for him to offer anything to the contrary as an empirical statement, since by definition bondage characterizes human society. However, if Rousseau intends to prove to us that bondage is empirically the case, then he should give supporting evidence for this view, showing bondage

---

[1] For example, see Ernest Nagel, 'A Formalization of Functionalism', in Nagel, *Logic without Metaphysics* (New York: Free Press, 1956), pp. 247-83.

in various manifestations, degrees, and so forth. Rousseau apparently means both at once, which makes the problem even worse.

Modern sociological formalizations face a similar problem in trying to determine what kind of explanation a theory actually gives. In Chapter 4, we saw that Homans made perfectly clear what kind of explanation he meant to give, and for this reason his theory seemed simple to understand. But it is not always clear, especially if functionalism is involved, whether the explanation is intended to be some variant of the causal type, teleological, or what. Consider the case of the 'self-fulfilling prophecy': if a thing is true in the mind of the actor, it is true in its consequences. Are we to take it from this that the acceptance of a prophecy in the mind of a person causes some succeeding event to occur? Is it that the actor, being under some impression, looks for something to happen and finds it? Or is the consequent action to be expected for other reasons, and the self-fulfilling prophecy simply irrelevant?

In addition to determining the kind of explanation in use, there is often a question as to what the author wants us to take as evidence for his assertions. Another way of saying this is that the methodology implied by the theory and the criteria for verification are either not explicitly stated, or are ambiguous, or both. Symbolic interactionism sins consistently in this department. Admittedly, it does not often try to explain rigorously, but it does make statements which are meant to be empirical. We would wish to have systematically explained why the empirical statements an interactionist chooses are the ones which elucidate the phenomenon under discussion. Criteria for doing this should come directly from unambiguous empirical generalizations contained in a theory. But symbolic interactionism offers no such assistance, and hence the interactionist is entreating us to believe two things:

1   that what he says is empirically true, and
2   that the explanations he gives are necessary and sufficient to account for the thing's being true.

Ordinarily, symbolic interactionist research provides neither the criteria nor the logical derivations from symbolic interactionist theory.

No theory is supposed to hold under all conditions, in all times and places. 'General' theory is rather comprehensive in scope, but even it has its limitations. For example, the functionalist theory of social stratification would not be expected to hold in the face of legal constraints setting the remuneration for jobs; the theory relies on a mechanism we call supply and demand. Usually it is not clear from theoretical statements exactly what the conditions are under which theory is supposed to hold. One might naïvely suppose that all conditions are covered by theoretical statements. But this is obviously not true; theoretical predictions of outcomes are sometimes wrong. If a prediction is wrong, do we say that the theory is defective, or that some unexpected condition intervened? If it is an unexpected condition, exactly what conditions were expected when the theory was invoked? If it is not possible to answer questions of this kind, then the theory is ambiguous with respect to the conditions under which it holds. Formalizations of theories attempt to clarify such issues.

Depending on the main objective of the formalization, various types of formal theory can be achieved. Berger *et al.* have noted that formalizations fall principally into three types.[2] First, the *explicational* formalization is intended to expose the central working concepts in a theory, and to relate similar concepts together, even though these may go by different names. Second, the *representational* formalization is intended to fully, abstractly, and clearly represent a range of theoretical ideas, observations, or both, resulting in a coherent pattern. Finally, the *theoretical-construct* type of formalization relies almost completely on systematizing abstract concepts in various explanatory systems in order to form a more inclusive theoretical statement about some phenomenon.

B. *Benefits of formalizations of theories*

In addition to clearing up problems of scope, conditions, and theoretical form, formalizations have other benefits. They can be used to pare down the sometimes considerable amount of verbiage in a theory, and they may produce the most parsimonious statement of the theory possible. Simple theory is always preferred to complex theory, if the explanations are of equal power, since the addition of complicating factors can have no purpose. If a simple theory works as well as a complex one, the general procedure is to choose the simple.

Sometimes sociological theory disguises explanations under a heavy cover of complication. It is then the job of the formalizer to expose the actual explanation by stripping off the extra increment of argumentation. If the resulting explanation is not really very simple by absolute standards, this cannot be helped. The important point is that, after formalization, the theory should be as simple and clear as it is possible to make it. In fact, the simplest good theory of social order may be very complicated indeed, but there is no use making it more so by unsystematic statement or ambiguity. Formalization of theories can provide the parsimony required.

A theory may appear to explain more than it actually does because its limitations are not obvious. Also, if various definitions of its subject matter are allowed to coexist, it is not always clear how the knowledge gained by use of the theory is to be cumulative. Formalization procedures that firm up definitions, clarify the conditions under which a theory holds, and remove ambiguity of various kinds can result in exposing gaps in the theory. There may be situations about which the theory is silent,

2 J. Berger, Morris Belditch, and Bo Anderson, *Types of Formalization in Small-group Research* (Boston: Houghton Mifflin, 1962).

for example, or points at which the theory gives two or more conflicting arguments. The exposure of things like this leads toward strengthening the theory.

The logic by which a theory proceeds is not always obvious. If we know that a theory makes some assertion, and draws a derivation from this assertion, the immediate question is, how does the derivation follow from the assertion? Amazingly, it is sometimes the case that the derivation does not follow in any standard logical way. In fact, some contrary assertion might follow better. This problem is complicated considerably when theories rely on analogies as mechanisms of explanation. The question always is, does the process implied by the analogy actually suit the social case being investigated? Is the analogy taken far enough to show what derivations are really implied by it? In formalizing theory, questions of this kind are always confronted.

C. *Formalization procedures*

Recent books and articles on formalization of sociological theory are generally in agreement on the benefits of formalizations, but differ on the way to proceed. Nevertheless, some basic rules can be laid down.

1. *Definitions*

It is particularly important to know exactly what is being theorized about. Hence, the most important definition in any theory is the statement of the subject matter. Since this definition is usually repeated several times in many contexts, and often not in the same words, the explication of the exact subject matter is really the first job. In addition, any theory will have several other key terms which are used in various places to describe or explain. These key terms are the subject of definitional studies. Usually a theory contains its own universe of discourse, at least in part, in which some terms are defined by others exclusively used in the theory. The problem here is to develop definitions to distinguish among the actual referents. Also, a term may have a partial referent to the empirical world and a partial referent to the theory itself. When this is the case, the formalizer will probably label the various meanings of terms to keep the senses distinct. For example, the term 'role' sometimes means a performance, and sometimes a particular relationship. These two senses of the term, if they appeared together in a theory, might be called Role-I and Role-II.

2. *Statements*

A theory consists of statements, some of which pertain to how we are to understand the theory *per se,* and some of which pertain to how we are to understand the world in the light of the theory. Usage on this point varies, but it might be acceptable to call the first kind of statement *analytic* because the subject of such a statement is not empirical but theoretical and internal to the theory itself. For a Parsonian to say that the cultural system and the personality system both have interfaces with the social system is to give an analytic statement, since he is describing how his theory works, and not at the moment telling what he expects empirically as a consequence of this.

The second kind of statement might be labeled *synthetic*, since its referent is the empirical world. The most easily understood synthetic statement is an assertion of empirical truth – something like 'The birth rate in Canada dropped last year by one half per thousand.' It is not, as it stands, a matter of theory that the birth rate behaved in this way. Yet this statement could enter a theory, while keeping its synthetic character.

Of particular interest are axioms and postulates. An *axiom* is a statement of the relatedness of two or more theoretical ideas or theoretical constructs. For instance, Durkheim's argument to the effect that the degree of normative consensus is related to the degree of division of labor is axiomatic. This relationship could be stated in one sentence, the subject of which would be theoretical terms themselves (normative consensus, division of labor). This would be an axiomatic statement because it is not there to be proven; rather, it is there as a starting point from which to think about interesting derivations. For example, what happens to normative consensus when the degree of division of labor changes?

Postulates are a kind of statement of a supposition about something that is empirically verifiable, at least in principle.[3] If it is axiomatic that normative consensus and division of labor are related in a given way, then postulate that division of labor is becoming exaggerated: what will be the theoretical prediction? In this question the two conceptual starting points (division of labor and normative consensus) were given, and then a postulate was added to the effect that some change was occurring. The postulate was the addition of something to the statement of original concepts by which it was possible to make a derivation from theoretical first principles. Several different postulates, and their justification on theoretical and empirical grounds, usually are found in theoretical works. Sorting out which statements are meant to serve in which capacity is of particular importance.

Now, the strange fact is that formalizations have been a great help in

---

[3] Gibbs says that there is conventionally no difference in usage between 'axiom' and 'postulate'. The difference is sometimes obscure. But keeping in mind that axioms are statements one starts with, and postulates are statements one adds in order to begin a deductive series helps to keep the two straight. See Jack Gibbs, *Sociological Theory Construction* (Hinsdale, Ill.: Dryden Press, 1972), p. 175.

making clear what theories say, but there is no agreement on how to reach the proper decisions when formalizing a theory. This is to say, while we may know what we want a theory to look like, it is not easy to give a set of rules by which we can make the formalization produce the desired result. Formalizers of theory have necessarily relied on their training in logic, their diverse knowledge of their field, and their insight to produce impressive formalizations. It is important to grasp that, depending on the complexity of the theory under study, the formalization might be either very simple or very complicated. Also note that formalizations are not always intended to explain what a particular theorist 'meant' by his work. In fact, the formalization often turns up things the theorist seems to have said either by implication or without knowing it. These derivations are another of the bases of criticizing and assessing theory.

III. *Theory construction*

Theory construction is related to theory formalization, but in construction the line of argument is just the reverse of formalizations. Whereas formalization starts from finished theory and works toward basic principles, theory construction starts from such principles and ends with finished theory. Theory construction is an attempt to rigorously develop theory according to some defensible plan, based on an understanding of axioms and postulates, the difference between synthetic and analytic statements, the divorce of definition from evidence, and the like. Theory construction as a special effort is aimed at making theoretical statements which have clear and logical antecedents and which imply an unambiguous methodological principle for empirical testing.[4]

In general, the techniques of theory construction have been applied by sociologists who are particularly sensitive to questions of methodology and scientific procedure. They are usually interested in developing theory to cover concrete problems which are often smaller than those attacked by general theorists. Hence, most theory-construction literature is organized around finding theoretical accounts for interesting data, working these accounts in with more general theoretical statements.[5] But never would a sociologist set out to build a theory of the scale, say, of Parsons', by using theory-construction techniques.

Theory construction and formalizations are most closely related in the beginning of the construction exercise. It is required that the constructor

---

[4] For example, see Gibbs, *Sociological Theory Construction*; Arthur L. Stinchcombe, *Constructing Social Theories* (New York: Harcourt Brace Jovanovich, 1968); Nicholas C. Mullins, *The Art of Theory: Construction and Use* (New York: Harper and Row, 1971); Paul D. Reynolds, *A Primer in Theory Construction* (Indianapolis: Bobbs-Merrill, 1971).

[5] Theory construction is often applied to smaller-scale theories, rather than 'grand theory'.

of a theory have at his disposal theoretical statements which bear on his problem. These must be parsimonious and in unambiguous form. In other words, a formalized rendition of existing theory is a first requirement for the further construction of sociological theories. The theory constructionist is not so much interested in making up wholly new theory as he is in finding out new combinations of theoretical statements which might lead to new explanations. Where new statements are required, the constructionist usually takes an inductive approach by generalizing from research findings, tentatively proposing these findings as general principles.

It is useful to watch these developments occur. If one theory suggests that A and B are related in some determinate way and if another theory suggests C and D have a characteristic relationship, this might become obvious in the process of formalizing. Evidence might turn up which suggests that B and C are related as well. Now, with the addition of this datum, the constructionist can create statements to theorize a relationship among A, B, C, and D on the basis of two theories and some datum. Note that the hypothesis leading to this new datum did not necessarily come from either theory. It might have been fortuitous circumstances which led to such a discovery.

It should be obvious that, to construct a theory, the constructionist should have some idea what type of theory he is creating. This has been a problem. As you know from preceding chapters, sociological theories not only say different things, but they say them in different forms. Theories may appear in deductive, hypothetical format, as internally logical patterns which are abstract analogies to social reality, and as perspectives which loosely define the social world in a given way and suggest an interpretive scheme for understanding it. Now, the theory constructionist must make some preliminary decisions about what he would like in the way of theory format. Most often in recent sociological literature, the decision has been in favor of the hypothetico-deductive form. In writing *Social Behavior*[6] Homans was engaged in theory construction, as he was trying to draw up a logically related set of definitions and propositions to explain a wide range of social action. Similarly, Miyamoto was doing theory construction when he combined certain aspects of symbolic interaction theory with some ideas from Parsonian work to arrive at an account of motivation in interactionist terms.[7] In Homans' case, the result was quite deductive and propositional; in Miyamoto's, it was not. One must not be led to think that theory construction is only done by those who engage in discussions of axioms, propositions, and the like. Although all theory can be rendered in those kinds of terms, there are several other ways of approaching the theory-construction problem.

[6] New York: Harcourt Brace Jovanovich, 1974, rev. ed.
[7] See above, Ch. 6, pp. 232-4.

A. *Concept formation*

Theory construction differs most from theory formalization in that constructionists engage more in *concept formation*. We may formalize or otherwise manipulate what has already been conceptualized, but there can be no formalization of concepts that are not already made. A concept is a name of a class of events or class of ideas. Concepts may be concretely relevant to observations or they may be completely abstract; of particular interest here are the former. But how concrete is the most concrete of concepts? Here lies a problem for the theory constructionist. Consider an example similar to one used by Gross.[8] A boy, Chris, is observed to take an apple from a grocery counter in a shop when the grocer has his back turned. This is the observation. How should we conceptualize this, especially if our objective is to explain the act, or acts of this kind? It is tempting to call the act 'theft' and Chris a 'thief'. Taking things against the will of the owner without due payment is theft. 'Theft' is a class name for a type of act which seems to include Chris' act; but note that 'theft' usually connotes other things as well – bad character, lack of moral self-control, or deficient socialization.

'Thief' is usually the concept used to describe people who take things against the owner's will. But normally, if Chris were a good boy of sound character, and from a good home, he would not be called a thief by most people, and most judges would let him off with a light reprimand. Of concern here is how to conceptualize an observation. We now have a case of Chris, who actually did take the apple, but who is in no other way similar to more ordinary thieves. Should the theory construction be carried on upon the ground that Chris is a thief because he took the apple, and the event be explained by theory designed to account for the activities of hardened criminals? Or perhaps, even though everyone knows that Chris took the apple, this observation will be disregarded and he will not be classed as thief. His activities will be explained in some other way. To what activities, done by whom, does the concept apply? What precisely are the defining characteristics of an activity, and by what criteria are activities allocated to conceptual categories? These are abstract considerations that interfere with placing crude observations directly into categories and calling them concepts. The boundaries around categories of action are fuzzy. What activities go in is not entirely a matter of pure observation. Theory construction, insofar as it establishes concepts as names of categories of activities, addresses the question of the boundary of these categories and draws up answers consistent with previous practice and theoretical clarity.

[8] Llewellyn Gross, 'Note on Selected Problems in Theory Construction', in L. Gross, ed., *Sociological Theory: Inquiries and Paradigms* (New York: Harper and Row, 1967), pp. 254-64.

B. *Linking concepts*

When a satisfactory concept is formed, it is linked to others in determinant statements. Suppose a satisfactory concept of theft has been formed, and it is proposed that thieves associate together frequently in a mental atmosphere in which theft is approved. Immediately, the precise idea of what 'associate' means becomes important, since these associations might form the basis of theories about how persons learn to steal. Hence observations of people's associations will be called for, and many problems of how to class these observations will arise. But if these problems are overcome, a tentative statement about the relationship between the concept class 'theft' and the concept 'association' could be made. And after this, the natural question would be, why is this particular pattern of relationship the case?

C. *Adding theoretical statements*

In answering the question 'why?' the theory constructionist might use constructs such as 'influence' (as in 'associations influence actions'). Since we do not observe influence, but only believe we see manifestations of it, a statement which answers the question 'why?' can be said to exist at a different abstract level from the statement about thieves and associations. This additional level answers a question about the statement linking 'theft' and 'association'. When different levels of abstraction are introduced, an acceptable route between levels must be established; logic holds the levels together. If we logically expect influence to explain the effect of associations on thieves, then the concept of influence must contain something in common with the concept of association. We might expect influence to be great under conditions of considerable associations and small among members who do not associate very much and zero when there is no association.

So far, we have a two-level theory containing two observational terms and one theoretical term. The concept of influence, the theoretical term in this example, has been cast in such a way as to be variable. Working in concrete cases of associations, it can run between zero and some maximum level. We should then be able to derive the hypothesis that, where criminal influence is great, thieves will be more prevalent than where criminal influence is zero. This influence is thought to work through the medium of group association – something we observed. We observed the association, not the influence. Hence, from an observation or two, a theoretical concept, and the logic of how one idea follows from another, we have built up a primitive theory of one class of behavior.

This simple example shows how complicated theory construction can be. What about other circumstances, sex differences, mass media influence, and sibling order? Or membership in other associations not conducive to theft? What about I.Q., natural temperament, or the size of the social complex in which all this happens? These, and more, require a logically adequate rendering in order to develop a more complete and more interesting theory of thievery. In principle, it could be done. To do it, the theory constructionist must pay strict attention to types and kinds of terms, clarity and precision of logical form, and details of definition. Above all, the theory constructionist wants to think straight, and his techniques keep him alert.

IV. *Ethnomethodology*

The rather ungainly term *ethnomethodology* attaches to a sociological viewpoint which has arisen in the last few years. Ethnomethodology is still in need of its definitive exposition, although Garfinkel's work is usually taken as the touchstone.[9] In the following discussion, the general theoretical ideas supporting ethnomethodology will be stressed, rather than its research procedures, although research will come into it. Various writers have stressed different aspects of the field, and the following description is gleaned from some recent works.[10]

A. *The problem of order redefined*

Ethnomethodology criticizes the standard way of tackling the problem of social order. Recall that, traditionally, the problem of order was taken in a scientific spirit. 'Order' was conceived as being 'out there'. It existed for some reasons which were its 'causes', and these causes were variously depicted by theorists. But the central point to which ethnomethodologists object is the idea that the order being observed has an existence of its own, independent of its being known or articulated by the participants. Ethnomethodologists suggest that order is attributed to situations by participants.

Let us examine this debate about the reality of order. Sociologists have felt for some time that the essence of social order was that it consisted of rule-following behaviors. How to account for social order? Account for the rules people follow, and you have an explanation of order in normative terms. What the social scientist gives in his account of rules is a description of action, from the 'outside'. The ethnomethodologist criticizes this approach for the very thing that scientists would praise: its detached and objective character. The ethnomethodologist

---

9 Harold Garfinkel, *Studies in Ethnomethodology* (Englewood Cliffs, N.J.: Prentice-Hall, 1967).
10 In particular the following are helpful: Aaron V. Cicourel, *Cognitive Sociology* (Harmondsworth, Middlesex: Penguin Books, 1973); Jack D. Douglas, ed., *Understanding Everyday Life* (Chicago: Aldine, 1970).

argues that, if the social scientist conceptualizes activity as being ordered because of rules which the participants followed, the sociologist makes an error. What in fact happens, says the ethnomethodologist, is that the participants pick up cues, discover meaning, articulate intentions, and so forth. The action is orderly because doing these things makes it possible for everyone to proceed along coherent lines of behavior. Accompanying this activity is a running line of talk, most of which indicates the acceptability of the activity to the actor and suggests that others ought to find it acceptable, too. Therefore, the main point of social research is to find out how people make it possible for each other to interact in orderly ways.

Note that this is similar to the interactionists' insistence that social order is created in interaction. Yet there are important differences between the interactionists and the ethnomethodologists. The interactionist would say that an order is created and has an existence once it is developed. The ethnomethodologist would not exactly contradict this – and here there is some difference of opinion – but he would be inclined to call social order a convenient fiction people allow each other to entertain so that mutual activity can proceed. Order is not 'out there' by virtue of any causes or processes. Rather, people come to feel that social life is ordered because their ways of describing action to themselves and others lead them to conceive of action as orderly.

An example of how appearances and behavior rules are understood and articulated will make this clear. Imagine, to take a case of research, that a receptionist in an institution has a formal rule system by which she is to refer clients to professionals whose help these persons seek.[11] We are interested in how the receptionist applies the referral rules. She does not abide by the rules at all! Rather, she understands the intent of the rule by divining the principle of organized action that the rule is supposed to facilitate, and then she actually either acts to the letter of the rule or departs from it, in order to keep orderly activity in motion.

The main point to notice is that it is not the rule which governs the action, but the intent of the rule. The rule is intended to promote orderliness. In fact, to preserve orderliness the receptionist may violate the letter of the behavior rule. Suppose too many clients come to her attention at once. Rather than taking them in rotation, according to the rule, she decides for herself which ones can be dispatched quickly and handles them first. By 'breaking' a stated behavior rule, the appearance of an orderly flow of action is maintained. The ethnomethodologists point out that only in the most rigidly formalized situations do we expect people to behave according to any rules of action. What we do expect is that they will behave in ways that conform to the intent of all the rules which we say govern the action.

11   D. Zimmerman, 'The Practicalities of Rule Use', in J. Douglas (ed.), *Understanding Everyday Life*, pp. 221-38.

B. *Talk*

The ethnomethodologist is interested in ways of articulating one's activities and feelings, to oneself and others. It is very important to get exact meanings, as far as possible, from respondents, since these descriptive sentences are really the main data of ethnomethodological work. The idea is that articulating an activity is a means of making that activity appear integrated into some on-going process which could be described by a rule of behavior. Note that it is the appearance of order that is being sought. It is sought because other people need to sense order so that they can make their activities understandable.

Here is the importance of talk in understanding how people come to view their social worlds as orderly, and how they communicate their ideas of order to others. In formulating and articulating a rule of behavior, or in discussing behavior of themselves or others, people articulate the features of action which lead to acceptable conduct in given situations. A lot of talk is needed, and actually there never is enough. People 'fill in' meanings to talk they hear by using the perspectives they share with those speaking. Garfinkel calls this the 'et cetera' practice people follow. He says that no matter how much talk passes between persons, it is never possible to completely and finally declare all the meanings that would have to pass between them for order to take place. So, each person draws on his own ideas of context, time sequence, empathy, and so forth to produce a closure in the talking. This way, the listener understands more than is actually said. The addition comes from the shared cultural context in which the talk is generated, not from the talk itself. Thus, in the example, the receptionist knew the rule, but she also knew the intent and the consequences of following or not following the rule in a given concrete case, and her activity was founded on all of this, not on the rule alone, or even the rule in particular.

Talk has a way of giving a cue to the acceptability of activities and utterances. Not what is said, but the way it is said, gives the cues. Cicourel calls these utterances 'normal forms'.[12] They allow persons to sense their environments and structure their perceptions as well as their activities. Activity that would seem perfectly normal and expected in one context would seem wildly chaotic and beyond understanding in another. It is not the activities that are ordered. Rather, the cued perceptions of activities and the judgments of appropriateness give the appearance of a socially ordered activity.

Hence, it is a sense of order, as manifested to persons acting in concrete situations, that ethnomethodologists are studying. This order is cast in the way action is described, and made to appear coherent, connected, or logical in sequence. This is not a 'discovered' order, but the manage-

---

12 Aaron V. Cicourel, 'The Acquisition of Social Structure', in J. Douglas (ed.), *Understanding Everyday Life*, pp. 136-68 (see especially pp. 147-53).

ment of affairs in a linguistic setting so that outsiders will recognize certain categories of actions as orderly. Participants are likely to describe, justify, or account for their affairs in language sounding to the outsider as if the action were rule-following in nature. By linguistically qualifying action as it goes, participants give other participants the idea that they are in action that is understandable, expectable, explicable, and ordered.

This may not strike the casual reader as particularly novel, especially in the light of symbolic interactionist theory, which sometimes sounds in secondary accounts like very much the same thing. But the difference between ethnomethodology and other social psychological ideas is that the ethnomethodologists concentrate on the procedures by which the accounting-for-action among the participants is carried out. They are not studying the rules of action, and they are not even studying the behavior *per se*. In principle, they wish to find out the ways that participants in action account for it linguistically and sublinguistically. They make no reference to norms, rules, behavior codes, moral constraint, and the like. They go into the field to look without an assumption of order. Instead, the question of a theoretical order or disorder is simply irrelevant to the point that, in practice, people make orderly situations possible by accounting for them to each other. It is the job of the ethnomethodologists to 'get inside' the contexts and meanings of these accounts, and to know from exposure what cannot be completely communicated formally, so as to understand the accounts and the associated actions. This departure from the concept of order as a theoretical assumption makes ethnomethodology something quite different from previous theory in sociology and in fact makes it something so different that it is perhaps not even theoretical in character at all. It contains theoretical ideas, of course; but as its name suggests, it holds these ideas as a minimum set of assumptions from which to select observations and understand them.

C. *Social structure*

The ethnomethodologist does not deny social structure. He recognizes it, but not in the ordinary way. Social structure becomes the enforceable conduct procedures articulated in expectations, laws, and the like. But remember, these are not the ways people really act. They are, in a fashion, pictures of the spirit in which people are expected to act, the manifest cultural ideas which accompany a community in activity. Their legitimacy comes from shared perspectives and commitment to them through action. Surrounding these social expectations and coexisting with them are actual situations. According to ethnomethodologists, persons in concrete activity are faced with a different question about how to act than other social theories suggest. Conventional theory asks the following question about the relationship between social structure and persons:

how do individuals come to know the norms, and why are they motivated to follow the rules? Ethnomethodologists ask: how do people
employ interpretive procedures to recognize the relevance of enforceable
rules in order to use them in defensible practical action? Recall the
receptionist and the clients. The receptionist was not penalized for
departing from rules when she made decisions facilitating smooth conduct. Somewhere between culturally validated rules and the actual conduct was interposed a gleaning of intent, interpretation of one's own
action, and a recognition of the rule. Out of all this, practical conduct
was fashioned.

Overlaying actual conduct is a running accounting of it in terms of
social structures – rules, expectations, motive, and so on. This account
gives the appearance of orderly rule-following activity. Cicourel has compared the function of social structure in conduct to the function of gener-
ative grammars.[13] Grammars make it possible for persons to arrange
words which could be used to express anything. The grammars are the
baseline principles which enable the speaker to order his utterances in
ways others have come to expect and which will make sense to them.
Grammars are so much a matter of everyday speech that no one thinks
about them when he talks. Similarly, the elements of social structure
which provide baseline principles people use in accounting for their
activities are so much a matter of common knowledge that they are not
normally on the conscious minds of the participants. They are 'what
everybody knows', and they are the principles relied upon implicitly
when vague, ill-formed, or incomplete sentences, or 'et cetera' usages, are
allowed to suffice in accounts of action.

D. *Research techniques*

Social structure, as the ethnomethodologist sees it, is the contextual features one relies upon when he interprets his and others' actions. We
cannot ask people directly about this, of course, since these things that
'everyone knows' are not usually consciously or articulately present in
most persons' minds. Similarly, we cannot directly ask about the
interpretive procedures people use to recognize the relevance of their
actions in situations. Two ways of finding out about both these aspects of
social life have been used by ethnomethodologists. One way is more
experimental and immediate, the second is less concerned directly with
activity and more concerned with written records and justifications of
action.

Everyday activity proceeds because of the appearances of order facili-
tated by people's verbal demonstrations. They articulate to each other
the perceived relevances of activities to some enforceable expectation so

[13] *Ibid.*

that the action in context appears orderly. One way to empirically discover what factors of situation, interpretive procedures, and contextual relevance are actually at work is to subtly disrupt ordinary activity so that the person under study is abruptly deprived of 'normality' in a situation. What does he do? He sorts through the situation to try to make sense of it to himself so that he might give some response. What does he look to in order to give the situation an appearance of coherence and orderly process? Whatever he looks to is the answer to the ethnomethodologist's question. In his information search the subject might ask questions, impugn the motives of the researcher, consult an oracle, ask for a repeat, label the researcher 'crazy', and the like. In constructing action in the artificially disrupted situation, the subject would build understandability out of the actual disorder. The construction itself would be most interesting to the ethnomethodologist, since it is this build-up of the ability to act which is the object of his study.

The student of organizations, work groups, agencies of government, and the like usually finds a large amount of written material available on rules of procedure, expected level of performance, objectives to be met, justification of the organization, policies to be followed. The ethnomethodologist would not likely take these documents at face value. He would seek a contextual understanding of them to reveal how the organization as a piece of social structure becomes a basis for interpretive judgment of action for initiated participants. Zimmerman and Pollner describe ethnomethodological study of organization as the search for the 'ways in which members employ organizational models as devices for analyzing, and making observable on particular occasions, an organization as an ensemble of coherent and unified actions'.[14]

V. *Formalizations, theory construction, and ethnomethodology as reactions to received wisdom*

Comparing the newer movements in the theoretical development of sociology, formalizations, theory construction, and ethnomethodology, it is clear that the first two are more than ever devoted to the scientific and objective mode of describing and explaining social life, while the last regards society as impenetrable by these methods and recommends instead that sociologists use the same modes of describing and analyzing society that ordinary people use in coping with it. Some of the problems unsolved in each of these areas will be pointed out below.

Formalizations of theory have often been quite impressive. They systematically lay out a theory, make what is being asserted as clear as possible, and often reveal where the conceptual muddles lie. Formalizations are a great help in research planning and interpretation, since clarity is of

---

[14] Zimmerman and M. Pollner, 'The Everyday World as a Phenomenon', in J. Douglas, ed., *Understanding Everyday Life*, p. 101.

particular importance. The formalizer is at considerable advantage over the theorist, since the strict formalization of a theory is hardly the creative effort theorizing itself is. Getting an idea and establishing it verbally is still the objective to be aimed for in theorizing.

Yet formalizations may be criticized on other grounds. By formalizing a theory, one often strips the theory of its arguments and interpretive context, making the theory appear more sterile and stark than it is. Formalizations take a point of view on what it means to 'explain' events – and this is usually the deductive format. Hence the formalizer pays particular attention to those statements in theory leading to a deductively derived conclusion. This mode of explanation is taken as the key to understanding the whole. While this accomplishes the limited objectives of formally deriving explanations, it denies that theorists theorize for a mixture of motives, and that explanation may be more than one kind of argument, pursued rigorously. Returning for a moment to the theme that sociological theory is an art form, rigorous renditions of explanations seem to take away the interesting insights that come with reading a theoretical work in simple prose. One of the accomplishments of explanations is that they bring the reader's mind to rest by forming a kind of closure around the problem at hand, sewing it up inside a satisfying quilt of ideas. Even if this is not important to explaining in a narrower sense, formalizers must realize that they remove something of value when they logically unstitch the threads that hold the quilt together.

More substantially, theory construction faces the standard questions that any theorist must confront. When action occurs and is to be explained by drawing up sets of categories to fit it, the theory construction question one hits first is: exactly which features of the situation pertain essentially to the action and which are irrelevant? When this is satisfactorily under control, one must reach some conclusions about what form the descriptive and explanatory sentences will take. Will they be the 'covering law' type, the statistical generalization type, the constant conjunction type, and so on? This is of crucial significance when one comes to evaluate what an explanation actually says and what it means as an assertion about the nature of the social world. Also of interest to most theory constructionists is the question of which methodological procedures are recommended or appropriate to the testing of theoretical sentences. Endless questions arise about the ways in which theoretical terms should be used in empirical research work. When one wishes to build up a theory which will be testable, he is hard put to prove that the procedures he suggests will be capable of testing his ideas.

Ethnomethodology does not share these problems; it does not make strong theoretical claims at all. Yet the central core of ethnomethodology can be questioned. Setting aside the methodological claim, we can ask simply whether the end product – an ordered social setting in which action fits in with a way of talking about it – is really very much different from what other sociologists speak about in other terms. No matter how people account for their behavior, the fact is that they are still doing something. However wrong it may be by ethnomethodological standards, it seems fair to say that sociologists with other theoretical models can, in principle, organize their observations into conceptual categories and relate these to other features of the situations and cultural contexts quite legitimately. Naturally, these other theoretically-minded researchers run into the problems of selective perceptions in observation, instability of categories, and the like. If they opted for ideal typical modes of characterizing the action, they would never actually see a pure enactment of their conceptual categories, but they would, we suppose, be able to understand the action at hand as approximations to some mental picture of it. These are acceptable ways of conceptualizing action.

The implicit radical departure of ethnomethodology is in the theoretical ideas invoked to justify its new focus, and in the claim that these new theoretical ideas are somehow more truthful than previous ones. The ethnomethodologists have a cogent point in saying that orderly conduct is behavior addressed to the contextually relevant and articulated meaning of behavior rules, not rule-following or principle-enactment *per se*. It seems that Parsons' characterization of social action as motivated behavior in accordance with general prescriptions of role-enactment is not really so far from the ethnomethodologists' concentration on appearances in contexts. Parsons' person, his actor-in-role, has certain standards by which he judges whether or not his activities are appropriate to given situations. It would be a misconstruction of Parsons' work to think that the actor is so completely constrained that the role determines his activities exclusively. Yet Parsons did not systematically address the question of how people convert the recognized rules of practical life into behavior, and the ethnomethodologists must be credited with exposing this omission and moving to correct it.

VI. *Conclusion*

New movements in the theory of sociology may all be seen as ways of reacting to the received wisdom of the founding fathers. Some have said that a field of study makes progress by rapidly forgetting the ideas of its founders. Of course a field ought not remain slavishly wedded to outmoded ideas. It ought not be slavishly wedded to any ideas. It ought to retain healthy respect for all serious contenders, whatever their era. It is a fact that no modern sociological theory could have been formed in the absence of previous thinking, even if the old work is entirely rejected by a modern theorist. More than anything else, theoretical study sets and develops the problems to be solved, and theoretical criticism dismembers these conceptualizations to see if anything is glossed over or omitted. This was as true previously as it is now, and aspirations to modernity ought not inhibit serious sociological thinkers from consulting whomever they wish in conceptualizing and theoretically solving the problems of social order. Hence it is appropriate to study the main theoretical positions to achieve basic literacy in the field, as well as to obtain a basis from which to evaluate new movements in theoretical thinking in sociology.

KEY CONCEPTS

theory construction	behavior rule
formalization	normal forms
explication	et cetera
postulate	verbal accounts
axiom	'what everyone knows'
concept formation	ethnomethodology

TOPICS FOR DISCUSSION

1 Compare ethnomethodology and theory construction by contrasting their objectives.
2 Formalizations can lead to theoretical criticism. How is this so?
3 Formalization usually precedes theory construction. Why?
4 Why are ethnomethodologists so particularly interested in what people say about what they do?
5 If we do not follow behavior rules, how do they influence conduct?
6 Can you think of any ways in which ethnomethodology resembles functional theory?

ESSAY QUESTIONS

Compare ethnomethodological and symbolic interactionist assumptions on the question of social order.

Discuss the difficulties of formalizing a theory which knowingly contained tautologies, or other non-logical constructions.

What are the main benefits, and some of the disutilities, of theory formalization?

Attempt a formalization procedure for functionalism, as found in Chapter 5 of this book.

Discuss the adequacy of explanation used by ethnomethodologists to account for social structure.

FOR FURTHER READING AND STUDY

Berger, Joseph, Morris Zelditch, and Bo Anderson. *Types of Formalization in Small-group Research*. Boston: Houghton Mifflin, 1962.

Cicourel, Aaron V. *Cognitive Sociology: Language and Meaning.* Harmondsworth, Middlesex: Penguin Books, 1973.

Douglas, Jack D. (ed.). *Understanding Everyday Life: Toward the Reconstruction of Sociological Knowledge.* Chicago: Aldine, 1970.

Douglas, Mary (ed.). *Rules and Meanings.* Harmondsworth, Middlesex: Penguin Books, 1973.

Garfinkel, Harold. *Studies in Ethnomethodology.* Englewood Cliffs, N.J.: Prentice-Hall, 1967.

Gibbs, Jack. *Sociological Theory Construction.* Hinsdale, Ill.: Dryden Press, 1972.

Gross, Llewellyn (ed.). *Symposium on Sociological Theory.* New York: Harper and Row, 1959.

(ed.). *Sociological Theory: Inquiries and Paradigms.* New York: Harper and Row, 1967.

Hage, Jerald. *Techniques and Problems of Theory Construction in Sociology.* New York: Wiley, 1972.

Mullins, Nicholas C. *The Art of Theory: Construction and Use.* New York: Harper and Row, 1971.

Nagel, Ernest. 'A Formalization of Functionalism', in Ernest Nagel, *Logic without Metaphysics.* New York: Free Press, 1956, pp. 247-83.

Reynolds, Paul D. *A Primer in Theory Construction.* Indianapolis: Bobbs-Merrill, 1971.

Scott, Marvin G. and Stanford Lymon. 'Accounts', *American Sociological Review,* xxxiii, 1 (February 1968), pp. 46-62.

Stinchcombe, Arthur L. *Constructing Social Theories.* New York: Harcourt Brace Jovanovich, 1968.

Index of names

General index